RELEARNING TO E-LEARN

Strategies for electronic learning and knowledge

M. S. Bowles

MELBOURNE UNIVERSITY PRESS

MELBOURNE UNIVERSITY PRESS
An imprint of Melbourne University Publishing Ltd
PO Box 1167, Carlton, Victoria 3053 Australia
mup-info@unimelb.edu.au
www.mup.com.au

First published 2004
Text © Marcus Bowles 2004
Design and typography © Melbourne University Publishing Ltd 2004
Designed by Polar Design Pty Ltd
0522 85126 6 printed in Australia by McPherson's Printing Group.

Marcus Bowles is licensed and possesses the rights to use the unique research and intellectual property in possession of the Unitas Knowledge Centre under a partnership with the Commonwealth Bank of Australia.

The LEGO name is used with the courtesy of the LEGO group.

National Library of Australia Cataloguing-in-Publication entry

Bowles, Marc (Marcus Stuart).
    Relearning to e-learn : strategies for electronic learning and knowledge.

    Bibliography.
    ISBN 0 522 85126 6. (paperback)
    ISBN 0 522 85130 4. (ebook)

    1. Internet in education. 2. Education - Computer network resources. 3. Computer-assisted instruction. I. Title.

371.334

Table of Contents

Supplementary Content

Supplementary content is available at the following web address:

http://www.mup.unimelb.edu.au/ebooks/0-522-85130-4/

Figures

Tables

Acknowledgements

This book is the direct result of government, corporate, university and community input into a major research project called Learning to E-learn. The project was conducted by the Unitas Knowledge Centre, a collaborative centre sponsored by the Tasmanian State Government in Australia, the University of Tasmania, the Commonwealth Bank of Australia and other strategic partners. This book is a product of the project and the research and literature sourced from around the globe.

While I am author of this book its contents represent a team effort. People involved in production of the book and with the original research are as follows.

Unitas project management team
 Anthony Baker — CEO, Unitas Company Ltd
 Julianne Blackaby — Project Director

Unitas Knowledge Centre research team
 Dr Marcus Bowles — Chief Researcher and Author
 Paul Wilson — Research Assistant
 Ginni Stieva — Research Assistant
 Beverly Goldfarb — Production Manager

The Centre for Research and Learning in Regional Australia (CRLRA) at the University of Tasmania provided support for methodology and structure, and contributions on learning communities, communities of practice and individual learning variables.
 Professor Sue Kilpatrick — Head of the Centre
 Helen Bound

The Centre for Teaching and Learning in Diverse Educational Contexts (CTLDEC) at the Northern Territory University provided support for overall methodology and contributed the research paper 'Designing Effective E-learning Interventions: What are the Practical Implications of Differences in Culture, Language and Literacy for E-learning?'
 Professor Ian Falk — Head of the Centre
 Dr Neville Grady
 Jo-Anne Ruscoe
 Ruth Wallace

The book editing team
 Jenny Lee — Managing Editor
 Marilyn Mackey — Copy Editor
 Hilary Ericksen — Editor
 Andrew Preston — Editor

Marcus Bowles, February 2004

Introduction

This book is part of a long-term research project, Learning to E-learn, which is sponsored through the Unitas Knowledge Centre, a joint establishment of the Commonwealth Bank of Australia, the Tasmanian government, the University of Tasmania and the Centre's research partners. This project has also produced a major report on the investigative research, a suite of tools, a manual, case studies and supplementary publications (see http://www.portal.unitas.com.au).

Relearning to E-learn focuses on how to implement efficient and effective e-learning in an organisational setting. It points to a number of solutions that can advance organisational learning and link it with major reforms to achieve service excellence, agility and the generation of new knowledge capital. To situate this discussion, the book deconstructs some popular misconceptions and re-explores some basic principles of managing e-learning for individual, business and community development.

The current debate on e-learning reflects both hope and doubts about the role that learning can play in economies and societies around the globe. This is especially true of corporate e-learning, which is the primary focus of the research that has led to this book. At present, the level of doubt is such that the future of corporate e-learning seems poised on a knife-edge.

Unfortunately, e-learning has widely been trivialised in order to accelerate its adoption. Many writers and service providers have tried to 'dumb down' the concept, narrowing their focus to particular activities such as the provision of online content, or treating e-learning as an extension of the most limited forms of skills-based training. In today's corporate world, the return on investment sought from e-learning typically focuses on reducing costs or speeding up the acquisition of skills to attain the minimum acceptable threshold for performance proficiency. This approach emphasises the acquisition of competence to perform.

The danger of this approach is that it risks simplifying the issues and offers inadequate foundations for the development of e-learning models and theory. These foundations will inevitably crumble as the hype and false promises that surrounded the initial promotion of corporate e-learning are unmasked and it becomes apparent that narrowly conceived programs are not capable of delivering sustainable, strategic business results.

Potentially, e-learning can be used to simplify complex communication processes, speed the flow of information and further embed knowledge-based attributes into a wide range of electronic transactions, bringing work and learning together in new ways. The opportunity exists for communities and businesses to develop a more viable basis for undertaking e-learning practices.

Organisations that pursue the opportunity to use e-learning effectively will be able to leapfrog their competitors, overcoming some of the barriers inherent in the approaches commonly advanced by e-learning vendors and those who promote supply-driven approaches to the provision of e-learning. Businesses that adopt a coherent strategic implementation model, backed by some simple tools and framed by integrated business processes, can make more effective and efficient use of e-learning to advance the generation and transfer of knowledge among individuals and groups and enhance the organisations' potential productive capability, agility and sustainable competitive advantage.

In a broader view, e-learning can be seen as a transformation process that must align with the organisation's capacity to deploy learning. In this scenario, technology is not an end in itself but rather fulfils an enabling role, maximising the effectiveness of the learning intervention. To achieve this, the e-learning technology needs to be secure, standards-based and designed for maximum flexibility and interoperability. When these conditions are fulfilled, e-learning technologies can enhance existing business processes and reporting systems rather than acting as yet another administrative overlay in an already-complex set of processes.

E-learning is a journey by different individuals, at different stages of progress and in different directions, with different capabilities and very few common elements to allow comparative positioning. This book does not pretend to provide a blueprint for every journey; to do this would be to deny the diversity that is the hallmark of this dynamic field of human endeavour. Rather, the aim of this work is to offer a broad view of the points of reference so that organisations involved in e-learning are able to move forward more confidently and explore its potential to achieve tangible benefits for individuals, organisations and communities.

What is Electronic Learning?

When the World Wide Web was launched in 1991, there was a surge of interest in the possibilities of electronic learning (or e-learning). The use of the Web as an educational medium was hailed as a harbinger of profound changes for communities, organisations and markets. By now, well over a decade later, one might expect that the concept of e-learning would be well defined and clearly differentiated from other forms of learning. Yet there is still a lack of consensus about what e-learning represents. For all the publicity it has received in recent years, e-learning remains something of an enigma, and its boundaries are far from clear.

E-learning intersects numerous fields of thought and practice, and cannot be trivialised into a simple formula for success. As Figure 1.1 suggests, writings on the 'theory' of e-learning encompass an array of academic perspectives: training and education, learning and knowledge, technology and the investigation of individual market segments. In this new industry, key concepts and understandings are still emerging. Any study of the effectiveness and efficiency of e-learning therefore has to engage with multiple issues, including the role of e-learning in knowledge and learning, its contribution to competent performance, its relationship to organisational transformation and strategies for embedding e-learning into other forms of electronic interaction.

Figure 1.1 Merging language and fields of study

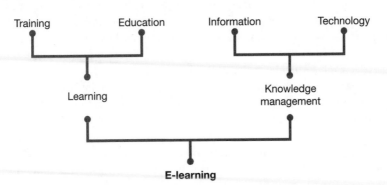

This chapter sets out to isolate the fundamental components that can be used to define e-learning. Here, it is important to separate 'technology-driven' perspectives from views centred on the learning process. Many of the definitional difficulties that have beset e-learning have arisen from an overemphasis on the mechanics at the expense of a commitment to improving the experience and outcomes of learning.

E-learning processes and systems

Although the focus of e-learning should be on delivering learning outcomes for people and organisations, much of the popular literature on the subject is preoccupied with the deployment of specific technologies. This section adopts a different tack. It begins by focusing on the crucial issue of how people communicate and learn in an electronic environment. This leads into an appraisal of some widely held ideas about the potential for creating modular 'learning objects', which in turn serves as background for a discussion of the terms used to describe the technologies that have been developed to implement and manage e-learning.

E-learning processes

Like any learning process, e-learning depends on effective communication of human knowledge, whether this occurs in a face-to-face classroom or across the Internet. Electronic technologies can no more guarantee effective communication than they can transform 'jxiqwop' into a meaningful word. The medium alone does not create the message.

The effectiveness of e-learning also depends on establishing two-way communication between teachers and learners, and among learners themselves. Unfortunately, when e-learning was first popularised, it was widely promoted as a means of minimising costs by delivering pre-packaged content to large populations of learners by means of electronic networks or CD-ROMs. Such an approach relies on one-way communication from teacher to learner, attenuating the learning experience. It views learners as atomised individuals and fails to take into account the social context in which learning occurs. Above all, it does not engage learners actively in the process of learning.

On the other hand, online technologies can also be used to foster interactive and collaborative engagement. This can be either synchronous or asynchronous: learners and instructors may either have regular, scheduled sessions whether they all 'meet' simultaneously online, or (more commonly) use electronic forums to exchange ideas in their own time.

The most familiar form of synchronous electronic communication is real-time two way text-based online chat, which is widely used in e-learning. More sophisticated forms of synchronous instruction include virtual classrooms, which use information and communication technologies to mimic a traditional classroom environment. This may involve video-conferencing or the use of shared electronic whiteboards, which allow learning materials to be created and modified in real time, either by the instructor or the learners.

In many cases, exchanges during synchronous instruction can be archived so that learners can review them later.

The use of virtual classrooms has considerable cost advantages for many organisations. The logistics of organising face-to-face classroom training can account for as much as 40 per cent of corporate training budgets (Koolen 2001: 5). On the other hand, virtual classrooms have several drawbacks. They require learners to have access to fast, reliable networks and reasonably sophisticated computing facilities. Learning in a virtual classroom also tends to be instructor-led rather than based on participatory, two-way communication. Above all, virtual classrooms share many of the limitations of the conventional classroom in that they require learners to be online at a particular time. This negates one of the major advantages of electronic communication, which is its ability to offer flexible access.

By contrast, asynchronous instruction allows participants to control their own timetables and fit learning around their other commitments. This is a major bonus, especially for adult learners who lead complicated lives. Many of the technologies used in asynchronous e-learning also permit two-way communication between learners and instructors, or multi-directional, collaborative communication among learners themselves. These are some of the communication technologies most commonly used in asynchronous e-learning:

- **Email** is the most common form of electronic information exchange.
- **Collaborative learning forums** promote learner interaction through **message boards**, where students can post questions and answers; **text chat or forums**, where learners can communicate outside the main classroom; and **threaded discussions**, where facilitators and students can discuss a given topic and review each other's responses.
- **E-boards** allow learners and instructors to create images, text and information and present them to other participants.
- **Application sharing** allows instructors and learners to work collaboratively on the same learning materials, either simultaneously or in sequence. Participants can see what is happening at all times.
- **Simulations or virtual laboratories** permit learners to work in teams to construct projects and complete them at their preferred pace.
- **Library/learning session cache access** provides access to archived text, presentations, video, audio and data files. This is especially useful for revision or for reviewing synchronous learning sessions a student may have missed.
- **Real-time tests and evaluation** can be triggered at agreed times or completed at the learner's own pace.
- **Video and audio streaming** can be used to disseminate information to learners, and can also enable learners to see and speak with the facilitator via the Internet rather than by telephone.

From the instructor's point of view, e-learning also offers classroom management technologies that permit instructors to log students into 'classes', establish work groups, manage interaction between students and receive feedback in real time. Other support services include real-time reporting on learners' progress, timetabling, tracking student and teacher activities, and authoring tools for generating content.

Asynchronous learning can be designed to develop both cognitive and performance skills, engaging learners in a 'cognitive apprenticeship' (Collins, Brown & Newman, cited in Brown, Collins & Duguid 1989b: 32–42). This supports an educational philosophy in which learners are active players in the process of learning.

Learner surveys consistently suggest that four benefits are seen as the critical deliverables when designing online learning as compared with other forms of technology-based learning. These are summarised in Table 1.1.

Table 1.1   Top four online learning benefits compared to other learning technologies

Online learning benefits	Computer/ CD-ROM	Electronic simulation	Tele-conference	Television broadcast	Video/ television/ radio
Learner control	Learner control of pace but not content	Reduced learner control; good learning retention	Reduced learner control	Reduced learner control	Reduced learner control
Accessible from anywhere, provided learner has Internet access	Reliably accessible, irrespective of bandwidth, but hardware-dependent	Consistent delivery, but may require high bandwidth	Consistent delivery, but requires high bandwidth	Consistent delivery; compatible with existing networks	Consistent delivery; compatible with existing networks
Available on demand	Available on demand	Just-in-time learning	Availability is time-dependent; affordable for groups	Availability is time-dependent; affordable for groups	Availability is time-dependent; affordable for groups
Personalised learning	Limited customisation	Customised to individual/ group context	Limited customisation	Limited customisation	Limited customisation

Based on Education Lifelong Learning Group 2001: 12

Learning content and learning objects

The major sectors that use e-learning — academic institutions, government, the corporate sector and the community and general consumer sector — approach it with different types of end use in mind. The approach to e-learning in corporate contexts is very different from that in formal educational institutions. Historically, learning in educational settings has been organised around self-contained subjects or course units. In contrast, many proponents of e-learning in corporate settings envisage systems based on much smaller units of content, known as learning objects.

The purpose of adopting this paradigm is to encourage the reuse of common elements, thereby decreasing costs, streamlining content creation and improving quality. The idea is to structure learning content into common building blocks that can be quickly found, reassembled and customised according to particular contexts and learner needs. Fast retrieval is achieved by tagging each object with metadata, including descriptive information on authorship, content and composition, as well as subsidiary information such as any prerequisite knowledge or special access conditions (Brennan, Funke & Anderson 2001: 4). Metadata can also be subjective, providing evaluative information such as how well an object works in particular learning situations. Hodgins has suggested that 'as personalization becomes the key element of learning, subjective metadata [will] become increasingly important' (2001: 15).

The assumption of this model is that e-learning systems enable effective reuse of content without compromising the context and themes of objects as they travel over various modules or courses. But as Table 1.2 indicates, the disaggregation of learning objects will affect what e-learning can achieve. Some kinds of knowledge lend themselves to being broken down and reassembled in ways that can promote the creation of e-learning content in short 'chunks'. Such content can be reused and accessed very flexibly. However, reducing *all* knowledge to bite-sized chunks that anyone can reassemble has risks, most especially in losing the integrity of instructional design and the situated meaning that some knowledge only possesses when packaged with other chunks of knowledge.

Table 1.2 highlights the spectrum of outcomes that e-learning can support. Disaggregating learning objects to their smallest form can greatly facilitate the reuse of one learning object for multiple learning activities. However, by definition, a learning object holds value because it supports learning that can enable knowledge transfer. If a learning object is disaggregated and dispersed to the extent that it loses its relationship to the instructional purpose or the applied outcome that can be assessed as a stand-alone outcome, then its real value is only as a form of data or information transfer.

Wiley has been one of the key critics of what has become known as the LEGO block analogy, suggesting that it threatens to 'control and limit the way people think about learning objects'. Unlike LEGO blocks, Wiley points out, learning objects cannot be combined indiscriminately, they cannot be assembled in any old manner, and it requires skill to put them together (2001: 15–16).

Wiley's alternative proposal is to regard learning objects as atoms, noting that:
- Not every atom is combinable with every other atom.
- Atoms can be assembled only in certain structures prescribed by their own internal structure.
- Some training is required in order to assemble them.

Furthermore, only experts can split or recombine atoms; in the case of learning objects, this role would fall to instructional designers and multimedia developers. An awareness of the advantages and disadvantages outlined in Table 1.2 should thus determine both the design of e-learning and the technologies required to complete it.

Table 1.2 Advantages and disadvantages of disaggregating learning objects to their smallest components

Activity	Information	Learning	Knowledge
Ease of design and reuse	Maximises ease of use and repack-aging for multiple purposes	More difficult to maintain instructional integrity because as the technology, context or person changes the pedagogy needs to be reviewed	Very difficult to achieve reuse because as tech-nology, context or person changes so should the knowledge outcome
Ease of use	Maximises port-ability and acces-sibility as anyone can 'grab and go' as required	Can be easier to access but integrity of relationship to learning outcomes in the given situation can rapidly be lost	Easier to access but without situated meaning and relevance to individual's needs it is just information
Ease of management	Once on a central database and meta-tagged it is easy to move, manage and track	Clustering into learning components (courses, curriculum etc.) can ease maintenance but it is hard to manage learning outcomes for one learning object that may relate to multiple learning components	Can use templates and database to store, retrieve and maintain objects but to hold knowledge value it has to demonstrate an applied outcome

The concept of learning objects underpins many of the advanced e-learning systems, and is now commonly seen as being central to the benefits e-learning systems confer. The concept's popularity has probably been fuelled by the promotional activities of the large vendors of IT and e-learning systems.

E-learning technologies

At present, e-learning technologies encompass three main areas of activity:

- **Content creation and management:** the sourcing, creation, storage and management of e-learning content – functions typically addressed by a learning content management system (LCMS);
- **Learning management:** the capture and application of information about learning resources, existing skills and learning activities to measure and manage learning outcomes at the organisational level – functions typically addressed by a learning management system (LMS); and
- **Learning activity:** the delivery of e-learning content, facilitating interaction and learning assessment – functions typically performed by instructors or trainers (Brennan, Funke & Anderson 2001: 10).

The three do not necessarily exist as discrete, identifiable systems. There is overlap and ambiguity in their functions and definitions. The term 'virtual learning environments' is also sometimes used to promote systems that have characteristics of all three. Put simply, an LCMS generates, stores, structures and delivers e-learning content (Brennan, Funke & Anderson 2001: 4), whereas an LMS is more an administrative tool that handles enrolment or registration, tracks students' progress, and records assessment scores and course completions.

Learning content is created through authoring tools (see, for example, Chapman & Hall 2001), which are generally part of the functions of the LCMS.

Brennan, Funke and Anderson (2001) identify the following key building blocks that a good LCMS will provide:

- easy-to-use content creation tools and support for reusable learning objects;
- flexible course design and delivery;
- administrative functions and assessment tools;
- open interface with an LMS or other enterprise system;
- communication and collaboration functions;
- security functions;
- facilities for content migration; and
- automated implementation processes.

By contrast, LMSs operate at the other end of the learning trajectory, supporting and analysing the learning transaction; their focus is on assessing learning outcomes and appraising the relationship of outcomes to investment. While LMSs have become a standard component of e-learning technology, Aldrich (2001) regards them as 'empty highways', and suggests that organisations often make costly investments in technologies that deliver little functionality. Ultimately, he claims, 'while we need learning management, we may not need learning management systems' (Aldrich 2001:1).

Aldrich also points out that as of 2001 the LMS market has had no clear leader. He believes that the competitive state of the market has increased buyers' frustration because different vendors promote such different approaches to managing e-learning. In a competitive market, e-learning technology providers are driven to differentiate and value-add their systems by offering unique features. This produces problems in establishing comparability, and therefore compounds buyer confusion. Aldrich summarises the problem as follows:

> As with most rapidly evolving industries, there's an inverse correlation between the suppliers with the largest customer bases and those with the best architecture. In other words, [clients] usually have to choose between stability and sophistication, or compromise their needs (Aldrich 2001: 1).

Even though some time has elapsed since Aldrich made these observations, it should not be assumed that the issues have been resolved (Egan 2002). It seems that although there is emerging agreement on what an effective LMS should do, there are still gaps between market expectations and the technologies on offer.

E-learning and communication technologies

Most forms of e-learning depend on access to electronic communication technologies. In general, the more interactive the approach, the greater the demands on the communication network, although the transmission of text is less demanding than the transmission of visual images and sound. Various e-learning technologies and their network capacity requirements are shown in Figure 1.2.

Many of the recent advances in e-learning have been driven by the expansion of fixed-line network capacity and the growth in Internet use. Of

particular interest to many in the e-learning field has been the emergence of
the World Wide Web, which offers a user-friendly graphical interface through
which learners can gain access to a huge range of information, including
images, data files and sound as well as text. More recently, there has been a
rapid growth of new mobile communications technologies that offer Internet
access while bypassing both the fixed-line network and the Web.

Any assessment of the potential of e-learning must accommodate all
these technologies. To state the obvious, some countries will have 'emerging'
technologies that other countries consider 'old'. At the same time, some of
these slow adopters will 'leapfrog' current technologies and adopt newer
ones. The following sections outline the current state of play, looking at the
changing global and regional patterns of Internet use and the emergence of
new mobile technologies. While we have used Australian examples as case
studies in several instances, our primary focus is on global trends.

Figure 1.2   Advancing network capacity and learning interactivity

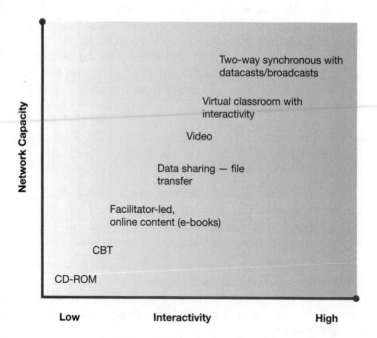

Global and regional trends in Internet use

The Internet is a major driver of e-learning advancement. Early estimates that
some 300 million people would access e-learning over the Internet by the end
of 2002 have since been revised upwards (see Kitchen 2002, slide 10). Various
estimates placed the global online population (i.e. people possessing Internet
connections and accounts) at a little over 600 million in late 2002 (Nua.com
30 January 2003; UNCTAD 2002). Based on growth trends, it seems that more
than 60 per cent of Internet users had connected in the previous eighteen
months. This saw worldwide Internet traffic double between 1998 and 2002.

There was sustained growth of more than 40 per cent in Asia and Africa over 2001–02, and of more than 30 per cent in Latin America and Europe. Table 1.3 shows Nua.com's figures for the geographical distribution of Internet users in September 2002.

Table 1.3   Online population by region, September 2002

Region	Internet connections (millions)
Europe	190.91
Asia–Pacific	187.24
North America	182.67
Latin America	33.35
Africa	6.31
Middle East	5.12
Total	605.6

Source: http://www.nua.ie/surveys/how_many_online/index.html (accessed 25 September 2003)

With the growth of the online population, there has been a corresponding shift away from English as the leading language used on the Internet. In 2000, SunTrust reported that English was used by 92 per cent of the global Internet community (Close, Humphrey & Ruttenbur 2000). In March 2003, Global Reach reported that English was the primary language of only 35.2 per cent of the online population. Chinese came second with 11.9 per cent, followed by Japanese at 10.3 per cent (Global Reach, 31 October 2002, sourced 30 January 2003 at http://www.glreach.com/globstats/index.php3).

The Asia–Pacific region has led the global growth in Internet connections since 2000. Within this region, Australia occupies a key position, with 58 per cent of the adult population having access to the Internet in mid-2002. Table 1.4 provides a granular view of the Internet-using population, comparing the Australian, Asian, US and world markets. A crucial feature of the recent growth in Internet use is that it is increasingly being led by mobile devices that do not rely on the fixed terrestrial network.

Table 1.4   Internet use and household computer access by region, 2001/02–2002/03

	Australia		Asia		USA		Rest of World	
	2001–02	2002–03	2001–02	2002–03	2001–02	2002–03	2001–02	2002–03
Internet users	7.2m	9.3m	150.5m	201.1m	142.8m	155.0m	192.5m	227.1m
House-hold PCs	10.0m	11.0m	132.2m	140.4m	178.0m	190.0m	201.7m	215.4m

All 2003 figures are to May 2003. Source: International Telecommunications Union (ITU) 2002 and 2003 figures at http://www.itu.int/ITU-D/ict/statistics (accessed June 2003); CIA Factbook, http://www.cia.gov/cia/publications/factbook/index.html (accessed 4 September 2003)

Accommodating emerging technologies

The emergence of mobile, wireless and satellite technologies is already impacting on e-learning. New Internet technologies are being used to support small-screen mobile and wireless devices. Satellites and mobile wireless devices can use TCP/IP (Transmission Control Protocol and Internet Protocol) to communicate on the Internet. In a field marked by such rapid evolution, we cannot assume that the Web as we know it today will remain the primary conduit for Internet-based e-learning.

Technologies such as telephone, television, the Internet and computing devices are increasingly converging. Given the speed of this convergence and the increase in the number of users, even the most conservative forecasters predict that massive changes will occur over the next decade. It took a century, from 1900 to 2000, to create a fixed terrestrial network connecting some 850 million telephone users globally. Yet it is expected that at least as many connections again will be required by 2015. By the end of 2003, the Asia–Pacific region alone is expected to have some 165 million Internet users, 400 million mobile phone users and 25 million mobile Internet users (reported in http://www.news.com from IDC 2003 Report, 6 January 2003).

By contrast with terrestrial phone connections to the Internet, which require a large social investment in infrastructure, mobile and wireless networks offer rapid connectivity and accelerated access. Around the world in 2002 there were estimated to be more than 790 million connections to mobile cellular networks and some 700 million wireless subscribers (Sabnani 2002: 3). Trends and forecasts for mobile and fixed network connections are summarised in Figure 1.3.

Figure 1.3 World subscriber forecasts and the impact of mobile communications

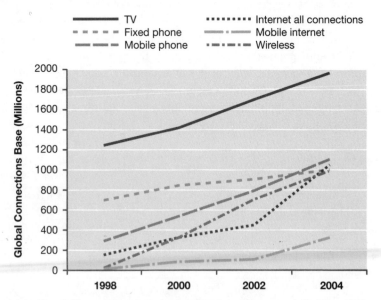

Chart derived from © Ericsson 2001, from Boston Consulting Group, Ovum presented in Kitchen 2002, slide 10; ITU 2002: 9; Lucent Technologies cited in Sabnani 2002

The advent of mobile and wireless connections has fostered a shift in how people and businesses can communicate and learn. Until the late 1990s, access to the Internet was dominated by those using fixed terrestrial phone connections, but now some 30 per cent of global users access the Internet by cable, satellite, wireless or mobile devices. As the use of mobile and wireless devices has expanded, their capabilities have converged with those of older network technologies.

Handheld devices

Handheld devices and personal digital assistants (PDAs) have been rapidly adopted by businesses in many countries. PDAs are basically small, handheld devices with computing, data storage and retrieval capacity. While PDAs were originally used for keeping schedules and address book information that could be synchronised with a computer, the newer devices have powerful scanning capabilities and can also record, transfer and interrogate data. They can scan bar codes, use scaled-down applications previously found only on more powerful computers, use wireless transmission to communicate and update central databases, and sort data required for immediate decision making. These devices are now capable of many functions once performed only by computers.

Mobile phone technology

Mobile technology is rapidly evolving to support data applications. Mobile phones can be used to send and receive short message services (SMS), take and send pictures, send and receive data files (music, text files, video), and browse the Internet. Third-generation (3G) mobile technologies such as CDMA-2000 and wideband CDMA (W-CDMA) can transmit data at speeds of up to two megabytes per second. At such speeds, mobile phones will be able to offer a vast array of new services.

Wireless technologies

Wireless technologies are also expanding their range of functions. Wireless communications are particularly useful for supplying data services to remote communities (and some urban areas) that do not have access to high-speed fixed-line connections. The use of wireless technologies to support networks has been hampered by differences in standards, which have hindered interoperability across networks by different devices. Increasingly, however, hardware manufacturers are producing devices that can adapt to either of the two major standards that utilise spectrums 802.11a and 802.11b (WiFi). While systems able to operate on these spectrums are certainly not the only or most likely long term options (i.e. 802.11g and 802.16 offer important alternatives), high speed, broadband connectivity between different wireless technologies is now possible. Wireless local loops (WLLs) centred on very small aperture terminals (VSATs) and satellite technologies now permit wireless and satellite connectivity at speeds of more than two megabytes per second both ways (upload and download). Within the network, data can be distributed at rates of up to fifty- four megabytes per second. Wireless technologies are now competitive with other mobile technologies, particularly 3G technologies.

The combined effect of all these changes will present huge new opportunities for communication. To take the Australian case, 3G infrastructure at present is still embryonic, but the deployment of CDMA-2000 is under way, and Telstra expects to offer W-CDMA by about 2005. At a cost of $1 billion, this will radically alter the types of applications available.

Bandwidth and access to e-learning

Bandwidth refers to the amount of information that can be sent or received at a point on a computer network: the greater the bandwidth, the greater the carrying capacity and speed of transmission. Bandwidth is a major issue in the deployment of e-learning. The higher the quality and quantity of audio, video, interaction and processing tasks, the more sophisticated the communications technology required. The bandwidths of various communications technologies are depicted in Figure 1.4.

Bandwidth also costs money, so there is a financial imperative to manage the amount of bandwidth used for e-learning, particularly where it is used to support remote and distance users who may not have access to fast data connections. The most common way of dealing with bandwidth constraints is to minimise the amount of information that is to be communicated, usually at a considerable cost to learning quality; strategies such as data compression and caching files are also used.

Figure 1.4 Bandwidths of different communications technologies

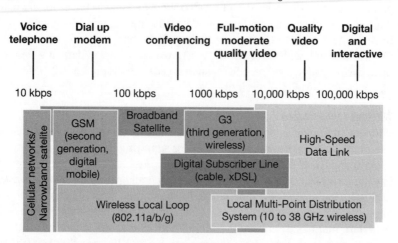

Modified from Sabnani 2002: 18

For users of the Internet, the content and services that can be accessed are dictated by the bandwidth available. Ideally, the connection should be broadband (high-speed data transmission), which is considerably faster than the standard 56.6 kbps dial-up modem speed. Table 1.5 depicts the range of communications available across different bandwidths, from mobile cellular-network voice connections at 9.5 kbps to the much larger 2400 kbps.

Table 1.5　Bandwidth and e-learning applications

Application	Bandwidth — speed kbps							
	9.6	14.4	28	64	144	384	2000	2400
Transaction processing								
Messaging/text								
Voice/SMS								
Text chats								
Still images								
Internet/virtual private network								
Database access								
Applications sharing								
Low-quality video								
High-quality video								

Key Indication of application performance

Nil capability ☐　Uncertain ▨　Preferred ■

At present, only the densely settled regions of affluent nations have access to fixed-line systems that will support the full range of functions outlined in Table 1.5. Delivery in rural areas is costly, difficult or impossible. Even in some affluent economies, the modernisation of fixed-line networks has proceeded more slowly than early projections suggested. In Australia, for example, the take-up of broadband connections has been slow. In 2002, only 10 per cent of homes had high-speed broadband connections over 56.6 kbps (NOIE 2002: 19).

At the same time, although the 'mobile Internet' is widely seen as offering an alternative avenue of opportunity for e-learning, it has several barriers to overcome. Not only are most mobile Internet devices unable to access the same amount of bandwidth as fixed devices, but they are smaller and tend to have less usable screens and keypads. As yet, no 'killer application' has emerged to define how mobile devices could be used for e-learning. The prospect of having mobile access to learning materials — in the 'right here, right now' context — is appealing, but it will require a substantial investment in applications to make use of the new technologies. On the other hand, given the astonishing pace of innovation in the past two decades, it would be rash to adopt an approach to e-learning that excluded developments in this area.

Setting the parameters for a study of e-learning

With communication technologies in a state of flux, it is important to adopt an inclusive definition of e-learning that can accommodate the widest possible range of technologies. Debate on this issue has not moved far since the late 1990s, when there was a spate of published works about e-learning markets in the corporate sector.[1] From the outset, e-learning was defined in relation to technology: as early as the 1980s it was used as a shorthand term for learning delivered using any electronic means, especially computers. This emphasis remains pervasive. For instance, the report of the US Commission on Technology and Adult Learning, *A Vision of E-learning for America's Workforce*, defined e-learning as 'instructional content or learning experiences delivered or enabled by electronic technology' (2001: 4). In July 2003, the Department for Education and Skills in the UK stated in its consultative document *Towards a Unified E-learning Strategy*, 'If someone is learning in a way that uses information and communication technologies (ICTs), they are using e-learning' (2003: 4). This broad definition, however, has not been accepted by all practitioners.

Some writers have specifically focused on the use of Internet technologies. Marc Rosenberg, for example, defines e-learning as 'the use of Internet technologies to deliver a broad array of solutions that enhance knowledge and performance' (2001: 28). He argues that there are three fundamental criteria for e-learning:

- It is networked, which makes it capable of instant updating, storage/retrieval, distribution and sharing of instruction and information.
- It is delivered to the end user via a computer using standard Internet and intranet technology.
- It focuses on the broadest view of learning — learning that goes beyond traditional paradigms of training.

The term 'e-learning' has thus come to encompass both the learning transaction and the technology used for producing and transmitting knowledge, with the emphasis on the latter. Discussion of the parameters of e-learning has also been confounded by the somewhat vexed relationship between e-learning and distance education or flexible learning.

E-learning, distance education and flexible learning

E-learning has historically been linked with distance education and flexible learning. In distance education, various technologies can be used to link learners, instructors and resources that are removed in time or space. The hallmark of flexible learning, as its name suggests, is its adaptability to learners' needs and circumstances. Burns, Williams and Barnett define flexible learning in terms of its flexible 'entry, course components, modes of learning and points of exit', which offer the learner 'control and choice regarding the content, sequence, time, place and method of learning', including flexible assessment processes (1997: 16). While e-learning may be seen as a form of flexible and distance learning, not all flexible and distance learning necessarily involves e-learning (Rosenberg 2001: 29). As shown in Figure 1.5, e-learning exists in a wider field of endeavour and has relationships that overlap with many different approaches.

Figure 1.5 Learning technologies, modes and relationships

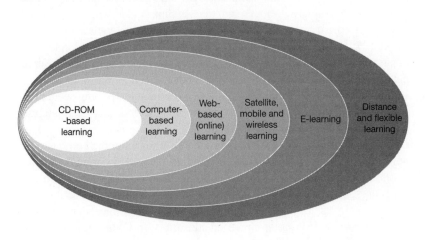

Based on Urdan & Weggen 2000: 9

E-learning has also been defined in terms of its social context and its ability to offer learners the option of working outside structured educational environments. In Canada, Doug Hum and Anne Ladouceur define it very broadly, suggesting it is 'using an electronic means to access information and learn about a topic, be it for personal interest, job at hand or career advancement' (2001: ii). Later, however, they refine their definition to 'training that takes place over a network, the Internet or an Intranet' (2001: 3). It seems unfortunate that self-limiting words such as 'training', 'network' and 'Internet' are introduced, though Hum and Ladouceur do acknowledge that e-learning must be adapted to the individual's situation, schedule and learning style.

The historical association between e-learning and distance education has had some unfortunate consequences. E-learning programs have sometimes been criticised for being boring, poorly conceived and designed, and unable to provide individuals with the knowledge they need. Distance and flexible learning are open to very similar criticisms; many of these programs have disappointed early hopes or promised more than they have delivered. E-learning seems to have inherited some of that legacy.

There have also been problematic relationships between e-learning and existing distance education and flexible learning programs. In some cases, online learning has been introduced to augment and improve existing practices, but in other cases the intention has clearly been to replace existing pedagogies with one-size-fits-all electronic solutions as a means of saving money. This seldom produces effective learning experiences, and has led some education and training professionals to view e-learning with scepticism.

Web-learning and web-based training

Some authors distinguish e-learning from web-learning (Beer 2000) or web-based training (Horton 2000). These authors emphasise the distinctiveness of the Web as an educational medium that can be used to transfer information and knowledge rapidly without restrictions of time or location, and potentially at a lower cost than alternative educational media or environments (Beer 2000: 4–5). Horton defines web-based training as 'any purposeful, considered application of Web technologies to the task of educating a fellow human being' (2000: 2).

Many authors who promote web-based learning or training seem intent on avoiding any association with e-learning. They tend to differentiate their practice by highlighting how Web technologies can enhance learning (Khan cited in Khan 1997; Beer 2000; Horton 2000). These authors emphasise the power of the Web to transfer information and knowledge rapidly, without restriction of time or location, and often at a lower cost than alternative educational media or environments (Beer 2000: 4–5). Horton describes web-based training as 'the confluence of three social and technical developments: distance learning, computer-conveyed education, and Internet technologies' (2000: 2).

Towards an inclusive definition of e-learning

As we have seen, e-learning is typically defined in relation to its use of specific technologies. The elements of many conventional definitions include:
- information and communication technologies;
- a network, including use of the Internet and the World Wide Web;
- delivery on time, at any time; and
- an electronic exchange of information for the purpose of learning.

This definition, however, is potentially limiting. To take only two of the available technologies, is a CD-ROM or a wireless-enabled learning exchange a form of e-learning?

For many organisations, e-learning simply means a CD-ROM and applications loaded onto single computers for computer-based training or instruction. These organisations do not need to use networks or web-based applications. Some e-learning practitioners and theorists argue that such 'platform'-based arrangements do not amount to e-learning.

Such territorial disputes are unhelpful. They are also increasingly irrelevant to e-learning practice, which is moving towards blending various electronic forms of communication with face-to-face instruction and elements of traditional distance education, as we will see in Chapter 3. Perhaps more significantly, to define e-learning in terms of its use of networks and the Web could be self-defeating, because it risks excluding emerging technologies that are not necessarily web-based.

To derive a foundational definition of e-learning, a set of logical statements can be advanced:
- E-learning encompasses any form of learning transacted by way of digital technologies.

- E-learning delivery systems are subject to the dynamics of socio-technological evolution.
- E-learning may be synchronous or asynchronous, self-paced or instructor-led, a process or a single event, online or offline, or any combination of these modes.

Taking these statements into account, we advance a broad definition of e-learning for the purpose of ongoing research: **Electronic learning** can be defined as a learning experience involving the acquisition or transfer of knowledge delivered or transacted through electronic means.

Conclusion

Even in the late 1990s, the mobile technologies that now carry 30 per cent of all Internet traffic had not been envisaged. Software applications, hardware capabilities and even fixed-line networks are in a state of flux. All these changes will have significant implications for e-learning.

According to both aggressive and conservative forecasts of business opportunities, learning is expected to be a major 'product and service' for many years to come. To restrict the definition of e-learning to Internet connections via networked computers is to ignore mobile devices and emerging forms of networks and wireless technologies. E-learning involves all forms of ICT, across all dimensions of the learning process. Restrictive definitions in terms of specific technologies are of limited long-term relevance to learning transactions in an electronic context. E-learning can be both a distinct area of study and part of the wider mosaic of learning, knowledge management and information exchange within an electronic environment. These interactions are the subject of this book.

Principle 1

E-learning encompasses a wide diversity of practices in a dynamic, rapidly changing field. It must therefore be defined to encompass all learning experiences involving the acquisition or transfer of knowledge.

[1] These works include Schank 1997; Masie 1997; Carpenter-Smith 1999; HRD Canada 1999; Block & Dobell 1999; Peterson et al. 1999; Urdan & Weggen 2000; Wentling et al. 2000a; Wentling et al. 2000b; McRea, Gay & Bacon 2000; Ruttenbur, Spickler & Lurie 2000; Learnframe 2000; Close et al. 2000; and Goldman Sachs 2000.

The E-learning Marketplace

While there is still debate about what e-learning is, the growth of the industry is unquestionable and its emergence as a force for transformation has become inexorable. For nations, industry sectors and major geographic regions, e-learning has become a significant vehicle for collaborating, building knowledge and increasing organisations' ability to adapt to change.[2] At this transitional stage, practitioners and researchers are focusing on the technology and its use to enable learning, but it is increasingly essential that an understanding emerges on how e-learning will facilitate the most interesting aspects of its role in converging effort across processes and networks.

The Internet has spawned new businesses and markets that trade in information and knowledge. In this New Economy, people have become major assets, their knowledge representing the wealth of organisations and societies. Just as the manufacture of machines and tools drove the Industrial Revolution, the learning industry in the current era enables knowledge industries and information technology (IT) to compete across all sectors of the market.

Various features of the New Economy reinforce the need to move knowledge across electronic networks (Bowles 2002c: 12). Perhaps the most pressing factor is the imperative of speed. As business cycles shorten and customers demand improved responsiveness, greater pressure is placed on businesses to develop low-cost, flexible approaches to providing services. The life cycle of knowledge too is shorter, placing a premium on the rapid transmission of continuously updated information about new developments. Other features underscoring the need to transmit knowledge across electronic networks include:

- the growing emphasis on the quality and reliability of products and services;
- the requirement that products be cost-effective throughout their life cycle;
- the need for access to knowledge on demand, as required, and adapted to the individual's needs and preferences using all available channels; and
- the requirement that systems be sustainable, not only in terms of effectiveness and competitiveness, but also in terms of their ability to evolve and satisfy all demands made of them.

E-learning, broadly defined, is an important part of this process. As more businesses deploy e-learning effectively, one would expect the 'bandwagon' effect — doing it because competitors or other major companies are doing it — to be replaced by deployment based on real understanding of the available options. This usually occurs as technologies mature. The growth stages through which technology-induced change tends to progress can be depicted as an S-curve (Christensen 1997: 44–7), as shown in Figure 2.1.

Figure 2.1   The S-curve of e-learning transition

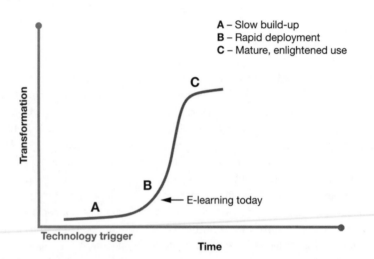

At the same time, it is difficult to formulate a clear picture of current and projected trends in the global e-learning marketplace, partly because of the definitional traps discussed in Chapter 1, and partly because predictions of e-learning growth have suffered from an excess of hype. Even at a national level, it is very difficult to elicit adequate data to assess the extent to which e-learning is being adopted, let alone more detailed information on its patterns of use within and across sectors. No doubt in time information will become more readily available, but at present the sheer pace of growth and the volatility of the e-learning marketplace make it difficult to extract a clear picture.

What this chapter sets out to do, therefore, is to examine what we know of e-learning in the marketplace and endeavour to make sense of it from the perspective of those investing in its future and selling its features. This study is not adopting the viewpoint of any particular discipline; it is not focusing on the technology alone, or on e-learning as an extension of the activity of learning. Instead we can examine it from a basis linked to its economic value, both as a commodity and an identifiable product and service that has value when deployed to enhance existing strategic imperatives.

Forecasting growth

Growth rates in new industries are generally more volatile and harder to predict than those in established industries with mature technologies and markets. In the case of e-learning, the market shrank after the 'dot-com' crash of 2000, experienced patchy growth over 2000–01 and picked up again in early 2002. Since then there has been very strong growth, partly because of the September 11 terrorist attack in New York and consequent political turbulence, and partly because of health scares such as SARS, which discouraged business travel and encouraged e-learning activity, particularly in Asia. In real terms, e-learning is replacing in-house education and training as the major force in corporate education, and is becoming a critical component of the global education marketplace.

As an indication of the uncertainty that surrounds predictions in this sector, one forecast in 2002 suggested the value of the global e-learning market would reach US$43 billion in 2004 (Reuters 2002). This seems extremely optimistic compared with other predictions of US$22 billion or US$25.3 billion in 2003 (Lawyer 2001; Connell 2001: 2). It is difficult to determine whether these forecasts were comparable, as it is not entirely clear what the forecasters included as e-learning-specific infrastructure, hardware, software, platforms, middleware and other services. In addition, the rate and volatility of growth make prediction a difficult matter. For the e-learning sector as a whole, the compound annual growth rate was between 35 and 50 per cent in 2001–02. According to research by International Data Corporation (IDC), a leading forecasting agency in the sector, content provision represented the largest segment of the market and had experienced the most rapid growth (IDC 2002). The fastest-growing companies in both the content and technology sectors reported revenue growth in excess of 400 per cent in the year to 2002.

In turn, corporate e-learning is the fastest-growing component of the global e-learning market. In 2001, IDC reported that the global corporate market had generated nearly US$2.3 billion in 2000 and was on track for a growth rate of more than 50 per cent, which would take it above US$18 billion in 2005 (IDC 2001). On the other hand, this was considerably less optimistic than IDC's forecast the previous year, which had suggested that the corporate market would reach US$23.1 billion by 2004 (IDC January 2000). If IDC's estimates are disaggregated, it seems that technology-based IT training accounts for more than half of total sales, with 'soft skills' trailing behind. Corporations such as Microsoft, Oracle, Novell, IBM, SAP and Cisco dominate much of this IT training.

IDC has also suggested that the US corporate market for e-learning would exceed US$7 billion by 2002, representing a compound annual growth rate of 98 per cent from 1997 to 2002 (IDC January 2000). In mid 2002, IDC revised this prediction upwards, suggesting that the US corporate e-learning market would actually reach US$13 billion before year's end (IDC revised data sourced 12 June 2002 from http://www.idc.com). This compares with a prediction by Brandon-Hall that the *total* US e-learning market would be US$10.3 billion in 2003 (cited in Adkins 2002: 3). Some of these discrepancies are probably accounted for by differences in what is being measured, which again raises the problem of defining the boundaries of e-learning.

The Asia–Pacific market is much smaller. In 2000, IDC estimated that the Asia–Pacific e-learning market was growing by 94 per cent annually and would be worth US$1.7 billion by 2003 (IDC January 2000). At the end of 2002, the Australian component of the market alone was reported to be worth some US$900 million. This figure was consistent with IDC's prediction that growth in the region would be largely driven by Australia, which would account for almost half of the e-learning market at the end of the forecast period. IDC subsequently predicted that the total value of e-learning in the region would reach US$2.34 billion by 2005 (IDC June 2002). Corporate e-learning represented a small part of the total, with expenditure projected to grow from US$83.5 million in 2000 to about US$233.6 million in 2005; this represented a compound annual growth of about 23 per cent (IDC 2001). It is noteworthy that IT training constituted more than half of the e-learning market in the region.

Market forecasts and value projections for e-learning are so ambitious that it is difficult to translate them into meaningful data at the enterprise deci-sion-making level. Cynical organisational managers often adopt the view that some research bodies think of a number over ten, place a billion after it and set it as a projected number of transactions or value for any 'e' market.

Many forecasters predicted that e-learning would 'come of age' at the beginning of 2003, when corporate e-learning would overtake revenue gener-ated from instructor-led, classroom-based corporate training (IDC January 2000; Urdan & Weggen 2000). These forecasters placed a value of US$7 billion on the threshold. In fact, the threshold was surpassed by 2002, but there was stronger than expected overall market growth, with the result that classroom-based instruction also generated some US$11 billion globally in 2002.

International market trends

The global marketplace for e-learning products and services differs widely from one country to another, with variations in the courses offered and tech-nologies used. These variations can be traced to differing cultural attitudes, communication resources and specific training needs, as well as the avail-ability of technical infrastructure and support and the impact of government policies (Mitchell 2000a: 11; Mitchell 2000b; 2000c).

The Organisation for Economic Cooperation and Development (2001) related e-learning growth opportunities to four different forms of learning:
- the early years and compulsory school cycle (representing opportunity for the transformation of existing business);
- initial tertiary and higher-education level, usually regarded as ages 18 to 24 (representing opportunity for transformation and extension of existing business);
- adult or continuing education (representing massive growth of new business in new e-learning modes); and
- whole-of-society learning (currently a diffuse, intangible market and vision).

Recent research on trends in e-learning within the US corporate market shows a growing trend towards e-learning through Internet and intranet connections. The same research reveals a shift towards 'blended learning', whereby a balance is sought between e-learning and instructor-led course offerings (Galvin 2001). This research, however, is not indicative of trends in all countries.

Hambrecht & Co. have identified the following trends in the US corporate e-learning market (Urdan & Weggen 2000). The research that formed the basis for this book suggests that these trends are also evident in Australia and parts of Asia:

- **An increase in competition:** Traditional training companies are moving into e-learning, and existing providers are likely to buy up smaller companies so that they can offer comprehensive training programs. In a highly competitive market, consumers are likely to opt for well-known providers to ensure high-quality, comprehensive training solutions.
- **Pressure for strategic alliances:** Alliances between e-learning companies are likely to increase; for example, content publishers will combine with educational technology vendors and training services suppliers.
- **An increase in outsourcing:** The outsourcing of training activities is expected to increase by more than 10 per cent each year.
- **Shorter development times:** With the increased use of templates and learning objects, content will be prepared more swiftly and assembled to meet customers' needs.
- **The adoption of standards:** Content and courseware will increasingly be reusable across the whole organisation.
- **A rise in blended learning:** E-learning is increasingly used as an extension of classroom learning rather than as a replacement for it. In this context, it offers instructor-led classes a sense of community, stronger communication, flexible delivery and supplementary materials.
- **The use of interactive and collaborative learning:** Web-based, real-time collaboration tools are supplanting static document delivery.

The mark of an advanced and market-differentiated e-learning provider will be its ability to integrate technology, content and services, allowing enterprises and users to migrate to the learning systems most appropriate to their needs. This is likely to be a highly responsive model, incorporating content-management capabilities with a range of options for learning delivery. E-learning content and services will be able to reside within a range of business applications, as well as in collaborative web-based learning and knowledge exchange systems.

Australian market trends

The absence of reliable data makes it difficult to offer a clear picture of the composition of Australia's e-learning marketplace and the trends that shape its growth. The material that is available can be both confusing and contradictory (Brennan, McFadden & Law 2001: 19).

'Pure' e-learning delivery — that is, learning that relies entirely on ICT — can be hard to isolate, as the technology is often used to enable other forms of communication, such as face-to-face meetings between learners and facilitators, video or telephonic conferencing or exchange of materials. The National

Centre for Vocational Education and Research (NCVER) believes that pure e-learning is rare in Australia; rather, blended learning is the usual approach (NCVER online 2002). Nevertheless, it is possible to provide an overview of what is known of the main e-learning market segments within Australia: the corporate sector, universities, vocational education and training, and the lifelong education sector.

Corporate sector

The transition to a knowledge-based economy has pushed corporate customers towards e-learning models. McRea et al. highlight the factors driving this move, including increasingly competitive global business environments, migration towards value-chain integration, rapid technological change, a lack of skilled personnel and the rapid increase in IT-vendor certification programs (McRea et al. 2000, cited in Mitchell 2000c). But while the imperatives of the knowledge economy compel organisations to engage in e-learning, there is still resistance within the business community.

In August 2001, TAFE Frontiers (2001) produced a report on the status of e-learning in Australia. The report was based on a survey of 1200 of Australia's largest businesses, in both the public and private sectors. While fewer than 20 per cent responded, the replies represented in Table 2.1 make it clear why organisations were not using, or planning to use, e-learning.

Table 2.1   Reasons for businesses not engaging in e-learning

Barriers to e-learning	Percentage
Not a business priority at present	20.2%
Budgetary considerations	14.6%
Lack of knowledge about e-learning	10.3%
Existing IT limitations	10.3%
No appropriate training product available	9.9%
Inappropriate for the organisation	9.4%

At the end of 2002, Monash University released a study of how 188 Australian manufacturing companies were deploying e-learning (Boulton 2002). The investigation confirmed that the predominant use of e-learning was to acquire IT skills and knowledge; this is supported by industry-sponsored reviews conducted by Bowles (2002b, 2002c). Major barriers to introducing interactive and live-expert e-learning sessions were issues of cost, bandwidth availability and a lack of suitable content providers. Because manufacturing operations run constantly and use multiple shifts, flexibility was a core issue in terms of learning design and access. On this count, e-learning was considered easier to organise than conventional training, and better for meeting individual learner needs. Boulton also provides insights into management confidence in e-learning and learner satisfaction (post-training) and perception (pre-entry), as summarised in Figure 2.2.

There is a striking gap here between learners' overwhelmingly positive responses and management's apparent scepticism. These results suggest that the management response was not solidly based in program evaluation. In fact, the report drew attention to serious deficiencies in the evaluation of e-learning. Between 48 and 70 per cent of the managers who responded did not know how e-learning was contributing to reductions in training costs, development time and competency transfer, cost per hour of contact time or overall return on investment (ROI) (Boulton 2002: 15). The research also supported anecdotal reports that many companies in Australia are focusing on short-term reasons for implementing e-learning, as Figure 2.3 makes clear.

Figure 2.2 Management and user satisfaction with e-learning

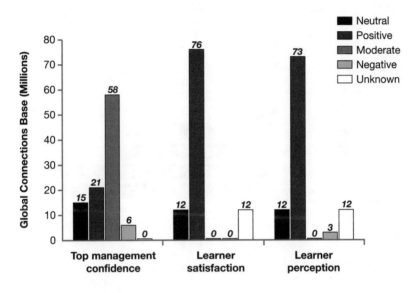

Extracted from Boulton 2002: 12, 6

University sector

The 2001 *Universities Online* report found that there were only 207 fully online courses at Australian universities (Bell et al. 2002). Of these, 90 per cent were at a postgraduate level, generally in specialised subject areas. More than a quarter were in management and commerce (fifty-five courses), a further thirty-five were in education and thirty-two in health. The remaining 85 courses were spread across a wide range of disciplines (Bell et al. 2002: ix).

At the same time, most universities and faculties were using web-based learning to support classroom-based teaching (Bell et al. 2002: 27). The most common learning systems were WebCT, used at some twenty-nine universities, and Blackboard at seventeen. Another twenty universities had in-house systems, but only four of these had implemented in-house course management and learning systems across all faculties.

Within a year of this review of Australian universities' online activities, however, major changes were already occurring. Many universities seemed to be searching for more open-platform systems with lower licence fees. Reasons for the move vary. Deakin University moved laterally from one proprietorial system, FirstClass, to another, WebCT Vista. Others moved to develop their own integrated solutions involving open-standards-based systems. These include RMIT's attempt to develop an integrated academic management system. Media releases in 2003 from universities indicated that many of those that in mid-2002 were using proprietary systems to deliver online courses were undertaking major online technology reviews. These universities included Charles Sturt University, the University of Southern Queensland, Adelaide University and the University of Tasmania.

Figure 2.3   Employer motivation for adopting e-learning

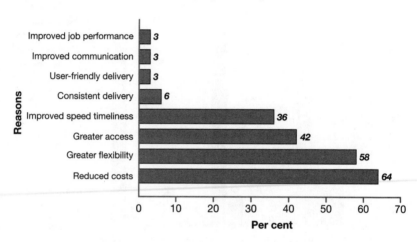

Extracted from Boulton 2002: 2

Vocational education and training sector

Governments and public education authorities have commissioned many reports on the use of e-learning in the vocational education and training (VET) sector in Australia.[3] Interestingly, though, these reports have not had a strong commercial focus. None examined the levels of activity across different e-learning modes (CD-ROM, computer-based or online) or within different industry sectors or market segments. Nor by mid-2003, despite reports commissioned to deal with the question, had NCVER sourced any definitive data on the overall size of the e-learning component in Australia and the South East Asia marketplace.

What the reports do reveal is the overall size and constitution of Australia's VET market. The apprenticeship and traineeship sector has experienced huge growth since 1995, with 136,000 training contracts growing to 334,370 by March 2002. The federal government's New Apprenticeships scheme accounts for half the number of individuals in training, whereas in 1995 apprenticeships made up only 10 per cent; and women constituted more than 35 per cent of all trainees and apprentices in 2002, against only 5 per cent in 1995. Growth is being led by areas outside the traditional manufacturing trades.

Throughout the VET sector, there is strong interest in the development of e-learning solutions. A large number of private e-learning providers are active in the field, and many VET institutions have developed learning materials and programs for corporate use. There have also been some large-scale collaborative initiatives to develop e-learning materials for use across the sector. In New South Wales, for example, the TAFE Commission has established a program called TAFE Connect, which in late 2001 was rolling out 450 e-learning modules for use in more than 400 VET courses in fifty-four fields of study.

Online lifelong learning and adult education sector

The advent of e-learning is breaking down the distinctions that have traditionally differentiated learning activities from work. Establishing the workplace as a place of learning aligns with a philosophical commitment to lifelong learning and adult education. In effect, e-learning is furthering the decline of the traditional 'educate-work-retire' life paradigm, and is accelerating progress towards fulfilling the needs and opportunities of individuals within a global knowledge economy.

Online lifelong learning and adult education, as precursors to the lifelong learning paradigm that appears likely to underpin the knowledge economy, provide significant measures of the status and progress of technological and educational reform. The Australian Bureau of Statistics reported that 26 per cent of the 3.9 million adults accessing the Internet at home in 2000 were doing so for educational purposes (ABS 2001). For the same period, NCVER estimated that between 1.1 million and 1.3 million people, around 8 per cent of Australia's adult population, were enrolled in some form of adult and community education (ACE) program, amounting to an estimated 25 million to 30 million hours of learning (NCVER 2000). More than 75 per cent of the students (with 80 per cent of all contact hours) received their training through non-TAFE organisations, including private providers and community organisations. More than 64 per cent of students were aged thirty-five and over, and nearly 70 per cent were female (NCVER 2000: 9).

Vocational programs accounted for almost half of all ACE students (49.8 per cent) and almost 70 per cent of program hours annually. These programs were designed to provide general training in literacy and communication skills, develop vocational skills and impart work-related knowledge. Figure 2.4 provides a breakdown of Australia's ACE market.

Adult and community education programs play an important role in individuals' continuing education. Through vocational training in particular, students come to acquire the skills necessary to enter or re-enter the workforce, to upgrade their skills or reorient them for a career change, or to gain a nationally recognised qualification (NCVER 2000: 7).

Figure 2.4   Participation in ACE in Australia by type, 2000

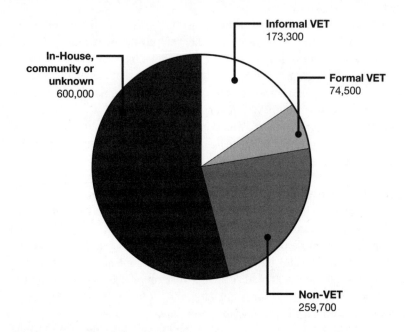

The Asia-Pacific market

Distance education is a key target segment for e-learning, and one in which Australian educational institutions have been extremely active. In 2002–03, the value of Australian education exports for students studying in Australia was A$4.17 billion, while offshore and distance education were estimated to have earned $1 billion (IDP, 17 September 2003 at http://www.idp.edu.au).

John Mitchell noted that trends in the Asian export market for e-learning differed from those in more mature markets (2000a). These were some of the factors he identified:

- There was a strong need for Australian providers to have on-site Asian partners, and to customise materials to suit local cultures.
- Some countries in the region had very small VET sectors, and greater prestige was attached to university qualifications rather than vocational training, which was seen as being for the poorer classes.
- At the same time, there was a growing need for training in vocational areas such as IT, business and language studies.
- Online learning was of greater value if combined with face-to-face support.
- Australian providers faced strong competition from Britain, Canada, Europe, the USA and other Asian suppliers, as well as from multinational companies.

Many students in the Asia–Pacific region are attracted by the perceived value of qualifications from universities in Australia, the USA, the UK and Canada. Higher education in Australia is of an international standard and has more overseas students per capita than in Britain, the USA or Canada. Most of Australia's overseas students come from the Asian region.

Australia has the opportunity to be a world leader in providing online education and training, particularly to Asia, but it must capitalise quickly on the first-mover advantage. The size and growth potential of education and training in the region is self-evident; numbers of students at universities in Asia are expected to grow from 28 million in 1998 to 45 million in 2010 (IDP 2001). The resources of bricks-and-mortar institutions in Australia will simply not be sufficient to meet increased demand.

The best solutions are to offer courses offshore (in students' home countries) and by distance education. There are significant limits on the number of overseas students who can come to Australia to study, as a result of language issues, high cost and entry prerequisites. A mix of offshore and onshore learning has been found to be highly effective in ensuring that overseas students have reached the appropriate educational standard before they enter Australia. Some components of courses are completed via distance and e-learning, or through partnerships with providers in the country of origin. The final course components are then completed at the host institution. This reduces time away from the country of origin and gives institutions greater confidence in the quality of the student's work. This blending of electronic with conventional learning is a sign of the growing trend toward viewing e-learning not as something that occurs in isolation, but as an effective complement or supplement to more conventional learning methods.

Conclusion

This chapter set out to reassess what constitutes e-learning by sidestepping a discipline-based or learning-activity viewpoint. To do this we examined the market view on what products and services constitute e-learning and the segments that purchase these services or products. What we see is that the absence of a clear definition of e-learning has precluded multiple market analysis around the globe to consistently frame what constitutes the e-learning market. Without substance for the term e-learning, the 'market' is delineated by inconsistent parameters and very broad descriptors of what technologies, content or services are e-learning specific.

While the definitional basis is once again obscuring application, this chapter confirms that significant transformations are occurring. The growth of e-learning is occurring against the background of far-reaching shifts, not only in information and communication technology but also in the organisation of people's learning and working lives. We can portray the current state of e-learning in terms of the interaction between a standard S-curve, representing the growth stages through which technology-induced change tends to progress (Christensen 1997: 44–7), and a 'hype curve' involving excessive expectations that are disappointed. The combined impact of these curves is depicted in Figure 2.5.

The S-curve illustrates how the first 'wave' of change in ICT and the Internet has spurred a second wave of change in e-learning. As the waves have progressed, they have begun to merge. The dot-coms that 'owned' the

Figure 2.5 The S-curve and hype curve of Internet-induced learning change

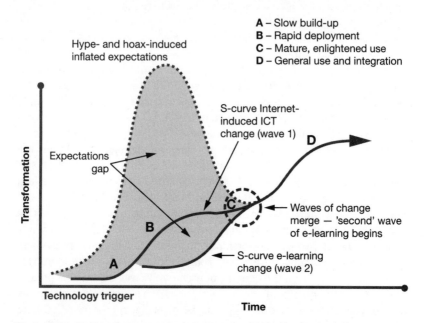

A – Slow build-up
B – Rapid deployment
C – Mature, enlightened use
D – General use and integration

first major wave of Internet and ICT deployment and shaped e-learning's first wave no longer have the field to themselves. E-learning has produced its own second wave of more mature approaches to learning, stimulated by educational practices and technologies that have focused on the individualisation of learning experiences, and increasingly driven by learner demand rather than 'top-down' programs or cost-cutting imperatives. In the process, the e-learning sector has also become more receptive to educators' expectations and ideas.

It seems almost inevitable that the second e-learning wave will augment the momentum spurred by the development of new Internet applications and the growth of a Web-literate user population. It is hard to predict what will happen when the waves of change combine. Earlier changes have had a ripple effect, generating a concatenation of breakthroughs that affect e-learning products, services and content. The changes to come will produce new effects, which may be in unexpected directions.

While one cannot see into the future, it seems highly likely that the combination of the waves will produce further convergence of technologies and markets. Change is occurring against the backdrop of convergence between the major ICT technologies that drive e-learning into traditional educational and domestic markets. Consider, for example, the market implications of advances such as Internet-connected electronic whiteboards in classrooms, and the convergence of computers and television technologies.

The convergence of the two waves may be marked by very rapid growth. E-learning in the twenty-first century is operating in a new environment, in that entire populations are learning to e-learn. New e-learning solutions now arrive in a marketplace in which most potential learners are familiar with core computer functions and the Internet. The resulting demand for on-time, flexible learning products is likely to reshape attitudes to all forms of learning and radically shift the markets for e-learning.

Principle 2

While global forecasts of the e-learning marketplace have suffered from a lack of comparability and reliability, e-learning seems poised for a major transformation driven less by providers' hype than by learner and educator demand.

[2] See for example the case studies commissioned for the Learning to E-learn project on Norway and New Zealand (Wilson 2003a and Wilson 2003b), the Australian transport and logistics sector (Whitby and Bowles 2003), and Pan-Canadian Health Informatics Collaboratory (Stieva 2003).

[3] These reports include Mitchell, J. G. 2000a, 2000b, 2000c, 2001; Mitchell & Wood 2001a, 2001b; TAFE Frontiers 2001; Brennan, McFadden & Law 2001; NCVER online 2002; Hill et al. 2003.

Promises and Pitfalls

The growth of investment in e-learning has led to the emergence of what could be described as an ecosystem of people and organisations, all interacting to develop, deploy and derive benefits from e-learning systems. Briefly, the ecosystem includes:

- organisations undertaking e-learning;
- technology providers seeking to develop and sell e-learning products;
- content providers seeking to develop and sell their own or other people's content;
- learning and human-resources professionals managing e-learning functions;
- users seeking to acquire and confirm capabilities; and
- instructional designers and those repurposing existing content to be used in e-learning.

At any point in time, the e-learning products available represent the ecosystem's best solution for meeting its members' individual and collective needs. This observation provides a context for evaluating the maturity of various e-learning technologies, by focusing on the gap between the needs the technology is currently meeting and the needs and opportunities that remain unsatisfied. It could be reasonably assumed that the technology will continue to progress rapidly for as long as the cost of developing new technologies is less than the value of unmet needs and opportunities. Technological developments, however, do not always move along a logical, linear pathway.

The e-learning ecosystem has not yet evolved to a point where a stable set of concepts and technologies has gained ascendancy. In a broader sense, just as ecosystems continue to change and evolve, so e-learning technologies are works in progress. E-learning lacks exemplars and stable descriptions of its domain, and this leads to uncertainty and competition between concepts. In short, there are inconsistencies in the explanations of what e-learning systems do and what they deliver. This presents a challenge to organisations evaluating their e-learning options. As Barron (2000: 1) describes it:

A frothy sea of competitors are jostling for dominance. Business and technology models are evolving at Internet speed. New products and capabilities are sprouting up weekly. Pity the training professional who must select a learning management system.

The research for this book suggests that the following issues can be seen as critical success factors for effective and efficient e-learning:

- continuity between the organisational needs and expectations and the e-learning strategy;
- continuity between individual learners' needs and preferences and the e-learning solution;
- continuity between the instructional designer's needs and preferences and the e-learning solution;
- continuity between educators' needs and preferences and the e-learning solution; and
- continuity between the expected return on investment (ROI) and actual performance.

The following sections outline the parameters of these issues in turn.

Organisational needs and expectations

Crowley (2002) identifies the following key drivers influencing businesses to consider e-learning technologies:

- **Cost:** E-learning can reduce costs of travel and lost productivity associated with face-to-face training, and can also reduce costs of content development because content can be reused and repurposed.
- **Scalability:** Networking or Internet capabilities permit content to be scaled up to larger numbers of learners, with multiple presentations of learning material to cater for differences between learners and variations in access to computers and networks.
- **Modularity:** The creation of e-learning content in short 'chunks' increases potential for flexible access.
- **Timeliness:** E-learning technologies can be used to enable learners to gain access on an as-needed, where-needed basis and deliver immediate knowledge required for performance-improvement needs.
- **Relevance:** Access methods and content can be customised and adapted to the learner's needs and context.
- **Accountability:** Evaluation can be enhanced by electronic mechanisms for providing feedback on the performance of learners, managers and e-learning developers.

Crowley translates these business drivers into the following design principles and implementation guidelines for e-learning architectures:

- **Open architecture:** Systems and architectures should comply with open rather than proprietary standards, thereby decreasing the costs of shifting technologies and migrating content to new or different e-learning systems.
- **Scalability:** While e-learning initiatives may commence with a small project, ultimately they can extend across the organisation to every

employee. Therefore an e-learning architecture must be designed with scalability in mind so that it is to some extent 'future proofed'.

- **Globality:** Content and technology should be portable globally.
- **Integration:** E-learning technologies must integrate with human resources, performance, finance and knowledge management reporting systems, while also being adaptable to changing business requirements and processes, technologies and vendor solutions.
- **Rapid and timely availability:** It must be possible to implement relatively straightforward information architecture in the short term and add more sophisticated systems over time.

In the late 1990s and early 2000s, when the growth of investment in electronic commerce (e-commerce) and information technology (IT) raised the corporate profile of e-learning, many corporations approached it with high expectations. Table 3.1 indicates some of the advantages e-learning promised.

Table 3.1   Early comparison of learning delivery methods by Bancorp Piper Jaffray

Criteria	E-learning	Instructor-led training	CD-ROM
Hardware and software requirements	◕	●	◑
Access to courses	●	○	◕
Instructor interaction	◕	●	○
Cost	●	◕	◑
Dynamic and fresh content (version control)	●	◑	◕
Scalability	●	◕	◑
Interactivity with other learners	◔	●	○
Immediate access to course updates	●	○	○
Performance/results tracking	●	◑	◕
Consistency (instructor and formats)	●	◑	●
Retention	●	◕	◑
Flexibility to learner (time etc.)	●	◑	●
Quality of content	◕	●	◑
Personalisation	●	○	◕

● = optimal

Source: Peterson, Marostica & Callahan 1999: 17. Reproduced with permission

Early investors were excited about the advantages e-learning promised over CD-ROM and instructor-led training, but definitional traps were being laid for subsequent studies. This can be seen from the categories used in Table 3.1, which seem to suggest that e-learning excludes CD-ROM and instructor-led training. If it does not, the distinction between delivery methods becomes less clear-cut. The confusion can be traced to the lack of definitional rigor discussed in Chapter 1. E-learning here is equated with 'pure' web-based training. This narrow definition influenced data collection and raised unrealistic expectations that learning could be provided without ongoing instructor involvement.

Businesses typically want education and training to have an immediate, tangible benefit. They are more likely to engage in learning when (Bowles 2002c: 26):

- it is completed in the workplace, and preferably supported by face-to-face, one-to-one coaching by an expert;
- online content, tools and resources can be accessed on demand to augment workplace coaching;
- learning is promoted as offering better performance, not just a pathway to qualifications;
- programs are learner-led, not facilitator-driven;
- sessions are tied to real outcomes and performance improvement;
- learning is available anywhere, at any time; and
- learning adds value to the learner's context and situation.

There have been some interesting Australian studies of what motivates business to adopt e-commerce and training in information and communication technology (ICT). A report in 2001 by the Victorian SkillsNet Association Cooperative (SNAC), e-Barriers, e-Benefits and e-Business, found that small and medium-sized enterprises (SMEs) in Victoria would adopt e-learning or e-business only if it offered full identification of implementation costs, enhanced competitive positioning, gross profit gains, reduced operating expenses and increased management effectiveness (McNicol Williams 2001, vol. 1: 15–18). The report also identified some major areas of business concern about e-learning:

- managers' ability to assess value for money and effectiveness of competing external service providers, including whether to opt for major suppliers or 'showcase examples' from small providers;
- professional support requirements;
- security;
- infrastructure problems, such as poor connectivity, low bandwidth and lack of appropriate hardware; and
- deficiencies in existing employee and management skills.

More recent studies have isolated other worrisome issues affecting smaller businesses in this field (Castleman & Cavill 2002: 43; Bowles 2002a: 7–9; Hall, Buchanan & Considine 2002; Kilpatrick & Bound 2003, vol. 1: 17, 21). These issues include:

- SMEs often lack the skill base to engage in e-learning.
- The adoption of e-learning has been hampered by the lack of access to 'credible' sources of advice on its commercial advantages or disadvantages.

- Many SMEs lack hardware and 'back-end' data-capture systems to evaluate the contribution of e-learning.
- Many SMEs view learning simply as a means of remedying competency gaps and expect short-term, tangible improvements.
- SMEs with limited time and infrastructure may have e-learning programs designed to accommodate these constraints, but ultimately their limited resources will frustrate the effective implementation of e-learning and e-commerce.
- Business training for SMEs has to be 'mass-customised' because specific enterprise requirements cannot be fitted into traditional occupational disciplines or 'courses'.
- Businesses prefer to use expert coaches or mentors who can assist individual employees or businesses as required, irrespective of the mode of delivery.
- SMEs prefer to work with training providers who understand their specific sectors, irrespective of the mode of learning delivery. In order of preference, they opt for professional and industry associations; local business advisers; federal, state and local government; registered training organisations; and finally contract service providers.

Taken together, these problems suggest that the adoption of e-learning in the small- and medium-sized business sector faces considerable obstacles, not least from SMEs' rather unsophisticated expectations of the outcomes of training in general.

Individual learners' needs and preferences

In the New Economy, learning is a powerful source of competitive advantage for individuals. There is particular value in acquiring, expanding and rapidly deploying knowledge assets that can improve performance. This places a premium on learning that is closely targeted and cost-effective.

Several authors have investigated the potential benefits that individuals look for in e-learning. Their findings can be summarised as follows (Block & Dobell 1999: 8, 44; Close et al. 2000: 12; CTAL 2001: 14–15):

Personal control: Individual learners can take responsibility for the pace and mode of their learning, be it instructor-led, self-paced, asynchronous or synchronous collaborative learning.

Availability: Individuals can access learning as required, independent of set times and locations, making it possible for adult learners to combine learning with work and family commitments. Key resources can be archived for on-demand access. A high level of availability is also vital to individuals and organisations seeking to keep pace with rapid change and shorter product cycles.

Personalisation: Personal needs and preferences can better shape learning processes and outcomes. Systems can draw on participants' previous records and on resource databases to generate individual education programs, so that the training takes each person's prior learning into account. Content databases can be used to track learners' previous courses, how well they did, what their job descriptions are, and which skills and what knowledge they most need. This approach is not always to be encouraged, but it does help to focus curriculum on skill gaps, saving learners and organisations time and money.

Interactivity: Interactive media can provide an active learning experience and avoid the linear learning dictated by textbooks and static text. Instructional media with rich content and design can offer problem-centred, scenario-based learning experiences, and collaboration can be encouraged through team projects, interactive chat and electronic discussion forums. Content and learning design can also be enriched by the use of audio and video.

Richness of content: Learners can choose between products by accessing a large bank of resources through the Internet host, while advisers can mix and match courseware to fit specific needs. Learners can preview presentations of different courses or access specific information swiftly.

Hands-on instruction: Instant messaging, chat rooms, discussion boards, electronic blackboards and emails allow participants to share information and collaborate in real-world tasks while permitting rapid information retrieval and review.

Rapid access to up-to-date information: The rapid rate of change in learning products and resources creates a challenge for conventional libraries. However, if an updated version of each product is kept on a host, users get instantaneous access to current information.

Improved privacy and anonymity: Some learners who are inhibited in a classroom setting may engage more freely online.

Improved certification and testing: Assessment and recording of results can lead to formal qualifications or certification by third parties. Individuals can also choose to maintain a 'skills' passport that can be securely distributed to employers, learning providers and others.

Various national reports have investigated the factors that encourage students in Australia to engage in structured vocational education and training (VET). These factors include:

- The courses offer clarity of assessment regimes and expectations.
- Students feel they need to achieve higher levels of proficiency.
- VET offers new pathways from schooling to further learning or careers.
- VET learning can lead to other qualifications such as school-leaving certificates and university entrance.
- Teaching staff are competent and have relevant experience.
- Providers have industry recognition.
- Content and processes take into account the fact that some entrants need assistance with literacy and numeracy.
- Access to teaching staff permits self-paced learning.

Clearly, learners tend to view continuing education in terms of their personal career and skills development. Significantly, this gives them a different perspective from teachers, employers and content providers.

In a study by Whiteman (2000), participants reported that the experience of e-learning was much more personalised and interactive than they had expected it to be. Hum and Ladouceur (2001) found that learners also valued the reduction of travel time and costs, and were pleased to have become familiar with the Internet, a skill they believed would help them throughout their careers.

Different user groups have various reasons for engaging in e-learning, and their priorities are often different from those of investors and educators. In a study of the use of e-learning in tertiary education, Williams (2001) noted that facilitators and students differed markedly in their perception and evaluation of e-learning, and students often dismissed advantages that were trumpeted by academics. Williams found that many students felt disfranchised by online options because they believed teachers were adding extra work online and did not appreciate the students' level of frustration over difficulties in accessing the network. Some also felt that teachers did not consider the cost of appropriate bandwidth and hardware, or other costs related to document sourcing and printing, which had been shifted to the student.

It would be unwise to ignore the existence of barriers to e-learning. Technology is still an important element. Volery and Lord (2000) identified the following technology issues:

- reliability of hardware;
- quality of software;
- richness of medium, including having both synchronous and asynchronous characteristics and a variety of elements (such as text, graphics, videos);
- convenience of access for students;
- speed of document exchange; and
- interface design, including ease of use and navigation, appropriate cognitive load, pleasing aesthetics and overall functionality.

Not all people with an Internet connection can or will access e-learning. Many potential users simply lack the means to access e-learning due to infrastructural or technological limitations. Instructors too may face technological barriers. Hum and Ladouceur (2001: 7–8) list the immediate barriers individuals have to overcome:

- The purchase of costly new equipment may be required.
- Technical difficulties may hamper students' and instructors' progress.
- Gaps in computer knowledge may require training in computer basics.
- Use of telephone lines and Internet providers may lead to high fees.
- The reliability of some Internet-based research material, and the issue of copyright, was questionable.
- Technological limitations, bandwidth and speed may not support the desired level of interaction, for example the use of multimedia.

Instructional designers' needs and preferences

Different e-learning technologies and approaches contribute differently to learning retention. Nevertheless, exciting and effective e-learning starts with good instructional design. Some studies suggest that without effective design, e-learning can be dull for those accustomed to classroom-based learning (Allen 2002: 6).

Six main design issues are highlighted in various reports on e-learning (see Falk, Grady, Ruscoe & Wallace 2003: 8–9). The first is that it is essential to build in opportunities for *social interaction*. In face-to-face learning, teachers and students can interact easily in a familiar context, but in e-learning, as Crawford points out, opportunities for interaction must be deliberately built into the process to 'simulate the learning community involvement that is lacking in the virtual environment' (2001: 69). NCVER online (2002) also found that students place a high value on opportunities to communicate and interact with teachers and other students through e-learning.

The second aspect concerns the nature of *pedagogy*. As Jefferies and Hussain (1998) found, student-centred e-learning environments are preferable to teacher-centred ones. Similarly, learning environments where learners are actively and collaboratively engaged are preferable to those that are conduit-like and individualistic.

The third matter concerns the *locus of control*. McFadzean (2001), for example, claims that virtual classrooms need to be designed to allow learners to take control of their own learning in a hands-on, experiential and collaborative manner.

The fourth aspect relates to the *provision of information to learners*. In face-to-face instruction, information can be imparted in an ad hoc way, but remote interaction can be daunting unless requirements are formally spelt out and communicated to students in advance. In a survey of students' expectations of e-learning, Choy, McNickle and Clayton (2002: 27–42) found that students placed very strong emphasis on the need for information, including:

- detailed information about courses, assessment requirements and enrolment procedures;
- security of personal details on the institution's database;
- helpful and timely feedback from teachers;
- availability of a variety of methods of communication with teachers, including email, online chat and face to face; and
- instructions on how to get help with computing problems.

These factors are reinforced by other international studies, including a case study specifically commissioned for this project (Gale 2003). Where e-learning is conducted entirely through remote contact, it has been shown that learners may need to be provided with support in installing software and learning to manipulate the computer interface. All these activities require that host institutions provide additional resources.

The fifth issue relates to *flexibility and convenience*. According to NCVER online (2002), 'what learners value particularly about online delivery is . . . the flexibility and freedom it offers; that is, learning that is "just in time, just enough and just for me"'. The stresses and strains of living and working in the twenty-first century mean that learners place a high value on learning what they need, when they need it and as they want it.

Of particular interest in this context is a study by Cooke and Veach (1997) drawing on Central Queensland University experiences in distance education. They assert that paper-based learning materials can actually limit learning. Learners are very selective in how they use their time, and many students excise 80 per cent or more of the reading material supplied to them. Cooke and Veach suggest that students reach a psychological threshold of 'too much' when they are presented with a multi-kilogram package of study materials in addition to prescribed texts. Gale (2003: 2) reports that learners want diversity but not quantity in their readings. The relevance of the material to learners' pre-existing 'world views' and personal development pathways is critical, especially where significant cultural differences exist (Wallace, Grady & Falk 2003: 3). E-learning can make learners' selection processes far easier and less guilt-ridden than traditional distance education methods. In a study of 45 final-year honours students in computing at a UK university, Jefferies and Hussain (1998) discovered that students cited the primary advantages of e-learning as being the ability to locate relevant material easily and the ease of communicating with fellow learners by email.

The sixth and final issue relates to the question: *How much e-learning is enough?* Jefferies and Hussain found that 72 per cent of students surveyed wanted less than 20 per cent of their course to involve e-learning, with just 2 per cent of students desiring full Internet delivery. This gives support to the practice of offering 'blended' modes of delivery, as discussed later in this chapter.

Educators' needs and preferences

In the early years of e-learning activity, educational practitioners issued strong warnings about barriers to moving education and training online. In particular, they pointed out that online learning would not resolve the problems associated with distance education. Educators stressed that more radical reforms to how students learn and how teachers interact with students was required (Hara & Kling 2000). They were especially concerned about:

- how students would engage in meaningful education and training in an online environment;
- the challenges in creating meaningful content and learning environments via the Internet;
- the need for investment in facilities and technologies to establish courses and support online learning;
- the implications for workloads when teachers are expected to provide support to students as required, when required;
- the balance and effectiveness of synchronous versus asynchronous learning; and
- overall learner and instructor satisfaction with the online environment, course administration and technologies.

Kathawala, Abdou and Elmuti (2002), who researched e-learning delivery of MBA programs, identified the following difficulties confronted by instructors:

- the time required to learn the technology;
- frustration when computers malfunction;
- long lead times in preparation;
- the time required to communicate in writing with students;
- encroachment on staff research time;

- lack of set-up funding; and
- the monetary costs of maintaining a home office.

On the other hand, time pressures are not new to staff who have experience in distance education. Cooke and Veach pointed out that in the mid-1990s the average lead time required for production of distance education material at their university had increased from one semester to more than two semesters per unit (1997: 204). They saw e-learning delivery as a means of decreasing these pressures.

Educators' early criticisms of online learning centred on its failure to engage students in meaningful exchanges, its high upfront investment for content development and facilitator training, and the seemingly poor results in terms of student retention — reports of drop-out rates exceeding 70 per cent in purely online learning were not uncommon (Bonk & Cummings 1998; Johnson et al. 1999; Hara & Kling 2000: 559; Simmons 2000).

More important, perhaps, are educators' instructional concerns. McFadzean and McKenzie (2002) express the widely held view that a good learning situation does not simply deliver pre-formed knowledge in an assembly-line manner. Rather, learners gain assistance to 'put flesh on skeletal concepts' through conversation, practical activity, negotiation and collaboration with others (see also Wallace et al. 2003). This has clear implications for pre-planning, support and post-course follow-up. With this in mind, McFadzean and McKenzie (2002: 474) state that the instructor must be attentive to:
- the learning tasks, procedures and structure of the learning process;
- development of teamwork among participants;
- team dynamics;
- participants' emotions and feelings; and
- participants' sense of trust.

One might add that this is what all facilitators do, regardless of the method of delivery. The point is that e-learning delivery is not merely a matter of technology — teaching and learning are at the heart of it.

An important question is who develops the online educators' and trainers' skills. Leu (2001) makes it clear that the instructor's role in orchestrating learning contexts becomes more complex with e-learning delivery, and that because of this there is a need for ongoing professional development for teachers and facilitators. Organisations of education providers also need to change if educators are to value the new instructional imperatives.

There is specific data about factors that affect teachers' abilities to provide flexible online VET. These factors include:
- the capacity to access and use technology;
- flexibility of delivery structures and timetables;
- availability of physical resources — especially financial, human and technological assets;
- interoperability of technologies, language and content between teachers, students, enterprises and third-party providers;

- the capacity of students to move between courses and organisations and progress to the next level of qualification (for example, the *IT Training Package ICA99 Review* (Bowles 2002b: 94) notes the Australian-wide difficulties experienced when students move from one sector to another's programs, such as moving from the school system into the vocational system); and
- availability of staff with competencies necessary to support self-directed e-learning, assess learners' skills and knowledge, devise and supervise programs focused on work-based competencies, engage in learning communities across multiple workplaces, provide customised learning resources within revenue constraints, understand the pedagogies related to various delivery modes and identify indicators of learning effectiveness.

As the list of requirements under the last point suggests, the skills necessary for effective delivery in an electronic environment are considerably broader than those involved in teaching by traditional means. Kathawala et al. (2002) have suggested that acquiring these skills would ultimately benefit facilitators in a number of ways. E-learning would help them to keep up with new educational methods and enhance their own computer literacy and it would offer staff greater employment security and the flexibility of being able to work from home.

Unfortunately, the implementation of e-learning has tended to focus on removing the more expensive forms of skills development and assessment processes. This focus has caused numerous problems, including:
- inconsistency in performance;
- variations in how individuals achieve performance;
- difficulty developing instruments to assess outcomes to an agreed standard across different learning modes;
- design of e-learning assessment tools narrowly based on measuring task competence rather than the acquisition of underpinning knowledge; and
- competing priorities between educators' views of learning outcomes and the performance requirements of organisations seeking to promote immediate task competence.

Assessment is a crucial issue. There seems to be a general belief that assessment tools for e-learning can be framed for technical skills performance or common knowledge and understanding, but not both. Equally, improved methods of assessing skills and knowledge through e-learning have been buried in the general debate. As the nature of work evolves, the business imperative to develop knowledge that underpins applied performance cannot be underestimated, but the assessment of e-learning may not always require demonstration in the physical world.

It is certainly true that many learning outcomes cannot be evidenced through e-learning and online assessment alone. That is why the blending of classroom and online learning has advanced so quickly through the 'connected' world.

Concerns about return on investment

The fifth of the critical success factors for e-learning noted at the beginning of this chapter is continuity between business expectations of ROI and actual performance. Many corporations have been disappointed in their initial hopes for e-learning. In one Australian regional project focused on resolving problems with flexible and online learning, studies of core customer groups revealed that several factors were repeatedly reported as key issues in e-learning implementation (Bowles 2002d: 18–20). The top five issues for business, government and educational users were as follows:

Employer/business users
- Technology of access (interoperability)
- Ease of access (price, technology and especially bandwidth issues)
- Cultural appropriateness (language, style and content relevance)
- Levels of interaction
- Linkages of learning to formal recognition that is portable and internationally recognised.

Government users
- Ease of access (price, technology and especially bandwidth issues)
- Technology of access (interoperability)
- Firewalls/security
- Branding (qualifications/content provider and ability to self-brand/ corporate university model)
- Overall ROI.

Educational users (schools, VET and university)
- Ease of translating hard content across to the Internet-based learning environment
- Ease of access (price, technology and especially bandwidth issues)
- Technology of access (interoperability)
- Levels of support by technology vendor
- Ease of navigation and assessment.

As these results make clear, the implementation of e-learning has been less than straightforward. Research suggests, however, that the problem has been partly a matter of organisations' having excessively high expectations and narrow procedures for evaluating e-learning, encouraged perhaps by the exaggerated claims of e-learning service providers. As Chapter 12 will discuss, more sophisticated techniques are called for if we are to evaluate the full impact of e-learning on organisations' capacity and effectiveness.

In the interim, e-learning practices continue to evolve rapidly. One of the most significant developments has been the rise of 'blended' learning strategies, which implicitly acknowledge the problems that have been encountered in early attempts to implement pure online instruction.

Blended learning

Blended (or hybrid) learning, as its name suggests, combines e-learning with other forms of delivery, such as physical, instructor-led, electronic, learner-directed. As Bielawski and Metcalf describe it, this involves 'blending classroom, asynchronous and synchronous e-learning, and on-the-job training' (2003: 71). Blended e-learning most commonly involves using computer-based instruction or online programs to support instructor-led, face-to-face training. It may involve providing content and learning resources online, using email, bulletin boards and chat rooms for interchange between students and facilitators, or even streaming video or audio presentations.

As Volery and Lord (2000: 216) suggest, blending online learning and assessment with classroom activities can merge the strengths of education and training to address the business imperatives to:

- expand access and participation;
- alleviate constraints imposed by reliance on bricks-and-mortar establishments;
- develop employees who can apply core skills to changing customer needs;
- offer a wider range of courses, content and assessment events;
- transfer common knowledge or generic competencies for new recruits or young people entering employment;
- promote lifelong learning for all staff in their own time; and
- permit rapid customisation of teaching practices and content.

The popularity of blended learning constitutes a tacit recognition that individuals and organisations often adopt e-learning gradually. Some organisations incrementally replace classroom-based learning or single-platform applications with more advanced electronic learning components. Others use e-learning to augment existing approaches so as to accommodate diverse learning styles, learning types, or means of delivery and assessment. Others adopt e-learning in a piecemeal way to limit costs and perceived risks, such as fear of failure, uncertainty about effectiveness or concerns about the stability of the technology, whether in terms of its obsolescence or its ability to integrate with existing infrastructure.

Voci and Young propose that blended learning combines 'the advantages of two learning modalities' (2001: 157). When classroom instruction is combined with self-paced instruction via the Internet, for example, the face-to-face contact makes for easy social interaction and allows for instant feedback. Meanwhile, web-based, self-paced learning offers consistency of content and delivery, respects differences in learning styles and pace, and offers flexibility and convenience: there are no waiting lists, there is no need for a student to postpone learning until a class is offered, and there is no time gap between when a student is motivated to learn and when learning takes place. Voci and Young conclude:

> The effect of these combined e-learning experiences with stand up instruction is potent; participants praise the curriculum in final programme evaluations, citing the sense of heightened teamwork and camaraderie. The blended

learning approach helps to create a shared understanding of concepts important to the learning culture and provide opportunities to reinforce them in a live classroom setting. Leveraging the convenience and accessibility of online components with traditional classroom instruction also expands the curriculum without increasing programme completion time (2001: 161).

Blended learning is also popular with instructional designers. Some learning objectives are much easier to achieve when supported by follow-up e-learning after an initial face-to-face session. Conversely, initial face-to-face sessions have been shown to be helpful for orientation or induction; students appreciate having the opportunity to meet peers and instructors and to familiarise themselves with the technology before having to concentrate on the online content/course material itself. This was noted in the several case studies commissioned for the Learning to E-learn project to validate research outcomes (Wallace et al. 2003).

Incorporating electronic technologies with traditional classroom methods seems to assist instructional designers and instructors to:

- balance learning to cover required attitudinal, cognitive and psychomotor outcomes;
- break learning into more effective sequences or pathways;
- deal with class size and resource limitations;
- overcome temporal and spatial constraints on collaboration;
- increase opportunities for offering experiences that translate into the real workplace;
- enhance the effectiveness of behavioural change through improved content (i.e. audio, visual, text, web-based tools, mobile applications such as SMS);
- develop innovative ways to assess emotional quotient (EQ) outcomes away from the classroom to see if behavioural change has been locked in;
- rapidly profile group and organisational EQ levels by analysing individual EQ surveys; and
- permit evaluation of individual and collective learning through use of more effective feedback and assessment mechanisms.

Blended learning can take many forms. In one study, for example, a provider teaching emotional intelligence online to work-based leaders developed a very effective procedure using short message service (SMS) assessment interventions (Bowles 2003a).

As Figure 3.1 indicates, blended e-learning today is likely to involve a mixture of e-learning technologies. Blending can also be applied to the reporting systems that evaluate outcomes and report on their business impact (Bielawski & Metcalf 2003: 20, 141). The functions and parameters of e-learning will continue to evolve as it is deployed to support organisational and societal change, and as e-learning technologies themselves evolve.

Conclusion

This chapter has outlined some of the recurring concerns expressed by learners, instructors and organisations involved in the development of e-learning. It is clear that these concerns need to be taken seriously. If organisations implement e-learning programs that, for example, impose heavy costs on participants (both as instructors/facilitators and students) or expect them to make the transition to e-learning unaided, they risk discrediting e-learning in the longer term.

Figure 3.1   Blending structured e-learning

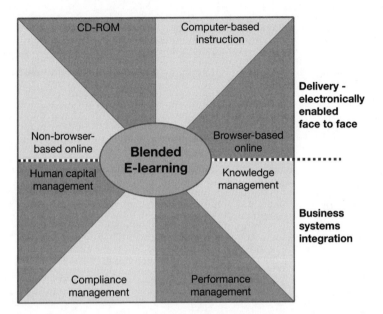

In the corporate arena, e-learning implementation is now progressing to a level marked by rapid deployment and a more mature, reflective understanding of what it requires and what it has to offer. This transition marks a second wave of e-learning implementation that is just beginning, as discussed in Chapter 2. At the same time, this new stage of development has required many organisations to modify their early expectations that existing training and education functions would be sidelined or superseded by 'pure' e-learning. The 'expectation gap' between promise and performance has compelled a re-evaluation of what e-learning entails and of how it relates to other modes of transmitting information and knowledge.

Principle 3

The effective and efficient implementation of e-learning relies on complex interactions between the needs and expectations of learners, facilitators and organisations, all of which must be understood in order to maximise systems-wide competitive outcomes.

From Comptetence to Capabilities

A major issue for organisations embarking on an e-learning strategy is the lack of consensus on how best to evaluate the effectiveness of particular learning interventions. At the same time, organisations increasingly look to e-learning to deliver outcomes that go beyond training. In the New Economy, employees' skills, knowledge and motivation have economic value because they enhance an organisation's performance and ability to adapt to change. In this context, the assessment of value has refocused on people, as they constitute the organisation's *human capital*. To quote Savage, the 'basis of wealth is shifting from that which is "possessed as a commodity" to the value of human capability' (1996: 12). E-learning has progressed from simply delivering learning outcomes to encompassing first knowledge management and now human capital management. E-learning must therefore be evaluated not only for its effects on individuals in various occupations and locations, but also for its contribution to the knowledge or intellectual capital value of an organisation.

A common 'currency' is needed to judge the success of e-learning and gauge its contribution to knowledge capital. Capability can provide that common currency. This chapter sets out the conceptual frameworks used to describe what is learnt and how it is translated into performance outcomes. The following chapters will address the factors that define the role of learning in an organisation's current performance and long-term strategic success.

The key point to be made here is that an employee's effectiveness cannot be determined solely by focusing on the development of task competencies, but requires learning activities supported by applied tools and a knowledge base that can integrate the individual's development with that of the organisation.

Competency-based models

When considering options for workplace-based learning, managers often begin from the desire to provide staff with the competencies they need to perform their work effectively. The essential question that confronts them is the level of competency required. We can distinguish between different levels of task-based competence:

- Unconscious incompetence: obliviousness to performance requirements that are far beyond the employee's work standards;
- Conscious incompetence: awareness of task and performance requirements but inability to achieve them;
- Conscious competence: awareness of standards and ability to achieve them with concentration, integrating most of the required skills, knowledge and behaviours but still requiring supervision and support in some conditions; and
- Mastery, unconscious competence: the ability to integrate all required skills, knowledge and behaviours consistently without full concentration. (This is where tacit knowledge gained from experience builds to produce excellent performance.)

While it is possible to teach competencies to the point of proficiency or conscious competence, mastery arises out of situated experience in applying skills and interacting with others.

Research into competence has undergone many evolutions since the early 1960s. The pursuit of competence has been seen as offering a behavioural form of pedagogy, a means of structuring work, and a basis for organisations to achieve competitiveness; it has also been the foundation for national vocational education and training (VET) systems.

In the corporate sphere, competency-based approaches to training, assessment and recruitment have been popular since the early 1970s. They remain prevalent today, partly as a result of the emergence of formal, national strategies to implement competency-based systems. In the mid-1980s, England and Wales started what became codified into the National Vocational Qualifications (NVQs) system. New Zealand and Australia followed suit between 1989 and 1992, establishing blueprints for VET based on competency standards. In the USA, the same ideas inspired the Secretary's Commission on Achieving Necessary Skills and the National Skills Standards (see http://wdr.doleta.gov/SCANS/).

In some cases the intention was simply to identify a small number of core or key competencies that should be achieved by all entrants into the labour market. Other proponents of competency were more ambitious, promoting it as a framework for reforming education, vocational training and industrial productivity. Many national advances were made in the UK, New Zealand and Australia by tying competency development to qualifications, workforce mobility, industrial reform and economic growth. Subsequently, other countries have embraced a competency approach as the basis of national training reforms. One case study commissioned by the Learning to E-learn project examined how Norway had married the competency reform with a national approach to e-learning under what is known as the NKN initiative (Wilson 2003a).

A major attraction of competency-based approaches to training and human resources is that they set a defined standard for both learning and performance outcomes, independent of the person, job or situation. Once a standard of competence has been set, it becomes a consistent basis for assessment. This clarifies what individuals need to know, and also permits greater mobility between jobs, locations and competency-based courses.

Critics, however, have pointed out that the competency-based approach has its origins in behaviourist theory, which focuses on the passive acquisition of specific, limited skills. Some have described competency as reductionist, narrow and inflexible, a 'one-size-fits-all' approach (Chappell 1996). It has also been criticised for failing to address attributes other than task-based skills (Bowles & Graham 1994b: 12). Nevertheless, competency-based approaches have become embedded in national, industry and organisational policies for the management of learning, performance and knowledge.

Limits of a competency approach

Most analyses of competencies draw on theoretical constructs developed by the earliest writers in the field, notably the early works by Argyris (1962) and Boyatzis (1982). The latter is of particular interest here because it betrays many of the shortcomings of a competency-based approach.

Boyatzis was specifically interested in competency-based approaches to management training, education and development. In simple terms, he saw effective performance as depending on three factors: job demands, organisational environment and individual competence (1982: 13). Unlike earlier theorists such as Mintzberg, who emphasised the different ways managers performed specific work (1973: 102–3), Boyatzis sought to *integrate* these factors into a *common* set of performance requirements.

Boyatzis sought to establish the characteristics of a universal concept of 'individual competence' that enabled managers to perform successfully (1982: 20). He examined the groupings of specific sets of competencies under different functions in an attempt to identify common or core management clusters. To assist differentiation, jobs were broadly grouped into entry, middle and executive level (1982: 217, 219, 222). Boyatzis identified clusters of management competencies as including:

- setting of goals and actions;
- leadership;
- human-resources management;
- supervision of subordinates;
- focus on others; and
- specialised knowledge.

The last category became a catchall for specific management competencies that did not fall into the other clusters. Under each cluster, Boyatzis suggested, one could define the tasks of a specific manager at a particular level of performance (1982: 215, 242).

This approach, however, omitted the following important considerations:

- The emphasis on generic functions and clusters of competencies had limited ability to explain or encompass variations found in many specific situations.
- The analysis did not differentiate between 'functional' skills and those that relate to 'roles'.

- The model concentrated on the individual's socio-psychological characteristics, traits, motives and generic skills rather than on knowledge.
- Although there was heavy emphasis on conscious and unconscious behaviours inherent in a manager's functioning, the model did not define what these behaviours were.

Later authors have attempted to accommodate some of these objections by emphasising the need for specific competencies that will contribute to the competitiveness of an organisation and its workforce (Prahalad & Hamel 1990: 79; Sanchez & Heene 1997: 5–6; Allee 1997: 21). Ultimately, however, competency-based models face a real-world dilemma: competitiveness cannot be generated from skills and knowledge that are readily available to anyone in the marketplace.

Defining capabilities

The movement to advance competencies was driven by the need to improve work processes, especially in the manufacturing sector. In the New Economy, however, organisations require more than process skills to remain competitive and adapt to change. In this situation, we need a broader measure of the factors that contribute to performance if we are to assess the 'bottom-line' value of knowledge to organisations.

This is where the concept of capabilities is useful. Capabilities define the range of performance that is possible, the potential capacity to perform. When individuals interact in teams, organisations and community groups, the context determines which capabilities an individual can apply to any given situation. The definition of capabilities therefore needs to encompass the human factors that shape performance capacity now and in the future.

In 1999, Bowles presented a framework for defining the variables associated with competency and capability based on work with major Australian corporations from 1993 to 1998. This framework integrates a competency-based approach to learning and performance with an effort to analyse outcomes by accounting for knowledge, or what is now most commonly referred to as intellectual capital (Bowles 1999: 52).

The framework begins by defining competence as the *knowledge* and *skills* that can be identified in an individual's performance:

Competence = Skills + Knowledge

But skills and knowledge related to task performance are only one aspect of overall organisational performance. Having the skills to perform does not guarantee successful deployment of those skills. Equally, a competency focus tends to emphasise skills and knowledge that are codified or explicit, while ignoring the bulk of a workforce's knowledge, which is uncodified or tacit. A further aspect, identity, was therefore added:

Identity = Cultural values or beliefs + Roles + Behaviours or traits

To establish the current performance capability in a given context, we must also take identity factors into account. The current performance capability therefore can be defined as:

$$\text{Capability} = \text{Competence} + \text{Identity}$$

Competence is the sum of skills and knowledge, and *identity* is the sum of cultural attributes, roles and behaviours. The concept of identity encompasses both an individual's inner sense of self and his or her relationship with the broader social and cultural environment. To understand the importance of identity in an organisational context, we must first investigate each of these dimensions.

Identity, meaning and belief

Fundamentally, *identity* is the source of meaning for individuals (Castells 1997: 6; 'conversation' with Rhonda Reger on organisational identity reported in Whetten & Godfrey 1998: 163). In the early 1990s, social researchers and management theorists began to examine identity in earnest, both for its contribution to individual consciousness and for its ability to encompass the human elements involved in individual and organisational performance (Dierickx & Cool 1989; Dutton & Dukerich 1991; Giddens 1991; Straw & Sutton 1993; Dutton, Dukerich & Harquail 1994). Several of their findings are relevant here:

- Many resources typically associated with individual or organisational performance are not 'tangible' or easy to transfer.
- People define themselves through their work.
- Many organisations do not value or manage the tacit beliefs and attributes of their employees, including individuals' motivation, commitment and identification with organisational goals.
- Organisations are not acknowledging how their collective identities are being shaped by individuals and their interactions.

In other words, individuals derive meaning from their roles at work, while organisations' identities are influenced by individual interactions both within and outside the organisational domain.

Identity is forged not only by the need to 'belong', but also by the ways in which people differentiate themselves from others. The crucial questions are 'who am I?' and 'who are we?' So identity is both a construct defining the characteristics of the 'self' and a basis for action, which in turn affirms and sustains a sense of identity (Gioia 1998: 19). *Meaning*, on the other hand, is more about the individual's 'symbolic identification' with the purpose of the action (Castells 1997: 7).

Individuals are more likely to identify with an organisation if they have a sense of its purpose, its traditions and the qualities they see as making it unique (Gioia 1998: 21). They may also identify with the organisation's core symbols and public persona. Their needs and expectations may become aligned with those of the organisation as it offers a pathway for them to fulfil their personal goals. Employees may respond to the reinforcement and recognition they receive as their relationship with the organisation evolves, and they may come to feel that the organisation endorses and validates their individual aims and aspirations (Castells 1997: 22; Gioia 1998: 17–33; Kim 2000: 317–19).

The reverse may also occur. Dis-identification takes place when organisational purposes, expectations and symbols do not align with employees' personal needs and aims. Individually or collectively, employees may rebuff the organisation's sense of meaning, consolidating an oppositional sense of identity. As new information flows emerge outside the purview of authority, people disaffiliate themselves from any sense of institutional identity. Old identities can be deconstructed and new ones generated (Castells 1997: 13).

Individuals engage with organisations through an already formed inner sense of identity, which may be more constant and enduring than the organisational identity. For instance, an individual may be influenced by deeply embedded cultural factors of language, belief and ethnicity. When they first relate to an organisation, its identity may be quite foreign to them, as its values and meanings may be difficult to perceive from outside.

How then is it possible to overcome these barriers and encourage individuals and groups to align with and reinforce an organisation's identity? The following sections will address this question by examining the social aspects of organisational identity.

Rediscovering the importance of organisational identity

The social rather than individual aspects of organisational identity are analysed here in terms of three core elements: roles; behaviours and traits; and organisational culture. This section focuses on the treatment of these elements in management research. The findings have to be extrapolated to encompass non-managerial employees and people interacting with an organisation from outside, whether as contractors, suppliers or customers.

Nevertheless, these studies are relevant here for two reasons: first, they highlight the importance of management and leadership strategies in generating a sense of organisational identity; and second, they emphasise the importance of communication and learning for organisational performance. For most organisations to perform effectively, they first require a culture that encourages communication and learning (Argyris 1993: 15). In this context, e-learning not only can help to orient individual actions towards agreed ends, but also has the potential to shape how individuals interact to generate new knowledge.

Roles

The roles allocated to individuals within an organisation are shaped by existing constructs of collective identity and purpose. At the same time, performing roles may contribute to reshaping collective identity. This is especially true of those occupying positions of leadership. In a stable environment the role of management can be almost ritualistic, but leadership at times of rapid change requires flexibility and commitment to shifting strategic goals. Management here has a role not only at the interpersonal and technical level, but also in setting and communicating common visions, values and beliefs.

The 'role approach' in management research has tended to focus on what constitutes an effective manager, beginning from observation of managers in the field. In the late 1960s and early 1970s, Henry Mintzberg made intensive observations of executives at work. The results exploded the notion that managers made decisions after careful planning and reflection. Mintzberg found that managers had little time for reflective thinking because they were so often interrupted. Rather, he concluded that they performed ten interrelated roles, which he grouped into three categories: interpersonal, informational and decisional (1973: 93):

Interpersonal
- Figurehead (performing ceremonial and social duties)
- Leader (motivating and activating subordinates)
- Liaison (maintaining a network of outsiders and contacts).

Informational
- Monitor (keeping informed about the organisation and its environment)
- Disseminator (transmitting information from subordinates and outside contacts to other organisation members)
- Spokesperson (acting as the public face of the organisation's policies and plans).

Decisional
- Entrepreneur (seeking out opportunities, initiating change and supervising major projects)
- Disturbance handler (taking responsibility for corrective action when unexpected problems arise)
- Allocator of resources (taking major decisions relating to budgets and expenditure)
- Negotiator (representing the organisation at major negotiations).

Subsequent research has generally supported this broad view of management and leadership roles, but it has been found that there are differences depending on the manager's hierarchical position, and especially between those who manage people to complete tasks and those who set directions. For example, the roles of disseminator, liaison, figurehead, negotiator and spokesperson seem to be more common in upper management.

In the late 1980s, Luthans led a team studying managers' roles from a different perspective. The team observed managers' roles by dividing their activities into clusters, and then calculating the percentage of time spent on each by three different categories of managers (Luthans, Hodgetts & Rosencrantz 1988). The team differentiated an average manager from a successful manager (one who achieves rapid promotion) and an effective manager (one who achieves performance outcomes on a sustainable basis while securing the support and commitment of subordinates). The results showed some surprising differences, especially between the latter two categories. Luthans found that task performance did not necessarily determine a manager's career success. See Table 4.1.

Table 4.1 Luthans's activities of managers

	Average managers	Successful managers	Effective managers
Activity	Percentage of time		
Traditional management	32	13	19
Communication	29	28	44
HR management	20	11	26
Networking	19	48	11

Adapted from Luthans et al. 1988

Such studies have helped to categorise the functions of management and establish the distinctive roles associated with leadership. A role-based approach assumes that contextual factors such as peer and community expectations will influence individuals' effectiveness and efficiency, both within the organisation and in its interactions with those outside. Relationships between individuals (leaders, managers, staff, peers and customers) need to be shaped if the organisation is to achieve its potential.

Behaviours and traits

Behaviour expresses an individual's identity in an action context, whether supportive, defensive or plainly hostile to the prevailing organisational identity. Research shows that employees who identify with an organisation's purpose also display behaviours that are beneficial to the workplace (Ashforth & Mael 1989; Dutton et al. 1994; Van Dyne, Graham & Dienesch 1994).

The study of behaviour in the management field has tended to concentrate on using behavioural-psychological theories to differentiate the behaviours of effective and ineffective managers, leaders and non-leaders. In 1961, a neo-classical theorist, Rensis Likert, completed a study investigating leadership behaviours that generated high levels of productivity combined with employee satisfaction and motivation. He found that higher productivity ensued when leaders emphasised the 'human aspects' of management. He concluded:

> in all interactions and all relationships with the organisation each member [should] . . . view the experience as supportive and one which builds and maintains his sense of personal worth and importance (Likert 1961: 104).

Higher productivity was achieved when employees were allowed greater autonomy in task management, while the leader focused on setting and achieving goals. Equally, staff felt greater ownership of organisational goals when they were involved in decision-making processes.

The effective leader, according to Likert, instilled goal ownership through collective decision making and by treating staff as human beings first and productive task-oriented resources second. The least effective managers were those who sought to control tasks and make all decisions. Likert suggested that the effective leader was able to complete interactions and relationships where 'each member will, in the light of his background, values and expectations, view the experience as supportive and one which builds and maintains his sense of personal worth and importance' (Likert 1961: 104).

If Likert typifies the behavioural approach, Douglas McGregor's Theory Y did much to entrench the approach in organisational practices (1960). Essentially, McGregor observed that management practices embodied two diametrically opposed assumptions about behaviour in the workplace. The first set of assumptions he called Theory X:

> The average human being has an inherent dislike of work and will avoid it if he can . . . Because of this . . . most people must be coerced, controlled, directed, threatened with punishment to get them to put forth adequate effort toward the achievement of organisational objectives . . . The average human being prefers to be directed, wishes to avoid responsibility, has relatively little ambition, wants security above all (McGregor 1960: 33–4).

The second set of assumptions, which he called Theory Y, began from the principle that work is 'as natural as play or rest'. Provided that people are committed to organisational objectives, they will work towards those goals of their own volition. Employees respond to the rewards associated with achieving objectives far better than to coercion or threats of punishment for non-achievement. Under the right conditions, 'the average human being learns . . . not only to accept but to seek responsibility'. Many people have the 'capacity to exercise a relatively high degree of imagination, ingenuity and creativity in the solution of organisational problems', but 'the intellectual potentialities of the average human being are only partially utilised' in modern industrial society (McGregor 1960: 47–8).

McGregor concluded that Theory X managers displayed directive and controlling behaviour, while Theory Y managers were facilitators and integrators. McGregor's theory had a remarkable impact; even today, managers are sometimes referred to as X or Y managers.

Blake and Mouton (1984), by contrast, tried to integrate personal and productive imperatives by locating management behaviour on a two-dimensional grid with two axes: concern for people and concern for production. The grid has nine intervals along each axis, creating 81 different positions into which a leader's style can fall. See Figure 4.1.

Blake and Mouton (1984) identified five key positions on the grid:

Cell 1:1 *Impoverished:* The leader exerts minimum effort to accomplish work.

Cell 9:1 *Task:* The leader concentrates on task efficiency but shows little concern for the development and morale of subordinates.

Cell 1:9 *Country-club:* The leader focuses on being supportive and considerate of subordinates to the exclusion of concern for task efficiency.

Cell 5:5   *Middle-of-the-road:* The goals are adequate task efficiency and satisfactory morale.

Cell 9:9   *Team:* The leader facilitates task efficiency and high morale by co-ordinating and integrating work-related activities.

Figure 4.1   Blake and Mouton's management grid

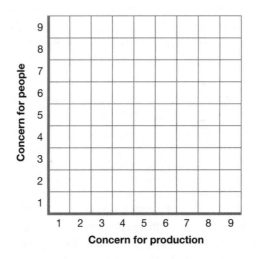

Subsequent studies of leadership traits have sought to isolate the characteristics that define good or even 'great' leaders. In many cases, employee behaviours have become a subordinate consideration. This gives some of the literature on traits a myopic quality.

A wave of popular 'how-to' books on the traits of successful people began with Dale Carnegie's *How to Win Friends and Influence People* (1936) and has boomed ever since. By the late 1980s and 1990s, the management and personal development sections of bookshops were full of works prescribing how the ordinary worker could become a great leader.[4]

Recent leadership theory has been influenced by the quest for a more holistic approach to organisational improvement. The change in emphasis is associated with the drive towards a more 'customer-driven' environment in which employees are expected to respond to client needs. This environment requires autonomy and flexibility, which can be enhanced by the formation of teams with 'ownership' of a process and problem-solving capabilities. This in turn requires more dynamic models of how employees' behaviours, traits and capabilities interact in the work environment.

Researchers and practitioners have begun to place greater emphasis on the context of leadership behaviour. The early situational studies of Edwin Hollander (1964; 1978) laid the foundations for this approach, and Avolio and Bass (1995) made an important contribution by distinguishing between transformational and transactional leadership.

Bass's study of transactional leaders (1985) emphasises the transactions that take place between leaders, colleagues and followers. Leadership is based on using these exchanges to achieve specific expectations. The leader uses the exchange process to guide followers' understanding and shape their behaviour by emphasising the consequences of their actions.

Transformational leaders, by contrast, motivate followers to achieve exceptional outcomes by setting and communicating visions that extend beyond individual self-interest to shared outcomes desired by the group. As Bass describes it:

> The transactional–transformational paradigm views leadership as either a matter of contingent reinforcement of followers by a transactional leader or the moving of followers beyond their self-interests for the good of the group, organization, or society by a transformational leader. The paradigm is sufficiently broad to provide a basis for measurement and understanding that is as universal as the concept of leadership itself. Numerous investigations (field studies, case histories, management games, interviews, and laboratory studies) point to the robustness of the effects of transformational and charismatic leadership (1997: 130).

This kind of leadership can be a powerful force in forging an organisational culture, which is the third element of organisational identity.

Organisational culture

Organisational culture can be defined as the 'general system of rules that govern meaning in organisations' (Smircich 1983: 339). According to Ernest Bormann, organisational culture is built on symbolic and shared purpose:

> A public consciousness is a crucial element in a group or an organization's culture. Culture in the communicative context means the sum total ways of living, organizing, and communing built up in a group of human beings and transmitted to newcomers by means of verbal and non-verbal communication. Important elements of an organization's culture include shared norms, reminiscences, stories, rites and rituals that provide the members with unique symbolic common ground (Bormann 1983: 100).

Bormann contends that these symbolic constructs can evolve into new patterns of reality. He argues, for example, that technological change is preceded by symbolic change. According to this argument, the preconditions for change are created symbolically before the technology is introduced. The organisation's response to new contingencies is built into how it already understands its core purpose and how well individuals can collaborate to achieve its aims.

Individual and collective identity can shape organisational cultures in different ways, depending on the individual's position and network of interactions. Owner–operators or entrepreneurial managers, for example, tend to 'imprint' the organisational culture with their personal beliefs and values. At the other extreme, a non-managerial individual's perception of an organisation's culture may be more distant, less intimately related to his or her sense of self. Looking outward, managers responsible for external customer relationships may be particularly attuned to how individuals inside and outside the organisation perceive its reputation, brand, promise or customer commitment — all identity factors that reinforce the value of the company's 'service culture'.

Identity is a valuable asset when individuals can align their beliefs and future with the organisational culture so that the individual is 'self-referential' with the organisation (Pratt 1998: 172). Individual identification with the organisation's identity assists the individual to:

- focus beliefs;
- reinforce a personal sense of worth through roles performed within the organisation;
- promote attachment to the organisation (the 'fit' between individual and collective purpose); and
- build self-concepts, beliefs, values and behaviours that match those desired by the organisation.

Blake Ashforth states:

> the process of identification is crucial because the nature of identity and the extent of identification are not determined by the pre-existing nature of the person or the organisation. Individuals, groups, and the organization mutually shape one another over time and become commingled . . . neither static nor discrete, neither independent nor autonomous (cited in Whetten & Godfrey 1998: 214).

Each organisation thus has a unique culture and identity, influenced by its specific context and history.

It has become increasingly obvious that communication and learning practices play a key part in organisational cultures, and hence in organisational capabilities. If communication and learning practices promote effective employee relations and build an organisation's human capital, its performance will be almost impossible for a competitor to replicate. Performance in this context is not a mechanical thing or a design for a product or service; it is embedded in how people want to work together from day to day.

Implications for e-learning

Increasingly, organisations see individuals as a capital resource. The New Economy has increased the emphasis on organisational agility and knowledge, driven by the need to develop individual capabilities and harness them, individually or collectively, to achieve competitive advantage.

There is also a growing recognition that if organisations are to develop their knowledge capital, they need new strategies to capture and mobilise individuals' experiential knowledge, the tacit knowledge on which mastery is founded. Strategies have to be developed to enhance individual employees' commitment to the organisational purpose to a point where they are prepared to transfer tacit knowledge to others. It is through these learning exchanges that overall performance capability can be enhanced.

Figure 4.2 Competencies, identity and capabilities

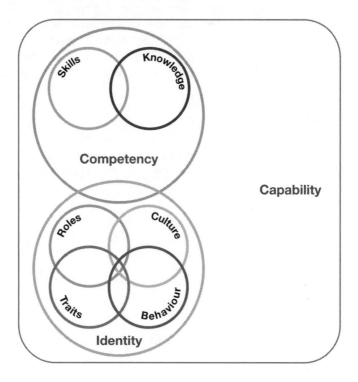

In this environment, effective learning can no longer be driven merely by competent performance of set tasks. It also has to be identity-oriented. To build compliant performance using explicit knowledge is not enough; organisational learning needs to leverage knowledge-sharing as a means of promoting the transfer of tacit knowledge.

E-learning has to maximise all the capabilities an individual, a group and therefore an organisation can deploy to be successful and survive. As Figure 4.2 depicts, each aspect may be undertaken in isolation, but a combination of competency and identity attributes provides a more complete view of the capabilities required to learn and perform: capabilities in effect form a 'currency' that can assist in the management of the processes of learning, performance, knowledge or change.

Conclusion

In the corporate world, e-learning has largely been promoted as a means of transferring codified, explicit competencies, but it can also contribute to interactions that build identity. Effective e-learning needs to:

- build collective identity founded on shared meaning;
- align individual identity with the common purpose; and thus
- improve productive capacity.

Organisations and teams need to explore the potential of e-learning as a strategic activity that can embed certain types of knowledge transfer into an organisation's culture. As the next three chapters will show, e-learning in such a context can be used to build identity attributes and hence expand an organisation's capabilities as well as develop the skills and knowledge necessary to improve performance at the individual, group and organisational levels.

Principle 4

Old paradigms based on e-training need to be revised to ensure that a focus on individual competence related to performance is augmented by targeting identity capabilities, which build purpose, shared meaning and a culture of collaboration.

---

[4] See for example Bennis 1989; Kotter 1990; Kouzes & Posner 1987; Manz & Sims 1987; Yukl 1989; Covey 1992; Bennis & Thomas 2002; Kouzes & Posner 2002.

Dimensions of Knowledge

The previous chapter has broadly defined the role of learning in contributing to the development of capabilities. This chapter looks more closely at the different forms of knowledge and the ways in which knowledge can be transmitted to form intellectual capital and help organisations to maintain their edge in a constantly changing environment.

There is a profusion of texts and perspectives on knowledge management, and the diversity of approaches has confused some of the simple messages concerning what knowledge management can and cannot do. To manage knowledge effectively, we need quite a sophisticated understanding of what knowledge is and how it works in different contexts. First, we need to look briefly at the processes by which knowledge is formed from data and information, and how it relates to the more philosophical notion of wisdom.

The basic building blocks of an information system are data — unstructured, discrete 'packets' of 'facts'. These building blocks are transformed into information when they are given structure and meaning. Information in turn gives rise to knowledge when it is shaped by its relevance to a particular purpose or set of values. The crucial point to note is that this is a matter of human agency: it is people who select the information and assemble it for a purpose, thereby transforming it into knowledge. Finally, wisdom is accumulated knowledge shaped by an individual's experience over an extended period of time (Katezenbach & Smith 1993).

In summary:

Data is the basis for forming information.

Information is data + structure + meaning.

Knowledge is data + structure + meaning + purpose.

Wisdom is data + structure + meaning + purpose experienced in a specific context and timeframe.

Knowledge therefore resides in individuals, alone or working in groups. This has important ramifications for the management of knowledge. Some organisations assume that they can manage knowledge assets as if they were physical or financial assets. There is a fundamental problem with this approach, for no organisation can own all the knowledge assets that contribute to its productive capabilities. In fact, most of this knowledge is not owned by the organisation — and does not need to be. It is owned by individuals and groups, many of which are outside the organisation's domain, such as computer software providers, specialist contractors or financial and accounting service providers.

This means that we can measure the 'value' of knowledge only by gauging how well individuals and groups transform information into knowledge that enhances productive outcomes. This is a process that involves learning, not only to absorb, transfer and expand existing knowledge but also to generate new bodies of knowledge in response to emerging demands on the organisation. Learning can thus be seen as a process of leveraging knowledge assets that an organisation does not — and in many cases cannot — own.

Tacit and explicit knowledge

Some forms of knowledge are more visible than others, and therefore easier to store and transmit. The success of Nonaka and Takeuchi's book *The Knowledge Creating Company* (1995) has created new interest in the phenomenon of tacit knowledge, a concept formulated by Michael Polanyi in the 1940s (1948; 1966). Polanyi drew a distinction between explicit, or codified, knowledge, which is formally set out in a way that makes it easy to transfer between individuals, and tacit knowledge, which arises informally out of experience, and is therefore highly personal and context-specific (Nonaka & Takeuchi 1995: 59). All human action requires both kinds of knowledge. Karl-Erik Sveiby emphasises the importance of the tacit dimension: 'Human knowledge is tacit, it is action-oriented, it is based on rules, it is individual, and it is constantly changing' (1997: 35).

Allen Tough (1999) suggests that only 20 per cent of lifelong learning is likely to be acquired by *formal transmission* or structured enquiry. Formal transmission includes various forms of purposeful, conscious telling, demonstration and guidance. Structured effort encompasses research, experimentation, self-directed enquiry or lifelong learning activities beyond those associated with formal qualifications (see Kearns et al. 1999). Some argue that up to 80 per cent of learning by an individual over the duration of an average lifetime is through *accretion* (Tough 1999), the subconscious or experience-based acquisition of social rules, behaviours and roles. A small component (perhaps 2 per cent) involves *tuning*, which results from patterning, structuring and accumulating new ideas and meanings that shape a person's creativity, wisdom and problem-solving capabilities.

In *The Knowledge Creating Company*, Nonaka and Takeuchi focus on how companies can gain a competitive advantage by managing both explicit and tacit knowledge. The book advances a theory of knowledge creation based on the assumption that 'human knowledge is created and expanded through social interaction between tacit knowledge and explicit knowledge'. Nonaka and Takeuchi analyse this process in terms of what they call 'knowledge conversions' (1995: 61). They suggest that knowledge conversions can take four main forms (1995: 62–70):

- **Socialisation:** consigning tacit knowledge by sharing experiences, mental models and technical skills. This is achieved through apprenticeships, mentoring or brainstorming.

- **Externalisation**: converting tacit knowledge to explicit knowledge by articulating it into a codified form. This may be achieved through group reflection on what makes certain processes work, or by the use of metaphor and analogy to codify practices that have been learnt through experience.
- **Internalisation**: converting explicit knowledge to tacit knowledge, achieved through learning by doing. This may involve experiential learning (deliberately exposing individuals to a wide range of experiences) or action-based learning, in which skills-based practice (explicit) reinforces individual behaviour (tacit).
- **Combination**: placing codified concepts into knowledge systems by reconfiguring existing information into courses, procedural manuals, marketing campaigns, strategic plans and so on.

Nonaka and Takeuchi argue that the transmission of knowledge and its conversion from tacit to explicit are central to an organisation's ability to generate new knowledge, encourage innovation and remain competitive (1995: 5–7).

By contrast, other commentators suggest that the codification of tacit knowledge cannot capture all the knowledge that dictates performance. If tasks require thinking, then solidified processes, rules and structures can actually inhibit the development of tacit knowledge that individuals use to achieve expert performance, intuition, creativity and innovation (Dreyfus & Dreyfus 1997: 33–5; Robinson & Stern 1997: 89).

Migratory and embedded knowledge

Another important issue for organisations seeking to harness knowledge is the extent to which knowledge is mobile. Managing the movement of knowledge is crucial to a company's competitive survival. Recent history offers many examples of companies that have recognised the importance of managing knowledge only *after* they have lost out to their competitors.

To this end, Joseph Badaracco has drawn a useful distinction between migratory and embedded knowledge. Migratory knowledge, as the name suggests, can be transferred from one firm to another and may be difficult to control and protect (Badaracco 1991: 34). Embedded knowledge, by contrast, 'moves very slowly, even when its commercial value is high and firms have strong incentives to gain access to it' (1991: 79). Badaracco describes firms as 'vast repositories of embedded knowledge' (1991: 80).

Different strategies are required to manage these two kinds of knowledge. To embed knowledge, organisations need to address internal factors such as craftsmanship, teamwork and communication, as well as the formation of external partnerships and relationships with the wider community (Badaracco 1991: 80–96). On the other hand, companies seeking to innovate need to allocate resources to attract migratory knowledge and prevent their own knowledge from migrating to competitors (1991: 56).

Harry Collins distinguishes between three types of knowledge embedded within individuals and societies (1997: 146–7):

- **Embodied knowledge:** Knowledge that resides in the individual body is highly specific to a particular person; for example, knowing that it is five steps to the door relies upon the individual's length of stride.
- **Embrained knowledge:** Knowledge that resides in the brain depends on the linkages individuals use to recall specific information, and these are different for each person. Language provides a common frame of reference, but the significance of information relates to the other memories to which it is linked.
- **Encultured knowledge:** Knowledge that resides in the cultural or social context relies on the linguistic and social frameworks that individuals acquire through interaction with others. Members of cultures or subcultures have their own language and frames of reference, which can influence interaction within the workplace.

The mobility of knowledge depends on the systems through which it is captured, stored, retrieved and used. There is a complex relationship between codification and the migratory properties of knowledge. Certainly the more explicit the knowledge, the more the factors influencing the migration of that knowledge can be determined; designs and blueprints can be legally protected, and barriers can be erected to prevent individuals from gaining access to knowledge unless they need it. In the longer term, the fact that knowledge can be replicated makes the organisation less dependent on individual memory and tacit practice.

Tacit knowledge is far more dependent on the individual than explicit knowledge. Because it cannot be owned by an organisation, one would expect it to move around with the individuals who hold it. On the other hand, because it is given meaning by interaction in a social context, it can be difficult to replicate in another setting. Take the individual out of the context, and the knowledge can diminish in value, meaning or relevance.

This is the crux of the problem. Making knowledge explicit can embed it into the organisation's processes and systems, but it also increases the risk that it will become migratory. Codified knowledge is easier to manage and convert within the organisation, but it is also easier to absorb, transfer and generate *outside* that organisation. Table 5.1 illustrates the dimensions of the movement of tacit and explicit knowledge within and across organisations.

It is difficult but not impossible for tacit knowledge to migrate. An example is the situation where workers who have been made redundant set themselves up as a new company, keeping their shared knowledge of corporate and production processes, working structures, skills and culture, even their hierarchy. Alternatively, the redundant workers may move to a competitor, which can then 'graft' their knowledge onto its existing capabilities. The new company thus secures both the explicit knowledge these individuals possess and their tacit knowledge of their craft, their working relationships and the relationships they have with suppliers and customers.

It is also possible to envisage scenarios in which companies may wish to recruit a workforce specifically for its tacit knowledge. As an extreme example, imagine that a manufacturer of quality furniture goes bankrupt and its workers are recruited by a company manufacturing high-quality boots. Although the furniture makers' specific skills are not relevant to the new context, the workforce may represent individuals with a personal commitment to quality products, who possess knowledge of the locality and potential players that can assist the export of high-quality merchandise. They may also be attuned to a culture where craftspeople work alone in an effective communication network. Recruiting from a pool of labour with pre-existing tacit knowledge but no explicit skills may reduce the 'start-up' time for their new company and add knowledge assets that would be difficult to create.

Table 5.1   Comparison of tacit, explicit, embedded and migratory knowledge

	Tacit knowledge (owned by the individual)	Explicit knowledge (owned by the organisation)
Embedded knowledge	Embedded tacit knowledge Non-transferable individual knowledge that affects how people think, how they do things and how they interact • Shared commitment • Mentoring relationships • Collective memory and wisdom	Embedded explicit knowledge Rules and codes that govern workplace conduct and interaction • Codes of conduct • Value statements • Documentation of context-specific processes
Migratory knowledge	Migratory tacit knowledge Knowledge that individuals hold but can take beyond the organisation • Craftsmanship • Social networks • Experience • Individual commitment • Individual customer/service relationships	Migratory explicit knowledge Knowledge owned and documented by the organisation • Procedural manuals/templates • Training courses/manuals • Process flowcharts • Service strategies • Systems architecture • Strategic plans • Market research

See Nonaka & Takeuchi 1995: 62–70

The *absence* of tacit knowledge may also affect a company's performance. Call centres, for example, are increasingly centralising customer service functions across large geographic regions. In many cases, this creates a deficit of tacit knowledge. The lack of local recruitment may weaken informal networks and service relationships with customers from other regions. Codified skills and knowledge may not be enough to build a sustainable service relationship with a customer or customer base (Frenkel & Donoghue 1996: 12, 15). For instance, if a service assistant has no understanding of a caller's regional frame of reference, their communication is likely to be at cross-purposes. The service provider will lack a basis for constructing shared experiences and an 'identity' with its customers (Frenkel & Donoghue 1996: 26).

These examples illustrate some of the complexities that surround any assessment of the value of knowledge, and hence the value of learning. For learning to be effective, it must be framed by an understanding of whether knowledge is tacit or explicit, embedded or migratory. As the following section outlines, the processes through which knowledge is formed and transmitted are an integral part of its value.

Knowledge and value

Knowledge has individual, social and capital value. Those who have knowledge value it as something that gives the 'owner' respect and authority, but organisations value knowledge for its strategic capacity to enhance productivity as measured in dollars. Knowledge held by individuals or organisations has a capital value that can be managed, evaluated and manipulated. Drawing on their experiences at Skandia, Edvinsson and Malone emphasised the role of intellectual capital in building successful organisations. They defined intellectual capital as 'the possession of the knowledge, applied experience, organisational technology, customer relationships and professional skills' to give organisations a competitive edge (1997: 44–5). They devised a formula for intellectual capital:

Intellectual capital = Human capital + Structural capital

This formula reinforces the centrality of human capital as the knowledge 'owned' by an individual and harnessed by a company to achieve strategic ends. Structural capital, on the other hand, is the knowledge possessed by the company or having only contextual value in the organisation (Edvinsson & Malone 1997: 46). This formula differs from an earlier version advanced by Edvinsson when working with Sullivan (1996), which also included relational capital: knowledge embedded in the organisation's relationships with the outside environment, including with suppliers, customers and communities.

Subsequent authors have modified the formula to replace relational capital with customer capital, which includes relationships, networks, value chains, customer loyalty, sales, supply and service alliances. This gives the formula:

Intellectual capital = Human capital + Structural capital + Customer capital

Not only do these different types of knowledge contribute to overall intellectual capital but, as Stewart (1997: 165) points out, they can be managed to support each other:

- Human capital and structural capital reinforce each other by establishing a shared sense of purpose, agility and entrepreneurial spirit.
- Human capital and customer capital combine to give individuals a clear understanding of customer expectations, a knowledge of customer relationships and a sense of responsibility for their part in the enterprise.
- Customer capital and structural capital support each other by allowing the customers and the company to learn from each other, establishing customer loyalty and developing a sense of ease on both sides so that formal processes become 'second nature'.

In this scenario, effective management of intellectual capital establishes a series of virtuous circles that lead to organisational agility and competitive advantage, buttressed by constant learning across all parts of the organisation.

Brooking suggests that what constitutes a competent employee encompasses more than the knowledge required to perform work. Employees require experience and the capabilities that enable proficiency. Organisational capability also requires transfer of knowledge between individuals. Codification of knowledge is therefore viewed as essential to the construction of structural assets (processes, management systems and so on) and the generation of intellectual capital. Managing knowledge as a corporate asset relies on managers considering the tacit or explicit dimensions of knowledge and managing each appropriately (Brooking 1999: 51–2).

In defining organisational intelligence, Sveiby differentiates between *focal knowledge* — 'the knowledge about the object or phenomenon that is the focus'; and *tacit knowledge* — 'knowledge that is used as a tool to handle what is being focused on' (1997: 30). If knowledge is a combination of both types, all action requires both aspects of knowledge. Building on Polanyi's work, Sveiby uses competence and the 'capacity to act' to differentiate tacit knowledge held by the individual from knowledge that is applied in a business context.

While the early writers on the subject of knowledge have strongly influenced works right up to the present (see sources used in major compilations such as Bontis 2002; Dieng-Kuntz & Matta 2002), it is worth noting that the authors who provided the foundations for the conceptualisation of intellectual capital observed that the creation, transfer and utilisation of knowledge are all implicitly affected by the organisation's capacity to learn (Choo & Bontis 2002: 16–17). The concept of organisational learning is explored in some depth in Chapter 10, but here it should be emphasised that learning is affected by the type of knowledge engaged. Learning is also a major force enabling the flow of knowledge across and outside an organisation.

Sources of knowledge

The acquisition of knowledge is a dynamic process, and as such is never complete. In practice, individuals and organisations may need only sufficient knowledge to achieve their strategic purpose, as long as they also know where to find additional knowledge as required. Tom Davenport and Larry Prusak (1998) have identified five types and related sources of knowledge within an organisation:

Acquired knowledge: This is knowledge sourced from outside the organisation. While it may be employed for the organisation's strategic purpose, its ownership remains outside the organisation's domain of operations. Commonly it is sourced or 'grafted' through training, contract work or consultancies, and sometimes through supply contracts (for example, between manufacturers and research organisations).

Adapted knowledge: Experience in a new working or operational context can result in adapted knowledge. In adapting to new situations and conditions, organisations and work groups increase their capacity to operate in the wider marketplace. This may occur when companies shift to online trading or move into markets in different countries and cultures.

Dedicated knowledge: When an organisation sets aside staff or resources to develop knowledge for a specific purpose, this results in dedicated knowledge. This strategy can generate specific competence in one knowledge set, while also ensuring that the knowledge can be integrated into the organisation's systems. Often dedicated teams are built to commercialise an immediate, short-term strategic opportunity.

Fused knowledge: This form of knowledge arises when people with different perspectives work on the same project. Their very difference may be the catalyst for generating new knowledge or insights. In some cases the purpose is simply to place individuals who hold tacit knowledge or highly specialised knowledge together in an environment where they can exchange ideas. Conflicts are not uncommon in such situations. The most common sources of this kind of knowledge are interdisciplinary work teams or project management teams.

Networked knowledge: This arises out of interactions and understandings created when people share information, formally or informally. It is one of the most important forms of knowledge within the corporate world, and one of the least understood. Networking, where professionals or communities of practice gather together or share a discipline, is most often viewed as the basis for networked knowledge. This is a limited view. The value of networked knowledge resides in its potential to utilise information from multiple sources to generate new and relevant perspectives. Networks are crucial in a world where it is impossible to allocate time and space to acquiring all the knowledge that may be important to an organisation.

A strong set of networks should include interactions with formal and informal groups outside the workplace. Networked knowledge also resides in the social fabric of the location, including characteristics such as political and social stability and the workforce's sense of well-being. Knowledge arising from these settings is often referred to as 'social capital'.

The role of social capital

A closer analysis of social capital helps to reinforce our understanding of the importance of tacit knowledge. Social capital is the shared values, networks and sense of trust that help people to interact productively. It is produced by strategic learning for a shared and worthwhile purpose. It helps to maximise individual knowledge assets by drawing on resources that extend beyond the boundaries of the organisation.

Robert Putnam defines social capital in terms of 'features of social organization, such as trust, norms, and networks, that can improve the efficiency of society by facilitating co-ordination of actions' (Putnam 1992: 167). Other commentators have noted that social capital has an elusive quality. It is context-specific and inherent in the structure of individual relationships. It cannot be embedded in structures or processes, and is impossible to bank or place on a balance sheet (Portes 1998: 7).

Social capital resides in humans; it is created through 'accumulated mutual obligations' and the societal need for reciprocity (Portes 1998: 7), and through relationships that promote group trust, norms and collective 'rituals' that govern behaviour and facilitate further interaction (Falk & Kilpatrick 2000).

Some commentators claim that social capital can produce negative effects such as conformity, 'group-think' and exclusion of 'outsiders' (Portes & Landolt 1996; Portes 1998: 13). Others contend that if the effects of interaction are negative, the interactions have failed to generate social capital (e.g. Falk & Kilpatrick 2000; Falk 1999).

In an earlier work that emphasised the value of networks of interaction, Bowles (1999) suggested a three-tier approach to the creation and management of knowledge capital. In this approach, structural, human and social capitals are viewed as dimensions or types of knowledge assets. Human capital is seen as focusing on skills and knowledge associated with operational outcomes – explicit knowledge – while social capital represents the stocks of tacit knowledge resident in individuals, networks, relationships and cultures (1999: 23). See Figure 5.1.

Figure 5.1 Types of knowledge capital

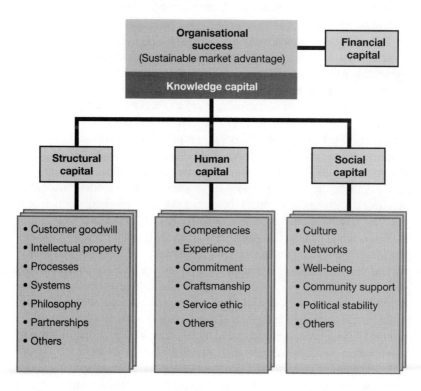

Reproduced with kind permission, Bowles 1999b: 24

The concept of social capital provides a mental construct that warns us, at the very least, to be aware that individual relationships and networks must be managed beyond the organisation's parameters if certain sources of knowledge assets are to be created and managed effectively.

E-learning, capability and knowledge capital

At this point, we can draw together the discussion of capability in the previous chapter and the insights derived from a broader and more articulated understanding of the transmission of knowledge. Knowledge is many-faceted, and its sources are often elusive. At the same time, it is an essential component of capital in the New Economy. Given that e-learning has become a significant factor in the transmission of knowledge and the formation of knowledge capital, a common 'currency' is needed to measure the effectiveness and efficiency of e-learning within, between and across organisations' operating domains. The creation of a structure and taxonomy for defining and measuring capability is essential to appreciate the contribution of e-learning to knowledge capital value.

As a construct, capability-based approaches to managing knowledge and learning can be extended to conceptualise how competency and identity attributes can be integrated, targeted, reported and analysed for their contribution to overall knowledge capital. We can term this contribution 'potential productive capacity', which represents both an organisation's current performance and its future ability to respond to change.

The sum of an individual's and a group's capabilities can be said to contribute to the organisation's total potential productive capacity. While capabilities may be used for purposes other than work, all capabilities held by an individual or group are potentially available for organisational outcomes. As discussed in Chapter 4, capabilities are not just about job performance; they also encompass how an individual creates and shares meaning and is motivated to perform. Without adopting a behaviourist approach, the term 'identity' can be used to group attributes that are not simply linked to skills and task performance in a given situation (occupational or functionally specific). Capabilities can therefore encompass identity-creating factors that involve interactions with others (cross-functional, cross-occupational) or in relationships the organisation does not own or always control.

The concept of potential productive capacity is not a static or 'bounded' term. It denotes an organisation's own definition of what is required to meet current strategic needs and to achieve sustainable market advantage through superior capabilities. E-learning employed to achieve productive capabilities is tied to knowledge as both a physical process and a human social process by which people capture, transfer and generate information. Knowledge is in turn created by these processes and shared by individuals through communication that involves physical, symbolic and interpersonal interaction.

E-learning can be harnessed by organisations and managers as the catalyst for transferring and translating communicated information into knowledge. As we will see in later chapters, this process is dynamic. It takes place in a setting where knowledge and activity occur through interaction between people at the level of the individual, communities of individuals (teams or groups inside and outside the organisation) and whole-of-organisation. The very ability of individuals to respond to new imperatives and embrace individual divergence represents a real value that an organisation needs to manage and report.

It should be emphasised, however, that most learning acquired by individuals in their workplaces does not occur through formal channels. To the modern e-learning practitioner or knowledge manager, this suggests it is insufficient to manage all individual and collective knowledge as codified knowledge found in procedures, manuals, training programs, job descriptions and so on. Fundamentally, organisations need to move beyond managing e-learning as a process for transferring explicit knowledge that contributes only to skills and knowledge (competence) that result in productive actions. Organisations also need to acknowledge how communication and identity can be interwoven into the e-learning process. Such an acknowledgement is necessary if e-learning is to stimulate collaborative learning and the learning that each individual acquires simply by participating in a transaction with technology, people or content.

E-learning must also be viewed as a process for building the potential productive capability required by an organisation. To build all aspects of knowledge assets available to it, an organisation needs to build e-learning frameworks that are as much about enhancing performance outcomes as they are processes that can add value to individuals' development of shared identity. This shared identity should hold meaning and generate the motivation to act.

The contribution of capability to potential productive capability can be extrapolated to underpin the valuation of an organisation's total knowledge capital (or intellectual capital). The contribution of e-learning has progressed from delivery of learning outcomes to encompass knowledge management outcomes and now human capital outcomes. The relationship has been expressed by the equation:

$$L + P + KM + HR = HC$$

In this formula L is learning, P is performance (which can be replaced by S for service), KM is knowledge management, HR is human resources, and they equate to human capital, HC. This formula can be modified to maintain its focus but incorporate the 'single currency' of capability presented in this chapter:

$$HC + IC + SC = KC$$

In this second formula HC is human capital (resident in performance and personal capabilities), IC is identity capital (social capital resident in shared purpose and relationships) (Formula based on Bowles 1999: 20), and SC is structural capital (capital resident in processes and physical resources) that together result in knowledge capital, KC.

Extensive review of the literature reveals no major research work to date on how e-learning will affect each component in the KC equation, or how such interventions will be measured and reported.

As Figure 5.2 illustrates, knowledge capital can take different forms. While there are many different ways of describing this, we distinguish here between human, identity and structural 'pools'. All can be managed to enhance the capabilities required to achieve performance outcomes.

Figure 5.2 Capabilities, potential productive capability and knowledge capital

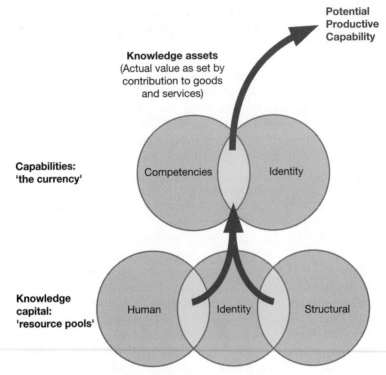

Reproduced with kind permission, Bowles 1999b: 140

As discussed in Chapter 4, knowledge assets resulting in applied outcomes or task completion (competency) are not necessarily the only contributors to performance. Identity capabilities (non-competency-based attributes such as culture, roles, behaviours and traits) hold equal value, and may be essential in order to achieve transformation to future performance needs as organisational purpose changes. It is the combination of competence and identity attributes that determines how effectively individuals, groups and organisations mobilise their knowledge resources for productive ends.

Note that the three circles of capital and the two for capability – competence and identity – have overlapping sectors. This indicates that productive outcomes at any given time do not draw on all the capabilities resident within individuals, teams or organisations. A key task for those who set out to maximise potential productive capability through managing knowledge assets is thus to address the organisation's untapped knowledge capital resources and capabilities, including its pools of tacit knowledge and identity attributes.

Conclusion

In the context of a rapidly changing economic environment, learning in general, and e-learning in particular, can be seen as playing a central role in organisational performance. If e-learning can be used effectively in an organisational setting to mobilise and transmit diverse forms of knowledge — not just the narrowly defined, codified knowledge that has traditionally been the domain of work-based training — it stands to enhance the organisation's knowledge capital at all levels. Where this is combined with a sustained program to foster positive identity attributes, the organisation will be far better able to realise its potential productive capability. As the following chapters will discuss, however, to achieve this requires a serious rethinking of learning strategies at individual, group and organisational levels.

Principle 5

The efficiency and effectiveness of e-learning as a strategic activity should be measured not only in terms of performance and learning outcomes, but also in terms of its overall contribution to an organisation's potential productive capacity and ability to adapt to changing circumstances.

Generating Knowledge Through Learning

If we accept that most knowledge is owned by people rather than organisations and draws its meaning from its use in a social context, then we need to look closely at how education and training can develop people's capacity to learn. This is vital to any organisational endeavour. To quote de Geus: 'The ability to learn faster than your competitors may be the only sustainable comparative advantage' (1988: 71).

Humans learn through every interaction with their environment, and especially through interacting with other humans. In essence, learning is a social activity. It cannot be simply switched on for as long as needed to transfer performance-related knowledge, and then switched off again. In any event, as we have seen, it is impossible to make explicit all the knowledge an individual needs in order to 'perform'.

This raises a fundamental problem with orthodox knowledge management approaches, which depend on codifying knowledge and making it explicit so that people know what they need to know and can transfer it to performance as required. Unfortunately, knowledge is not that simple. Often *we do not know what we need to know until we need to know it.*

Learning in all its forms has to be encouraged to ensure the capture, transfer and generation of knowledge that people need to work and to collaborate. E-learning is an increasingly important part of this equation.

Traditional approaches to learning

The differences between education and training are a definitional minefield, but the debate about delineating the two is secondary to our concerns. Training and education have complementary but distinct roles, and e-learning crosses the boundary between the two. Education is a process of transmitting facts and 'training' individuals to think and learn; training is the act of acquiring knowledge and transferring it into action.

The retention of knowledge – essential to its application in an organisational context – is a central issue for both training and education. The problem with conventional education in schools and universities is that students often retain knowledge only for as long as it takes to pass exams or complete academic assessments. Equally, training activities do not always develop learners' capacity to engage in the required actions without supervision or to understand the principles underpinning successful completion. Clearly, learners' physical and mental capacities must be harnessed together to maximise the effectiveness of learning and provide a context for the knowledge they acquire. Learning therefore encompasses both training and education.

Work-based training

Because our focus here is on adult learning in a workplace environment, it is worth surveying the field of work-based training. A variety of approaches can be adopted to implement training, and it is important for organisations to select the right method to meet their needs and those of individual learners. The advantages and disadvantages of each method are detailed in Table 6.1.

On-the-job training: This is widely used to teach employees specific job-related skills. Generally, the learner carries out tasks under the direction of a supervisor, mentor or fellow employee. The trainer is able to model the required new skills and ensure that the trainee can apply all aspects of the new skill set. This training method is particularly suitable for less complex technical skills used in the everyday work environment.

Off-the-job training: When people within the organisation do not have the desired skills or are not in a position to pass them on to others, training will need to take place off the job. This may take the form of conferences, short industry-based courses or classroom-based activities at universities, colleges or technical and further education institutions.

Classroom-based training: Undertaken either on or off the job, classroom-based training enables a large number of students to access learning material at the same time. It also allows students to learn from their mistakes without suffering serious consequences. Often this is important when students need to perfect their skills away from the supervisor's critical eye, or when mistakes can cause damage to people or property.

Self-paced training: This involves individual employees learning by themselves or in small groups, using resources such as CD-ROMs, online or distance education, books, periodicals and learning modules. This form of training is especially beneficial if conducted in partnership with networks of other learners and with input from mentors or coaches.

Coaching and mentoring: This one-on-one training and development is often provided for employees who are new to an organisation or are moving into unfamiliar roles.

E-training: This encompasses using electronic technologies in a workplace context to transfer skills and knowledge to individuals or groups. E-training is in effect the electronic distribution of self-paced training to accentuate and accelerate skills transfer.

The use of on-the-job training is nothing new. What is new is the emphasis on providing it with a stronger structure and better resources. *Off-the-job training* is not in danger of being replaced, as it still plays a vital role in the formation of competencies that fall outside normal work-based activities, but it has been recognised that both trainees and organisations benefit greatly from 'learning and doing' within the place of work.

Table 6.1   Advantages and disadvantages of training methods

Training type	Financial cost	Time-frame	Best for	Not recommended for
On-the-job	Low	Short	Small-scale, job-relevant skills	Complex skills that require in-depth analysis
Off-the-job	Moderate to high	Short to long	Broad-ranging, complex skills that require outside expertise	Skills that are relevant only to the organisation
Classroom-based	Moderate to high	Medium to long	Training a large number of employees in skills that require practice or interaction with others	Small-scale, specific skills that are applied directly in the workplace
Self-paced	Low to moderate	Short to long	Conceptual skills that require outside expertise, especially for employees with limited time	Small-scale, specific skills that are applied directly in the workplace
Coaching and mentoring	Low to moderate	Long	Skills that require complex understanding and gradual implementation	Small-scale skills that may be quickly acquired
E-training	Low to moderate	Short to long	Skills and knowledge required to comply with operational, legal or competency standards that need to be transferred to many individuals within a given timeframe	Operational skills only able to be demonstrated in a work-based context

In this context, the potential of e-learning extends far beyond e-training. In an e-learning context, instructional technology and electronic media should not be viewed simply as a learning stimulus or a mode of 'delivery' along a single channel from instructor to learner and back again. E-learning is more than an electronic means of distributing knowledge in formal, structured programs. It can also provide a medium for transactions that draw on the individual learner's experience, memory and 'mental models' to establish what may be described as an individual learning trajectory.

E-learning is very effective in promoting learning through unstructured processes. This is critical, as most of the learning completed by individuals over their lifetimes is not structured. Research has suggested as little as 20 per cent of lifelong learning is likely to be acquired by formal transmission or structured learning (Tough 1999). Formal transmission here is defined to include information, knowledge, ideas and skills taught through purposeful, conscious telling, demonstration and guidance. It also encompasses individuals' attempts to acquire knowledge through research, experimentation, self-directed enquiry or lifelong learning activities, not only those associated with formal qualifications (see Kearns et al. 1999).

Rumelhart and Norman (1978) distinguish between three forms of learning: accretion, structuring and tuning. Accretion is the addition of new knowledge to existing memory. Structuring involves the formation of new conceptual structures or schemata. Tuning is the adjustment of knowledge to a specific task, usually through practice. Rumelhart and Norman suggest that individuals use a mix of these approaches to learn. Some argue that up to 80 per cent of lifetime learning occurs through accretion, or the subconscious or experience-based acquisition of social rules, behaviours and roles (Tough

1999). A small component (perhaps 2 per cent) involves tuning, which results from patterning, structuring and the accumulation of new ideas and meanings that shape a person's creativity, wisdom and problem-solving capabilities.

The real value of e-learning then is the ability not only to address the transfer of explicit knowledge in structured frameworks, but to provide collaborative processes and pedagogies that can address the 80 per cent of knowledge an individual can acquire through unstructured or tacit means. Appropriate e-learning strategies can thus enrich the process of transferring both explicit and tacit knowledge, particularly if it involves a learner-centred approach to learning.

Learner-centred approaches to learning

Many of the current models of e-learning have been dominated by the acquisition and management of off-the-shelf courses. This approach is derived from educational paradigms that are similar to traditional classroom-based instruction, implemented to provide just-in-time learning, customised to multiple users, at a lower cost per unit. Often, the prospect of cost savings is the driving force. In all cases the focus is on the transfer of knowledge in structured or explicit packages of information.

A central problem with this approach is that it tends to reduce the learner to a passive recipient of pre-determined content – the proverbial 'empty vessel' receiving instruction from above. This approach is at odds with the cognitive orientation to learning, which sees learners as active participants in learning, 'sources of plans, intentions, goals, ideas, memories, and emotions actively used to attend to, select, and construct meaning from stimuli and knowledge from experience' (Wittrock cited in Woolfolk 1993: 237). Cognitive theorists believe that learning is the result of people's attempts to make sense of the world, initiating experiences and seeking out information to solve problems (Bandura 2001), and that education and training should be designed to reinforce and extend an active approach to learning.

There is no intrinsic reason why e-learning cannot adopt approaches that are aimed at stretching traditional instructor-led methods and promoting the transfer of unstructured or tacit knowledge (see Chapter 5). These 'alternative' types of learning include action learning, situated learning, scenario-based learning, and serendipitous learning.

Action learning

As its name suggests, action learning aims to reinforce the synergistic relationship between learning and action. Professor Reg Revans (1982) initially advanced the concept, advocating that learning should be based on individuals sharing and comparing real work problems. He proposed that this sharing and comparing take place in small groups, which he called 'action learning sets'. This process enables participants to question current assumptions and continuously renew individual and organisational knowledge. The final stage involves reflection and making sense of the facts presented, along with evaluation of individual, group and organisational outcomes and of the process itself. Action learning commonly utilises the formula:

$$L = P + Q + R$$

Here, Learning (L) equals Programmed instruction (P) plus Questioning (Q) plus Reflection (R).

The action-learning model has been influential in formal education and work-based training. As Dilworth puts it, 'Action learning is strategic . . . It is a marriage of action with reflection that produces the result' (1998: 6). The perceived benefits of action learning include the following:

- Organisations can deploy problem-solving exercises that result in collaborative learning, which, in turn, generates solutions for operational problems.
- Individuals retain learning, because real problems or challenges enable them to develop their own frameworks for problem solving that can be repeated in the workplace.
- Once learning becomes interwoven in the problem-solving process, individuals can learn outside structured contexts, collaborate with others and learn about themselves and their perceptions.

Situated learning

Situated learning emphasises the social dimension of learning. It is based on the belief that knowledge is inseparable from the contexts and activities in which it develops: that 'knowing what' is integral to 'knowing how'. Brown, Collins and Duguid refer to situated learning as 'authentic activity' – planned, completed and reviewed under real-world conditions (1989a: 38–42). When someone is learning a language, for example, it is not enough to read the dictionary for definitions of unfamiliar words; definitions alone do little to help the learner understand how the words are used or establish the different meanings they may acquire in different contexts.

Advocates of situated learning argue that the most effective learning relates to the individual's situated role (Clancey 1995: 63). It begins from the assumption that it is virtually impossible to assess everything people know, because knowledge is complex and multi-dimensional. The learning process must therefore be open-ended: it must not only lead learners to certain outcomes but also encourage them to continue to learn, developing further knowledge and skills.

It is collaboration, above all, that provides the opportunity for situated learning. Collaborative activity in real-world contexts also 'enculturates' the learner; social interactions in a specific environment develop shared meanings – a frame of reference or belief common to the people and place where learning occurs. Pedagogies that emphasise interaction among learners and encourage them to construct their own meanings can improve individuals' capacity for problem solving and critical thinking (Oliver & Omari 2001; Holt et al. 1998).

Situated learning is based on a social constructivist theory of knowledge, according to which learning is about making meaning. Individual learning is not about cognition in isolation; it is the process of making meaning of the social situation and context in which the individual operates. At a fundamental level, then, learning is a social process (Wenger 1998). The benefit of e-learning for this approach is that it can offer an alternative learning environment that is under the learners' control, drawing on their individual mental models and learning styles.

Scenario-based learning

Scenario-based learning places specific, structured learning into a 'real-life' framework. It thus integrates features of action learning and situated learning. The use of scenario-based approaches to e-learning is becoming increasingly popular. Here, the use of the electronic environment for learning is coupled with assessment and evaluation designed to confirm the learners' progress, allowing them to make an immediate association between actions and outcomes. Scenario-based learning is designed to encourage learners to:

- share experiences;
- reflect on their own experience before or during learning;
- judge their personal ability to handle scenarios;
- shape scenarios to actions and a context relevant to the real situation; and
- refine the learning objectives so that they reflect learners' personal orientations and behaviour.

Serendipitous learning

Serendipitous learning acknowledges that the human search for knowledge may occur by chance, or as a by-product of the main task. Often the greatest lessons occur without conscious thought or even rational understanding of the 'need to know'. In an environment where everyday tasks or careers are constantly changing, workers need access to up-to-date knowledge on demand. They have to be able to search for solutions to problems that affect them *now*. This requires information to be highly situated and immediately available (Nichani 2001: 1).

The search for immediate knowledge often triggers broader understanding. For instance, an online search may take the individual on a tangent that proves to be more productive than the original query. In this case, serendipitous learning has occurred.

The retention of knowledge acquired by serendipitous learning is very high, because the motivation resides with the learner (Nichani 2001: 2). This learning may occur through 'legitimate peripheral participation' when new members join existing communities and modify their behaviours (Wenger 1998: 100). Equally, the learners may 'steal' information from one source and 'reinvent' it in their own context (Brown & Duguid 1992). This kind of learning is most effective when learners perceive that they control the process of acquisition or have a 'unique' perspective (Cerri et al. 1999: 19). In this sense, serendipitous learning promotes structured informal learning.

All these approaches to learning can be described as discovery-based, in that they actively engage learners in an active role, tackling real-world problems. Table 6.2 summarises how such discovery-based approaches develop interactivity, tying learning to the individual context and avoiding the reliance on transferring generic, explicit knowledge to all learners. In simulation-based learning especially, the driver decides which vehicle to use, which accessories to add and what route to take to the destination point – before taking off on another adventure.

Table 6.2   Comparative approaches to learning and instruction

	Instructor-led training	Action learning	Situated learning	Scenario-based learning
Knowledge source	Scope of learning set by experts who examine the subject, establish its components and establish right and wrong answers	Problems are carefully selected, and relevant to the situation	Learning based on context-based situations/case studies	Experts initially model domain knowledge and learning strategies
Learner contribution	Explores and completes task or subject to be mastered	Develops critical knowledge to solve problems, alone or with group	Creates meaning through exploratory activities that can be applied in similar situations	Develops situated knowledge within a real context and may build collective identity through group exercises
Instructor contribution	Facilitates process, provides mentoring support and assesses outcomes	Provides guiding questions, resources, exercises and frameworks for learners to interact and develop their own solutions	Creates opportunities for learners to transfer knowledge into real-world challenges	Provides initial scenario and may coach along the way until learners attain self-directed competence
Community contribution	Ranges from no interaction to complex interaction to support learning	Provides source for content and context for problems	Provides experts' input and feedback on real events	Provides mentors or experts able to support learners' explorations

E-learning in the learning continuum

Using technology in an electronic environment to mediate the learning transaction may be a departure from previous practices, but this does not mean that it is somehow separate from them. E-learning practitioners can learn from both conventional and innovative approaches to learning. The attempt to isolate e-learning from learning in general has disfranchised many educators and made the transition from the known to the 'unknown' more difficult. Fox and Herrmann describe a spectrum of views among educators:

> Some have deep-rooted concerns about changes in work practices, and others see the huge gap between the rhetoric surrounding technology and the realities of educational settings, while others boldly embrace new media with seemingly little critical pedagogical concern (2000: 73).

It is therefore worth emphasising that e-learning development must be educationally sound. The challenge is to engage educators and learners in the design process and ensure that e-learning builds on optimal learning and instruction methods. The transition to an electronic environment requires a wide range of skills. As Oliver and Dempster write, 'engaging staff to make educationally sound changes to their teaching requires a genuine understanding of curriculum development and change management' (2002: 1).

The relationship between e-learning and pedagogy has also recently become a popular topic in discussions of educational theory. For example, Martin Weller (2002: 79) suggests that online learning draws from six main pedagogies:

- constructivism;
- resource-based learning;
- collaborative learning;
- problem-based learning;
- narrative-based teaching; and
- situated learning.

These pedagogies for online learning are all derived from the pedagogies used in conventional learning. Furthermore, while there are continuities between the pedagogies for e-learning and non-electronic learning, e-learning must use a combination of methods, as no single pedagogy can satisfy all online learning needs. The pedagogy also has to reflect diverse or emerging technologies, even where the curriculum, content and audience remain the same. New combinations and modulations of established pedagogies are therefore likely to emerge.

Clearly, how e-learning is designed and packaged is a major consideration. Old content simply transferred into an online environment does not improve learning. New packages are desirable, and they have to be labelled so that users can access the information and knowledge they need.

All the innovative learning approaches discussed above place the learner at the centre of the process. The immediate rationale for learning may be to acquire specific skills and knowledge, but further learning generated as a by-product is a driver for personal achievement and strategic success. A process that actively engages the mind elevates learning above an instrumental status. Learner-led learning requires individuals to make the learning meaningful to *themselves* and thus to extend their existing potential. This moves away from a force-fed or supply-driven approach to learning (push), towards a demand-led one (pull).

John Seely Brown highlights the Web's unique ability to help learners achieve this kind of autonomy. Other media forms, he comments, are 'one-way propositions: they push their content at us. The Web is two-way, push and pull' (2000: 12). The Web permits designers and instructors to give learners an 'experience' that they can immediately relate to the real world. This is essentially a form of experiential learning. At the same time, learners can tap into experiences beyond their ordinary reach – flight simulators or three-dimensional tours of ancient buildings, to name just two. This type of activity involves self-discovery, problem solving and 'sensemaking' strategies that develop the cognitive frameworks essential to cope with current and future problems (Werkman & Boonstra 2002: 1). Online engagement supports all these forms of learning. To quote Brown again:

> Most of us experienced formal learning in an authority-based, lecture-oriented school. Now, with incredible amounts of information available through the Web, we find a 'new' kind of learning assuming pre-eminence — learning that's discovery based. We are constantly discovering new things as we browse through the emergent digital 'libraries' (Brown 2000: 14).

Simulation-based training combines many of the features of alternative approaches to learning. Combining visual, textual/numerical and interactive media in online simulations simultaneously develops the 'what', 'how' and 'why' of learning (Rieber 2002: 3). The instructional design can also encompass group learning, enhancing collaborative skills. Lloyd Rieber suggests that online simulations permit learning to address individual self-efficacy issues while building learning patterns that encourage the use of 'deeper cognitive processing' (2002: 6).

In a corporate context, what is most important is that effective knowledge transfer through e-learning must translate into improved business productivity and profitability. It seems clear that corporate e-learning can achieve this outcome if management can escape a 'skills' and performance mindset and implement learning processes that develop situated meaning and identity.

E-learning, assessment and knowledge creation

Assessment has been a thorny issue for educators in all fields, partly because the assessment of *educational outcomes* has had a different focus from the assessment of *training outcomes*. From a cognitive perspective, educators have questioned trainers' use of assessment criteria that relate strictly to performance and not to critical thinking skills. Furthermore, many educators have criticised forms of educational assessment that require students to regurgitate materials provided during class activities and lectures. This often falls short of fully evidencing a student's deeper understanding (Entwistle 1992: 39).

Traditional assessment methods were based on ranking students according to the knowledge they had gained. The assessment instruments were designed to let students demonstrate their knowledge in ways that could be measured easily, to facilitate comparison between them (Nightingale et al. 1996: 6–8). These assessment methods are often inadequate for evaluating applied knowledge, because the knowledge assessed may not reflect the performance or critical thinking capacity required in real-world conditions (Nightingale et al. 1996: 9).

In recent years, there has been a shift away from these methods of assessing knowledge. The pressure for change has emerged from three key imperatives:

* recognition of the need to develop a broader range of learning outcomes and student abilities than can be assessed by attenuated instruments designed for easy comparison;

- pressure to maximise the value of the assessment process in enriching the learning process and encouraging greater feedback; and
- emphasis on developing students' capacity to practise independent judgment and evaluate their performance (Nightingale et al. 1996: 6).

At the same time, assessment issues raise the deeper question of how learning outcomes are framed. Here, it is helpful to revisit Bloom's taxonomy of educational objectives (1956), which focuses on three main 'domains' of learning:

- **Cognitive:** concerned with the acquisition and application of knowledge, understanding, thinking/creativity and intellectual abilities; for example, defining a term, describing a topic or reading a technical drawing;
- **Psychomotor:** concerned with performance based on the application of motor and other skills; for example, typing a letter, driving a car, communicating with staff or developing a film; and
- **Affective:** concerned with developing motivations and self-awareness; for example, taking responsibility for health and safety, showing concern for fellow employees' feelings or developing sensitivity to environmental problems.

These domains can serve as reference points for the assessment of a wide range of outcomes. In the context of work-based learning, the cognitive domain is particularly relevant, because traditional training pedagogies have often neglected cognitive approaches in favour of narrowly defined skills development. Bloom's taxonomy can thus be used to revisit the wider issue of the pedagogies adopted for workplace learning.

Table 6.3 summarises Bloom's typology of different levels of cognition and highlights how the assessment of learning outcomes can be framed in a manner that is appropriate to each level.

This taxonomy can be used to ensure that the design of learning activities and assessment tools addresses skills and knowledge appropriate to the various levels of cognition. For organisations developing an e-learning strategy, the crucial question is the level of competency required as an outcome of learning. Is the aim to achieve an immediate threshold of proficiency for a new employee? If so, the process needs to recognise that individuals may not have sufficient cognitive awareness or tacit knowledge to mobilise their skills. When individuals progress in a job, they develop the understandings and insights necessary to improve their performance. It is situated experience that builds mastery.

The provision of new modes of assessment is a key area of development in e-learning. Electronic delivery creates unique opportunities for learners to use self-assessment programs that offer immediate feedback as a study aid and revision tool, as well as for marked tests. Significantly, electronic feedback from learners can also be used to evaluate learning processes. At the same time, through self-evaluation, learners can critically assess their own participation, evaluating how they learn and work with peers. Self-reflection and self-evaluation also promote problem solving by giving the learner control over processes and outcomes. These developments, combined with the immediate capture of data and the provision of feedback in real time, represent a major advance for all forms of education.

Table 6.3 Levels of cognition and assessment criteria

Levels of cognition	Illustrative instructional objectives	Illustrative terms for assessing outcomes
Knowledge: The remembering of previously learnt material, ranging from specific facts to complete theories	Know common terms Know specific facts Know methods and procedures Know basic concepts Know principles	Define, describe, identify, name, list, match, outline, select
Comprehension: The ability to grasp the meaning of material	Understand principles Interpret verbal material Interpret charts Translate verbal material into mathematical terms Estimate future consequences	Convert, distinguish, estimate, explain, extend, give examples, paraphrase, predict, rewrite, summarise
Application: The ability to use material in new situations	Apply concepts, laws and principles to practical situations Solve mathematical problems Construct charts and graphs Demonstrate correct usage of a method or procedure	Change, compute, demonstrate, manipulate, modify, operate, predict, prepare, produce, relate, show, solve, use
Analysis: The ability to break down material into its component parts so that its organisational structure may be understood	Recognise logical fallacies Distinguish between facts and inferences Assess the relevance of data Analyse the structure of a work (art, music, writing)	Break down, diagram, differentiate, distinguish, infer, outline, analyse
Synthesis: The ability to put parts together to form a new whole	Re-present learnt material in a coherent written or spoken form Produce original creative works Propose a plan for an experiment Integrate learning from different areas into a plan for solving a problem Formulate a new classification schema	Compose, create, devise, design, generate, modify, reconstruct, reorganise, review, rewrite
Evaluation: The ability to judge the adequacy of material for a given purpose	Assess written material for consistency Judge how far conclusions are supported by data Appraise the value of a work (art, music, writing) by use of internal criteria	Appraise, compare, conclude, contrast, criticise, discriminate, explain, interpret

Based on Bloom 1956

Conclusion

To restrict e-learning to a training paradigm is to vitiate its real potential for transforming the learning process and extending it far beyond the narrow band of skills traditionally associated with work-based training. Traditional learning processes tend to reduce learners to the status of passive recipients of information from on high, while evaluating 'achievement' through simplistic, standardised tests of knowledge retention and performance skills. Both these characteristics have a tendency to limit the types of knowledge that learning engenders.

By contrast, e-learning that deploys learner-centred pedagogies and continuous self-evaluation can be used to transmit a far wider range of skills and knowledge while remaining relevant to organisational needs. Pedagogically innovative e-learning can develop critical faculties that can be applied effectively in real-world situations. Ultimately, effective e-learning has the potential to raise the stakes for learning of all kinds by offering an unprecedented level of autonomy to self-paced and self-directed learners. If the outcome is a learning process that is led by learner demand rather than by supply-driven force-feeding, this will be to the benefit of all parties, from individuals to organisations to societies.

Principle 6

E-learning has maximum strategic impact when it deploys
pedagogies and assessment procedures appropriate to the individual
learner while enhancing situated performance and strategic thinking.

Individual Factors in E-learning Performance

Every individual learns differently, but an individual's capacity to learn can be extended or limited by the learning experience itself. Knowing why people learn in different ways is crucial for the design of e-learning if it is to develop its potential to meet individuals' needs. This chapter begins by reviewing some useful interpretations of the factors affecting individuals' predispositions to learn, then explores a range of strategies for developing an inclusive approach that accommodates individual differences.

Self-efficacy and e-learning

Numerous studies have established a strong link between individual personality characteristics and learning success. Research by Holton and Naquin, for example, reveals that personality traits are directly related to the successful completion of a learning task or activity. Extroverted and conscientious people tend to have high educational achievement, especially in interactive settings (Holton & Naquin 1999: 651). When extroversion is combined with a positive outlook – enthusiastic, vigorous and sociable – or a positive perception of the learning task, people generally are motivated to learn and have strong work-related behaviours and values.[5] Yet the question remains: what specifically makes people want to learn, and what impact does their motivation have on individual performance?

Psychologists use the concept of self-efficacy to describe the process people go through when making choices or approaching a new task. Faced with a certain degree of risk, people generally want to weigh up their options. They want to determine 'what's in it for them' (the personal benefits and rewards) and the effort required to gain the rewards (Brown, Collins & Duguid 1989a; Bandura 1986, 2001; Schunk 1981). This perception creates a frame of mind in which the individual is favourably or unfavourably disposed to attempt the challenge. A positive mental outlook helps to mobilise the cognitive, motivational and behavioural capabilities essential to carry out a new task. This is an important point, as self-efficacy factors can also directly relate to an individual's success in e-learning. Figure 7.1 summarises the factors that determine different levels of self-efficacy.

Employees who perceive themselves as highly efficacious have a dispositional perspective described as positive affect. Their level of motivation

Figure 7.1   Determinants of self-efficacy

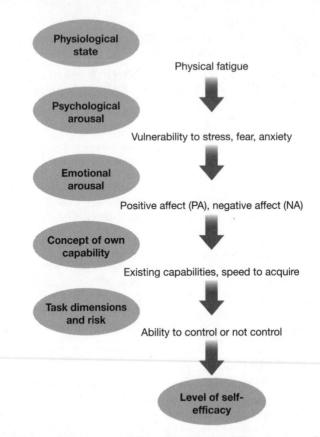

permits them to learn successfully and embrace different ways of learning. Those who view themselves as having low self-efficacy are likely to have increased negative affect, resulting in high levels of anxiety. This tends to make their efforts to learn disjointed, and can precipitate failure or non-completion. Anxiety also makes it more difficult for learners to mobilise the behaviours required to adopt new learning methods, as when shifting from facilitated classroom-based instruction to e-learning.

Self-efficacy partially explains why some learners succeed in e-learning and others do not. An individual who is anxious before engaging in e-learning will find it more difficult to use the learning experience to build new meanings, behaviours and capabilities. Without these, individuals disengage from the process and feel threatened. They resist learning to e-learn. It is vital that the initial engagement with e-learning is designed to eliminate factors that are likely to promote negative affect and diminished self-efficacy. The rewards or perceived benefits must have a stronger impact than the perceived problems.

Self-efficacy and work-related performance

Self-efficacy also impinges on individuals' performance in organisational settings. Research by Stajkovic and Luthans (1998) confirms that there is a strong relationship between 'frame of mind' and work performance. Work-related performance improves when organisations foster a positive predisposition to act and acquire knowledge. This can be achieved by refocusing existing approaches to learning, even while using standard methods of communication, planning and appraisal (1998: 260–1).

There are numerous advantages in promoting self-efficacy and overcoming negative affect. A positive predisposition helps to translate learning into performance that is beneficial to both the individual and the organisation, assisting people to co-orient themselves to a purpose that holds meaning for themselves *and* for the group. Self-efficacy also helps individuals to draw on past experience and make the benefits of learning explicit within an agreed future outcome. Etienne Wenger labels this a known learning trajectory (1998: 153–5). In the process, organisations can assist in the formation of a 'social concept' of identity and develop the individual's ability to recognise the factors that contribute to self-efficacy (Wenger 1998: 190). To this extent, a positive outlook can become self-reinforcing.

Self-efficacy is subjective and driven by personal perception. Individuals' perceptions shape their reality in their private lives as well as at work. The individual's cognitive capacity plays a key role in the ability to make judgments and build self-efficacy. This has implications for the design of e-learning, which is both a practice requiring new capabilities and a means of building those capabilities.

Self-efficacy and technology use

Not surprisingly, many studies have shown that people's use of technology is related to their beliefs about their ability to use technology successfully. Research by Compeau, Higgins and Huff confirmed that adopting new technologies was not just a matter of 'selling the technology' by convincing people of the benefits they would gain from it, but also involved 'coaching, teaching, and encouraging individuals to ensure that they have the requisite skills and confidence in their skills to be successful in their use' (1999: 1). Recognising and mobilising the prerequisite skills may require a deeper level of knowledge than that required for performance alone.

Conventional approaches to learning may not develop the higher-order skills needed for successful e-learning (Beer 2000: 33; Horton 2000: 15–16; Chung & Reigeluth 1992: 14; Gale 2003: 2–3). For example, where learners have a strong fear of failure, a negative affect can occur in which poor understanding generates spirals of anxiety that magnify learning difficulties at both individual and collective levels (Lindsley, Brass & Thomas 1995). In an e-learning environment, it is particularly important that learners identify with the purpose of learning, construct their own meanings, interact with others in collaborative activity and resolve problems associated with the learning (Kilpatrick & Bound 2003: 22; Ross, Powell & Elias 2002; Wang, Hinn & Kanfer 2001).

As Leu points out, new forms of information and communication technology require new instructional practices to assist learners to acquire new forms of literacy (2001). In today's society, technologically based information literacy is increasingly essential. Oliver and Towers (2000) summarise the generic skills this involves:

- resource/socio-structural literacy (for example, understanding the nature and location of information);
- research literacy (for example, the ability to analyse, extract and use information);
- communications literacy (for example, the ability to format, communicate and publish ideas electronically);
- problem-solving literacy (for example, the ability to organise and classify information); and
- technological literacy (for example, the ability to determine the efficacy of new methods and adapt to changing technologies).

These new literacies are essential prerequisites for e-learning, and need to be explicitly built into the design of the learning process if the process is to foster participatory and positive approaches to acquiring new knowledge. This is particularly important when dealing with culturally diverse populations that include adult learners who may have had negative experiences with conventional classroom instruction.

Cognitive and metacognitive skills

Building cognitive capacity involves individuals purposefully accessing learning; selecting, processing and evaluating information; re-evaluating the choices they have made; and building a sense of purpose and meaning. Cognitive approaches acknowledge that learners are active players or, to use Bandura's term, social theorists, whose experiences, social networks and beliefs guide their actions and interactions (2001: 3).

Cognition and constructivism

A cognitive orientation to learning holds that learning takes place within the individual mind. In this view, learners are 'sources of plans, intentions, goals, ideas, memories, and emotions actively used to attend to, select, and construct meaning from stimuli and knowledge from experience' (Wittrock cited in Woolfolk 1993: 237). Cognitive theorists believe that learning is the result of people's attempts to make sense of the world by using all the mental tools at their disposal. Learning is influenced by how people think about situations and by their knowledge, expectations and feelings. People are understood as active processors of information, who initiate experiences, seek out information to solve problems and reorganise what they already know to achieve new learning (Woolfolk 1993: 237–9). Woolfolk claims that knowledge is more than the end product of previous learning. It guides new learning, because what people bring to a learning situation – what they already know – largely determines what they will learn, remember and forget.

Neo-Piagetian proponents of constructivism have also drawn heavily on the work of Lev Vygotsky, who viewed development as a complex dialectical process characterised by periodicity, unevenness and metamorphosis or qualitative transformation of one form into another, based on an intertwining of external and internal factors and adaptive processes (Vygotsky cited in Cole et al. 1978: 122).

As Brown, Collins and Duguid point out:

> learning is a process of enculturation . . . the activities of a domain are framed by its culture. Their meaning and purpose are socially constructed through negotiations among present and past members (1989a: 34).

From a constructivist epistemology, then, learning is about making meaning. Individual learning therefore is not about cognition in isolation; it is the process of making meaning and using as a social process able to engage the learning in constructing new meaning (Wenger, McDermott & Snyder 2002: 33–37). Cultural artefacts such as tools, social structures and language provide the means through which learners interact with and act upon the world, which in turn interacts with and upon the learner. Socialisation is critical to the development of higher cognitive functions.

Social cognition refers to the way people think and reason as a result of the interactions they have with others. Through interaction over time, people come to share common ways of thinking and using language. Another sociocultural perspective on learning is the theory of situated activity as previously discussed in Chapter 6 in relation to learner-centred approaches to learning. This theory argues that knowledge is inseparable from the contexts and activities in which it develops and challenges the assumption that learning which occurs in one context can automatically be transferred to another; rather, it states that the activity through which knowledge is developed and used is inseparable from learning.

Social cognitive theory, efficacy and technology use

Social cognitive theory seeks to examine how pre-existing beliefs and experiences influence individuals' learning behaviour, independent of the desired outcomes. In collaborative learning scenarios, group attainments – or what Bandura calls 'collective efficacy' – may transcend the individual self-efficacy of individual learners. As Bandura succinctly states:

> Because the collective performance of a social system involves transactional dynamics, perceived collective efficacy is an emergent group-level property, not simply the sum of the efficacy beliefs of individual members (2001: 12).

Self-efficacy is critical to engagement in technology use. People's beliefs about their capabilities to use technology successfully are related to their prior experiences, their decisions about whether and how much to use technology and the extent to which they are able to learn from training.

Social cognitive theory suggests that the relationship between self-efficacy and the environment is reciprocal. While self-efficacy is important to accelerate and encourage technology use, the environment can influence cognitive beliefs, which in turn influence attitudes and behaviours (Compeau et al. 1999: 1) that underpin individuals' adoption and use of computers and computer-supported collaborative learning (Hill, Smith & Mann 1986; Weller 2000; Wang et al. 2001). The more successfully an individual's expectations are realised, the greater the increase in positive affect and individual capacity to make judgments on self-efficacy. Over time, the distinction between acquiring capabilities and having the confidence to deploy them diminishes or disappears.

E-learning models that address self-efficacy and cognitive beliefs can positively link individual learning experiences with real-world performance. Equally, the inverse can occur: poorly designed learning processes can lead to poor understanding or a failure to reinforce positive factors involved in individual learning. This, in turn, may embed spirals of anxiety and dispositional perspectives that magnify learning difficulties on an individual and collective level (Lindsley et al. 1995).

Cognition and metacognition

Metacognitive skills are also essential for successful learning. Sometimes described as 'thinking about thinking', metacognition involves an awareness of how I learn and what I need to do to control *my* learning and thinking processes. The value of improving metacognitive skills becomes obvious when we consider that organisations are complex environments in which effective performance often requires 'a command of a body of knowledge that exceeds the average person's mental capacity' (Wiig & Wiig 1999: 2). Preparing workers for such an environment necessitates a focus on building conceptual, metacognitive capabilities.

The initial study of metacognition is generally attributed to John Flavell (1979, 1987), who divided metacognitive knowledge into three categories (summarised in Livingston 1997: 1):
- **Knowledge of personal variables:** how people learn and process information;
- **Knowledge of task variables:** what people know about the task, the demands likely to be placed upon them and the options available; and
- **Knowledge of strategic variables:** awareness of how to use the knowledge and its likely impact on those involved, the context and the individual.

Individuals' metacognitive capability strongly influences their attitudes, levels of motivation and resulting behaviour in terms of tackling new tasks at hand.

Sensemaking

On a day-to-day basis, individuals are required to make sense of unpredictable situations that arise. To do so, they draw on their previous experiences and their stores of knowledge. This process is called 'sensemaking'.

Sensemaking is crucial to individuals' ability to meet new contingencies, because it enables them to transform their knowledge into a form that can address the new situation and speed up their adaptation to it. This is an invaluable capability in terms of both individual achievement and organisational success. Making sense of the non-routine or unknown often requires making tacit knowledge explicit. This re-emphasises the importance of cognitive and metacognitive capacity (Davenport & Prusak 1998).

Generating positive emotions when transferring current learning and experience into new situations has a positive influence on performance, particularly when people are under pressure or facing large-scale change (Weik 1995: 229). The more negative the stimuli, the less opportunity the individual has to learn from experience; and the more inconsistent the trajectory of the planned change process, the more likely it is that individual sensemaking will fail. Sensemaking is itself an evolving process, influenced by random and unpredictable factors (Weik 1995: 15, 153).

Encouraging individuals to recognise their own sensemaking activity can help them to escape the constraints imposed by explicit knowledge structures (the baggage of cultural and work-based perspectives). This may be enabled by forms of learning that promote self-reflection and metacognitive growth. The aim is to encourage self-direction to a point where learners make sense of their own learning while reflecting on and evaluating the experience.

Yet cognitive and metacognitive skills are far from being the only forms of intelligence that are mobilised in a work-related or learning context. To account for the full diversity of individual responses to learning, we need to consider other aspects of intelligence and differences in learning styles.

Learning styles

Keefe defines learning styles as 'characteristic behaviours . . . that serve as relatively stable indicators of how [learners] perceive, interact with, and respond to the learning environment' (1979: 4). Conversely, individuals who are aware of their own learning styles are better placed to manage their learning experiences and understand their strengths and weaknesses.

The design of learning, whether by physical or electronic means, needs to consider the wide range of factors that are likely to facilitate how each individual will transfer the learning into applied practice or behaviours. Awareness of learning styles allows managers, instructors and instructional designers to design, develop, implement and assess individualised learning experiences. In the simplest terms, learning styles reflect individual preferences for learning. These differences can be classified in a number of different ways. Once again the broadest classification could be an individual's preferences for:

- **Visual:** learning by seeing (text and image);
- **Auditory:** learning by hearing (audio files); and
- **Kinaesthetic:** learning by doing ('touch and feel', practice or projects).

A great deal of literature exists on learning styles and the dimensions that shape individual learning preferences. Table 7.1 outlines and provides a point of comparison for five of the better-known frameworks in use around the globe: Kolb's Learning Style Inventory, the Gregorc Style Delineator, the Myers-Briggs Type Indicator, the Honey and Mumford Learning Styles Inventory, and Solomon and Felder's Index of Learning Styles.

It is widely recognised that online learning needs to consider differences in learning styles (see for example Brennan, McFadden & Law 2001: 31), but research on how to achieve this has produced mixed findings. Although there are significant numbers of research projects investigating the impact of learning styles on computer-mediated learning, the research parameters and definitions of e-learning varied so much that the studies, taken as a whole, must be regarded as inconclusive. Even when studies dealt with comparable variables, their findings on how different learning styles affected e-learning were incompatible. As Brennan, McFadden & Law suggest, interactions between users and technologies are as varied as the range of learners and their preferences.

Table 7.1   Comparison of some learning-styles classifications

Theorist	Description	Range
Myers-Brigg (1975)	Katherine Briggs and Isobel Briggs Myers' Myers-Briggs Type Indicator (MBTI®), which assesses personality types, is based on the types and preferences of Carl Gustav Jung, who wrote Psychological Types in 1921. Developed in World War Two, it was not until the mid-1970s that the MBTI® became the most widely used tool for classifying individual, group and organisational attributes.	Extroversion–Introversion (E–I) Sensing–Intuition (S–N) Thinking–Feeling (T–F) Judging–Perceiving (J–P) See http://www.knowyourtype.com/
Kolb (1981)	David Kolb's Learning Style Inventory measures four learning modes.	Concrete Experience–Abstract Conceptualisation Reflective Observational–Active Experimentation See http://www.hayresourcesdirect.hay group.com/Learning_Self-Development/ Assessments_Surveys/Learning_Style_ Inventory/Overview.asp
Gregorc (1982)	The Gregorc Style Delineator is a self-scoring battery-based questionnaire on mediation theory that states that the human mind has channels through which it receives and expresses information most efficiently and effectively. According to Gregorc, mediation abilities describe a person's capacity to use these channels.	Concrete Sequential (CS) Abstract Sequential (AS) Abstract Random (AR) Concrete Random (CR) See http://www.gregorc.com/gregorc.html
Honey & Mumford (1986)	Peter Honey and Alan Mumford's Learning Styles Inventory is based on Kolb's concepts. However, their set of inventories was developed specifically to help students and teachers identify the diversity that exists in any group of people.	Activist Reflector Theorist Pragmatist See http://www.peterhoney.co.uk/main/
Felder & Solomon (1999)	Barbara Soloman developed the Index of Learning Styles (ILS) in conjunction with Richard Felder. It has evolved from other 'learning indexes' and places a deliberate emphasis on metacognitive knowledge as a key factor in learning styles.	Processing (active–reflective; ACT–REF) Perception (sensing–intuitive; SEN–INT) Input (visual–verbal; VIS–VRB) Understanding (sequential–global; SEQ–GLO) See http://www.ncsu.edu/felder-public/ ILSpage.html

It is not obvious which factors need to be considered when shaping e-learning interventions to accommodate individual learning styles. Despite mixed findings in both early and recent studies, Wang, Hinn and Kanfer suggest that 'students with all kinds of learning styles would benefit from delivery media that promotes flexible learning in both individual and collaborative learning' (2001: 75). The assumption here is that the learning is designed and delivered to accommodate or target different styles.

It is also important to reflect on how e-learning promotes learning and instructional strategies that can influence or change the prevailing learning style of an individual or group (Cohen 2001; Ross & Schulz 1999). Learning styles can be dynamic, and so can the design of learning interventions. For instance if learning is not just endeavouring to transfer the ability to perform manual tasks, but for example is seeking to build problem-solving capabilities or communication and collaboration skills, adapting the instruction to individual learning styles may provide a framework to model a more personalised intervention. The discourse on learning styles and e-learning also embraces the multiple intelligences approach, which suggests there are different forms of intelligence that shape the individual's learning.

Multiple intelligences

Intelligence is widely presumed to be a universal, probably innate, capacity to make use of linguistic and logical symbols. This notion was challenged by Gardner, who developed the notion of multiple intelligences that are distinct but complementary. His list includes:

- **Logical–mathematical intelligence:** the capacity to discern patterns, work with numbers and engage in higher-order thinking;
- **Linguistic intelligence:** sensitivity to the sounds, rhythms and meanings of language, and hence the capacity to communicate effectively in writing or orally;
- **Musical intelligence:** sensitivity to the realm of sound and vibration, with their powerful consciousness-altering effects (hence some would prefer to call it 'auditory/vibrational intelligence');
- **Bodily/kinaesthetic intelligence:** the ability to control one's body movements and handle objects skilfully;
- **Spatial intelligence:** understanding the relationships of objects in the space–time continuum, including directionality, recognition of specific patterns and designs, and the spectrum of colour and texture;
- **Interpersonal intelligence:** the capacity to discern and respond appropriately to the moods, temperaments, motivations and desires of other people; and
- **Intrapersonal intelligence:** the capacity for self-consciousness, the ability to reflect on oneself and learn from such reflection (Gardner & Hatch 1993; Vincent & Ross 2001; Gardner 2002).

Gardner recently added another category, naturalistic intelligence: the recognition, appreciation and understanding of the natural world (Vincent & Ross 2001). These multiple intelligences develop differently depending on individuals' cultural and personal contacts. The intelligences rarely operate independently of each other, but are used together and complement each other (Vincent and Ross 2001). Vincent and Ross (2001) have developed a set of pedagogical strategies that draw on Gardner's theory.

Gardner's work has been driven by two main concerns. On the practical side, he was concerned about the almost exclusive emphasis on linguistic and logical–mathematical symbolisation in school environments, while on the theoretical side, he was interested in the development and breakdown of cognitive and symbol-using capacities (Gardner & Hatch 1993). He found that individuals may be more talented in one form of symbol use than in others, and that there is not necessarily any carry-over to other forms of symbol use.

An appreciation of multiple intelligences can guide educators in enriching learning experiences and enabling learners to exercise different kinds of intelligence. Some commentators have pointed out that strategies such as story-telling use a number of intelligences, because they involve negotiating and renegotiating meanings to solve complex problems (Jonassen & Hernandez-Serrano 2002). Similarly, Veenema and Gardner (2000) include the example of using a CD-ROM to tell a story through eyewitness accounts, offering close-up views of sites and artefacts. Here, electronic technology can present pictorial, aural and textual renderings from different perspectives, assisting students to 'form rich representations of an event and cultivate deeper understandings'. Learners can then display their understandings in different ways: some might use language to argue, question and make connections; others might work out a narrative of events; still others might produce a play, or create a series of sketches, a video or a piece of music.

The theory of multiple intelligences helps to explain why forms of e-learning that require individuals to work alone suit only a small number of participants. It also highlights the advantages to be gained from collaboration and the use of multiple strategies and media in designing e-learning experiences.

Emotional intelligence

Using Gardner's interpersonal and intrapersonal intelligences as a starting point, Salovey and Mayer developed a theoretical account of emotional intelligence, which they defined as:

> The subset of social intelligence that involves the ability to monitor one's own and others' feelings and emotions, to discriminate among them, and to use this information to guide one's thinking and actions (1990: 189).

These ideas were publicised by Goleman in his book, *Emotional Intelligence: Why can it Matter more than IQ?* (1995). He suggests that the skills involved in emotional and social competence include monitoring and controlling emotions, coping with frustration and stress, social problem-solving, effective communication, controlling impulses, working cooperatively with others, and initiating and maintaining friendships.

Ross, Powell and Elias emphasise the importance of social problem solving and decision making. Success in these areas, they suggest, requires the skills of noticing and understanding people's feelings, determining and selecting goals, generating alternative solutions, selecting appropriate solutions and reflecting on the process (Ross et al. 2002: 43).

How different individuals cope with stress is also a much-researched area. Slaski and Cartwright (2002) note that experiences of pressure or negative emotions can be moderated by the way individuals use emotional intelligence to appraise their relationship with their environment. Their study of 320 middle managers working with a major British retailer showed a significant link between emotional intelligence and health and performance.

Skills sets that include emotional intelligence have become increasingly popular when used as consulting tools. According to prevailing opinion and anecdotal evidence, emotional intelligence can increase performance and productivity (Thi Lam & Kirby 2002). It has also been suggested that emotionally intelligent individuals are capable of setting priorities, leading to increased commitment to the organisations in which they work. Abraham's studies of customer-service representatives and health professionals found that emotional intelligence had a tighter relationship with organisational commitment than did job satisfaction (Abraham 2000).

It would be interesting to investigate the correlation between emotional intelligence and e-learning.[6] Goleman includes focusing on clear, manageable goals as one of the guidelines for emotional intelligence training (1998: 252), and highlights the need for performance feedback, the opportunity for practice, and the provision of models, encouragement and evaluation. Having the necessary emotional intelligence to accept and provide feedback, to empathise with others and to listen is also part of building metacognitive abilities (Goleman 1998). Although these suggested strategies relate to emotional competence, the same strategies are applicable to other forms of learning.

Because non-standard problems are typical of work environments, problem solving (usually done in groups) is a feature of most contemporary learning approaches. Some studies suggest that e-learning has certain advantages in encouraging problem-solving activity. For example, in a study of learners dealing with non-routine problems, Jonassen and Hyug found that computer-mediated learners generally took longer and experienced greater frustration than face-to-face groups, yet their problem solving was of a higher quality. Jonassen and Hyug also suggest that this environment is conducive to 'deep and reflective thinking' because social problem solving and decision making are an intrinsic part of the process (2001: 35).

The skills involved in emotional and social competence – coping with stress and frustration, social problem solving and decision making, communicating effectively and working cooperatively with others – are aspects of emotional intelligence that enhance learning in any environment. People with this predisposition would seem to have many of the cognitive and metacognitive skills required for effective e-learning. Figure 7.2 provides an overview of the factors that shape not only an individual's predisposition to complete e-learning, but also the individual's sense of identity.

By shaping e-learning to accommodate individual differences, we can not only improve learning outcomes, but also assist individuals to develop the capacity to translate learning into a given situation, whether for personal, learning or work-related purposes.

Figure 7.2 Individual e-learning variables

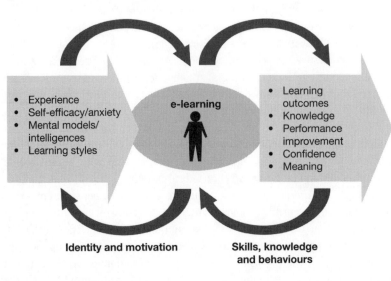

Identity and motivation | Skills, knowledge and behaviours

Cultural differences

Conventional classroom-based instruction involves dozens, scores or even hundreds of students interacting with a single instructor. E-learning, by contrast, offers opportunities for different modes of interaction involving many more people from diverse cultural backgrounds. This involves a new set of literacies, which require both teachers and learners to read and think more self-critically, and 'develop new insights about far more cultural traditions and ways of knowing than we have ever experienced' (Leu 2001: 16).

In face-to-face situations, instructors are all too ready to give priority to 'getting through' the set material, even when students of different cultural backgrounds are struggling. It is also difficult for a sole instructor to take account of cultural differences in the tempo of communication. Among traditional Indigenous people in Australia, for instance, interactions have a rhythm that is very different from the Western norm:

> Many people may speak at once; attentiveness is not shown either by maintaining silence or by maintaining eye contact with the speaker; adults tend not to talk down to children; it is not considered polite to ask direct questions or to move too quickly from social to 'business' talk; and . . . silence is an acceptable response on the part of someone who has been addressed (Malcolm 1998: 130).

On every count, this places Indigenous people at odds with the conventional Western approach to classroom instruction. This was reinforced by a case study on this topic commissioned for the Learning to E-learn project (see Falk et al. 2003).

Some of the difficulties in conducting cross-cultural e-learning also derive from differences in how participants of different cultures collaborate with other learners, or with the instructor. To accommodate these differences, learning processes need to encompass more than one 'world view' or socially constructed sense of what holds meaning (Falk et al. 2003: 2).

Cultural differences may be exacerbated by e-learning approaches that rely heavily on written communication. A study by Goodfellow et al. (2001) pointed to the difficulties experienced by non-native speakers when they are expected to produce timely and intelligent written comments in a foreign language. Similar problems are likely to be experienced by native-speaking adult learners who are not confident of their written communication skills.

McLaughlin (2001) argues that e-learning environments should be designed to be culturally responsive by promoting shared understandings and flexible thought; situating learning in the students' context; and emphasising active, collaborative, conversational, reflective learning. Ideally, learning in cross-cultural settings should be a conversation within a community of inquiry. Strategies to achieve this include story-telling, viewing differences as strengths and developing a learning environment where people, rather than content, are the focus (McLaughlin 2001). Just as any team needs to be nurtured through appropriate group development processes, so there is a need for conscious development of an e-learning community in which the instructor acts as a facilitator, not the focal point for knowledge transfer (Gunawardena et al. 2001).

Conclusion

It is often claimed that e-learning is somehow more democratic, collaborative, interactive and driven by a person's learning style and preferences than classroom-based instruction, but this is not necessarily the case. These qualities have to be designed into the learning process. Furthermore, individual learners have to acquire preparatory skills if they are to respond to the opportunities available in the electronic environment. Learning to e-learn requires individuals to make explicit and conscious use of new capabilities (Kilpatrick & Bound 2003: 19).

The design of e-learning needs to be responsive to the differences between individual learners. It must also build strong relationships between learners, organisational personnel and learning facilitators. An integrated e-learning design should use technology and the learning environment to accommodate the individual, not the other way around. E-learning needs to be a process that can encourage reflection and develop forms of knowledge that extend beyond mere information content. To maximise performance outcomes, it is often necessary to build capabilities and literacies that are peripheral to the transfer of operational skills and knowledge.

Everyone acquires and uses knowledge differently. If this seems obvious, why do so many learning programs ignore individuals' differences and limitations? To have maximum effect, e-learning processes must encourage self-efficacy, self-reliance, flexibility, reflection and strategic thinking. This can be achieved only if the learning process is designed to accommodate individual differences and take learners' perspectives into account. Addressing individual needs and perspectives can then directly translate into how well we undertake e-learning to meet collective imperatives.

Principle 7

Effective e-learning requires innovative approaches to the design and delivery of learning programs to accommodate individual differences and actively engage learners in developing their ability to acquire knowledge.

[5] See, for example, Levin & Stokes 1989; McFatter 1994; George & Brief 1992; all cited in Holton & Naquin 1999: 651.
[6] See Bowles 2003a, a commissioned case study on the role of e-learning in EQ training; note: emotional intelligence, or EI, has been popularised as EQ, or Emotional Quotient, to parallel IQ, or Intelligence Quotient).

Toward Collaborative E-learning

Collaboration should be central to the design of e-learning. Effective learning is based on collective experiences, and assists the flow of both tacit and explicit knowledge. Any e-learning system that inhibits this flow or narrows the sources of knowledge transmitted will limit its development of human potential and ultimately its potential productive capability. But how can learning be targeted to mobilise collaboration among learners and engage their tacit as well as their explicit knowledge?

The acquisition, transfer and generation of capabilities are part of an individual journey, but repeated individual action and interaction can translate individual capabilities into collective capabilities shared by the group, team, organisation or community. Appreciating that the journey is shared is an important aspect of understanding that e-learning is also a means to orient collaborative endeavour and meaning. As well as transferring new competencies (the means to perform), e-learning can match competencies with identity attributes (individual and collective sense of purpose). The widespread failure to appreciate this has limited how we deploy e-learning. Figure 8.1 suggests how a sense of collective purpose can co-orient competency and identity attributes.

Virtuous circles

Borrowing from the economists' lexicon it is possible to use the concept of 'virtuous circles' to explain how learning can contribute to a strategy that is mutually beneficial to the individual and the organisation. Michael Porter's writing on competitiveness and cluster development suggests that particular economic strategies can establish a self-reinforcing virtuous circle of increasing productivity, competitiveness, excellence and value creation (1990). In simple terms, this means that more and cheaper production by a skilled workforce, oriented by a guiding development strategy, can lead to more innovation and learning, even lower production costs and greater sales.

The term 'virtuous learning circle' is used here, not as an economic construct, but to denote a mutually advantageous relationship between individual learning and group or organisational outcomes. The circle metaphor suggests that the knowledge flow is reciprocal, not linear. Two examples can be used to flesh out this concept: learning to change while undertaking change; and learning to service customer needs while providing service.

Figure 8.1 Orienting individual performance and motivation with collective purpose

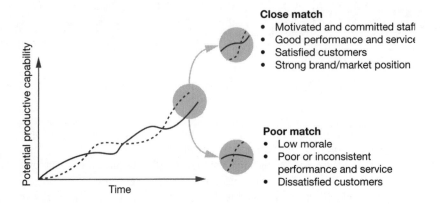

In the first example, e-learning may be used to train individual employees to respond to a specific change. A virtuous circle exists when learning promotes the capability not only to change, but also to learn through the change processes. This can then lead to greater capacity to undertake change. The 'smaller' issue of learning to change is placed in a wider, more sustainable context of agility and responsiveness.

In the second example, both the staff member and the customer in a service relationship can be treated as learners. Investment in teaching customers and staff how to improve service exchanges becomes 'virtuous' when the exchanges themselves reinforce positive mutual expectations, competencies and behaviours. The interests of all concerned (staff, customers, managers, owners and shareholders) are best achieved where learning builds relationships so that customers choose to be serviced by the organisation. The result is that loyal and valued customers become sources of knowledge on what represents service excellence. This in turn enhances reputation, credibility, trust, brand and market position (see Chapter 11 for more on this point).

Reinforcing a virtuous learning circle may simply involve making the individual learner aware of the link between learning and the benefits they will enjoy as a result. These benefits go beyond the certificate of completion, better job-related skills or even a qualification. They include customer loyalty, organisational growth, improved job security and stronger career prospects.

While situated learning processes that address real workplace problems and accommodate different learning styles lend themselves to producing a virtuous learning circle, it is above all the linking of individual learning to collective processes that builds awareness of mutual needs and offers the best longer-term results for all involved.

Facilitating collective e-learning

An effective e-learning community is unlikely to develop of its own accord. Facilitators need to develop this community in much the same way as sporting coaches develop teamwork among players. Traditional information-providing behaviours (the 'sage on the stage' model) need to take second place to promoting interpersonal relationships and group development.

Teaching in e-learning environments requires both pedagogical and technological knowledge. Those involved will often need support in developing the necessary skills and knowledge to design experiences that incorporate interactivity, dialogue, reflectivity, student control and collaborative learning (Eastmond 1998; Khan 1997). It may be necessary to establish teams of teachers, including individuals with expertise in the specific subject and others with technological know-how, supported by administrative staff (Harper et al. 2000: 23; Schrum 1998: 60). Developing effective e-learning is a resource-intensive process; Muhammad Betz has estimated that every hour of web instruction costs about a hundred hours of preparation (cited in Brennan, McFadden & Law 2001: 49).

Studies of e-learning practice have highlighted numerous issues facing instructors and designers. Lally and Barrett found that e-learners needed time for group interaction and a sense of group identity to emerge (Lally & Barrett 1999: 155). Participation in chat rooms, in particular, is slow to start and requires formal structures to encourage involvement (Snewin 1999). It can also be time-consuming to provide meaningful feedback using the Web, and some students resist participating in collective discussion, preferring one-to-one contact with the instructor (Khan 1997; Gale 2003). Students especially value interaction with instructors when they respond quickly, keep the class discussion on track and are readily available for individual attention (Eastmond 1998: 37; Gale 2003). Teachers need to take an active role to keep the dialogue alive and provide discussion points that assist in the creation of a socially cohesive group (Weller 2000).

E-learning seems most effective when it is employed within a framework of 'co-operative goal structure', whereby individual students can attain their personal objectives only if they work with their fellow students towards shared goals (Lally & Barrett 1999: 153–4). In this environment, student interaction becomes an integral part of learning.

Accommodating learner differences

Heterogeneous learning communities are characterised by variations in learning orientations, linguistic skills and cultural imperatives, to name just a few. Accommodating diversity is often difficult in classroom settings; by contrast, online learning can provide opportunities for alternative approaches designed to accommodate individual differences and facilitate the sharing and transfer of knowledge within a learning community.

Technically, it is possible to offer all learners a high degree of flexibility in the way they engage with e-learning materials. In an ideal situation, with no restraints on resources, one student could have learning materials translated instantaneously into Bahasa Indonesian while another could read the same materials in Mandarin. One could access a graph to illustrate a point, while another might download a photograph. One learner might spend thirty minutes on a task that took another several hours.

While it would be costly to build this kind of flexibility into learning programs across the board, the World Wide Web constitutes a huge repository of resources that can be used to facilitate flexibility. The scope for participation by non-native English speakers is also increasing as the Web becomes more multilingual.

Barrett and Lally's early study of e-learning (1999), even though a small sample size, found that there were gender differences in participation and collaboration, with men contributing more and longer messages than women. On the other hand, the women who participated were making more effective use of the interactive potential of the medium. The opportunity to read an entire sequence of postings before composing a response in a web conference can act as a stimulus to reflection. In a study of online learning conducted by Holt et al. (1998), it was found that reading and reflecting on other students' responses helped participants to evaluate their own beliefs and feelings.

Using Web resources effectively requires an approach that is primarily process- rather than content-oriented. For example, learners in an architecture course who needed to understand the stresses within roof structures could search the Web for roof styles characteristic of different cultures. Here, learners might need to understand certain content, but their instruction is primarily related to process: how to obtain the necessary information. Learners might also visit buildings, construct model roofs, engage in online discussion with experts in the field and use computer-aided drawing programs. These approaches promote engagement with other learners and with people who have experience to share. Conversations about the required competencies, what they mean and how they can be acquired take place as an integral part of learning.

Collaborative learning places responsibilities on learners as well as facilitators. Learners need to take responsibility for understanding their needs and searching for ways to accommodate those needs. This develops participants' capacity for self-directed learning (Schrum 1998).

Strategies for fostering collaboration

Teachers in fully online environments need to contextualise and monitor learning activity to compensate for the absence of physical cues. For example, students' participation in online discussion will often need to be monitored to ensure that all are participating constructively and understand the meeting mode. Instructors may need to intervene to resolve problems and offer comments that summarise the state of a discussion and provide a sense of accomplishment and direction.

Collaborative learning may require learners to reorient their values as well. In a study of sixteen first-year medical students participating in e-learning through email, asynchronous computer discussions and readings on the server, Lally and Barrett (1999) reported that some participants remained passive; that is, they did not participate in discussions. Online groups were not supportive of all participants, and discussions sometimes became more competitive than collaborative. Lally and Barrett conjecture that this may have been due to 'communication anxiety' or to a lack of familiarity with cooperative approaches to learning. They suggest that the learning community needs to accommodate such anxieties and provide a 'safe' framework for those who experience a fear of online communication.

Hill (2001) suggests the following strategies and techniques for collaborative e-learning:

- Establish a 'failure-safe' space in which to work and communicate.
- Assist the learner to set expectations and overcome information overload.
- Establish where to find information and materials on the Web and when to anticipate various types of communication.
- Encourage an atmosphere of adventure.
- Assist with time-management strategies.
- Encourage the setting of priorities in reading messages.
- Remind learners that someone is 'out there' by creating multiple ways for them to keep in touch.
- Establish a well-organised structure to facilitate efficient interaction.
- Minimise technology 'glitches' and provide training for coping with them.
- Establish the importance of community — that is, why it is important for learners to contribute to the learning experience.

Making the role of group members explicit enhances group participation. Oliver and Omari (2001) suggest it is necessary to define intermediate steps in the problem-solving process and relate these to defined roles. It is also important to provide a private bulletin board for each team within the group and a means for students to record members' roles and activities. Other studies recommend introducing students to the course and each other in a traditional mode before moving to electronic modes, or at the very least using face-to-face or telephone contact early in the course so that students can 'get to know each other' (Snewin 1999: 321; Gale 2003: 2; Wallace et al. 2003).

In short, e-learning interventions need to be designed so that learners can interact with each other in productive and trust-building ways. Facilitators can achieve this by involving students in planned, sequential, problem-solving experiences that require high levels of mutuality and 'guarantee' individual and joint success (see, for example, Carrier & Sales 1987; Damon & Phelps 1989; Hooper 1992). These collective experiences must be directly related to the learning purpose and reflect the stage the learning has reached.

Group-development experiences fall into two broad types. The first type relates directly to content. For example, a set of e-learning tasks in an environmental studies course might include developing an interview schedule to gather information from a sample community, writing a letter to the appropriate city council authority, designing a facility such as a community garden and obtaining a quotation from a landscaping contractor. This type of exercise allows each participant to take a leadership role in one of the tasks, to assist in refining the 'deliverables' and to work on drafting the required documents. The mediator helps to guarantee success by providing constructive feedback at all stages.

The second type of experience is synthetic and generic in content. Many simulation exercises fall into this category. Here, the primary focus is on learning how to build emotional intelligence. The task becomes secondary to the effort and subsequent reward when individuals are working with others and being assessed on their ability to apply new behaviours in the workplace (Bowles 2003a). Equally, the very act of e-learning may provide a means of building communities with the interest and the capacity to utilise information and communication technology for purposes other than learning.[7] In face-to-face learning contexts, it is usually easy for participants to see the benefits of teamwork. Online learning provides far fewer visual and kinaesthetic cues, so facilitators need to offer plenty of opportunities to develop trust and communication.

Research suggests that well-designed collaborative e-learning can have numerous benefits for learners:

- It can develop teamwork skills (Oliver & Omari 2001; Schrum 1998).
- It can improve students' information technology skills (Maki 2000).
- It can increase participation by giving learners more time to formulate responses and build on others' contributions (Holt et al. 1998: 49).
- It can develop critical and reflective thinking (Holt et al. 1998:49).
- It can challenge learners to reconceptualise their identity as learners (Harper et al. 2000: 25).
- It can reduce the sense of isolation often felt by distance learners (Lally & Barrett 1999; Harper et al. 2000).

Well-supported, interactive e-learning can ultimately lead to the development of a strong learning culture within the group, facilitating the transmission of both explicit and tacit knowledge. This culture in turn can underpin the formation of strong learning communities or communities of practice.

Learning communities and communities of practice

While many researchers agree that it is important to develop a sense of community among online learners, the definitional and conceptual frameworks applied in this area are still evolving. Tu and Corry (2001) have strongly argued that research and literature relating to online communities has failed to develop a paradigm beyond what would apply to traditional communities. In effect, many studies simply 'transferred the traditional community model to an online environment', thereby clouding the meaning of online community (McIsaac & Gunawardena 1996 cited in Tu & Corry 2002: 7). Elsewhere, Tu and Corry (2002) distinguish between a learning community and community learning. A learning community is generally dependent on the community collectively undertaking learning exchanges in which participants learn together through horizontal interaction. By contrast, community learning can involve both horizontal and vertical interactions.

There are considerable differences in terminology from one study to another. Boyer (1995) uses the term 'community of learners', defined as 'a group of people with a shared purpose, good communication and a climate of justice, care and occasions for celebrations' (cited in Mentis, Ryba & Annan

2001: 2). Mentis et al. use the terms 'learning community' and 'community of learners' interchangeably, and suggest that these communities are drawn together through the principles of commonality and interdependence.

Kaplan supports the view that learning communities are a vehicle for 'connecting to other people's stories and experiences', mentoring and sharing tacit knowledge (2002: 1). The importance of this process can be gauged when we consider that, according to Kaplan, approximately 70 per cent of what employees need to know to do their jobs successfully is learnt outside formal training.

The learning community approach also has parallels with the concept of a community of practice. Some authors have used the terms interchangeably (see, for example, Bowles 1997: 90; Goss, Cochrane & Hart 2002) while others suggest that a community of practice is one of the elements required for a learning community (Tu & Corry 2002). Lave and Wenger define a community of practice as a set of relations that develop over time among a group of people as a result of shared experiences, language, values, tools, processes and procedures (1991: 98). Dunphy and Griffiths describe communities of practice as informal work groups that link individuals anywhere and at any level of an organisation on the basis of shared interest (1998: 160). As Snyder notes, they are 'soft' structures that not only accelerate individuals' professional development but also develop the organisation's capacity in specific areas of knowledge (cited in Dunphy & Griffiths 1998: 160). Communities of practice can thus help to establish best practice both vertically and horizontally.

Learning in communities of practice involves sharing experiences, developing trust and participating in dialogue and argument. In a study of the interactions between abstract knowledge and situated practice, Brown and Duguid observed a community of practice that evolved among technical support representatives in a large organisation (1991). Learning in this context often took the form of sharing stories of previous machine breakdowns and using narratives to solve problems. This example, an act of converting tacit knowledge into an explicit form, highlights individual learning and the collective learning of the community of practice as integrally linked.

Collective practices, developed over time, reflect the social relations within the community (Wenger 1998: 45). In the previous example, the sharing of stories and the joint building of narratives to diagnose a non-routine problem establish a virtuous circle of mutual engagement, trust and support. These interactions provide the opportunity for joint enterprise — a shared outcome in the form of solving the problem. At the same time, the group or 'community' is connected by much more than performing a task. Group members choose different ways of solving the problem, but ways that also fit the mental framework of the group. The shared 'vision' is to get the job done.

Wenger describes communities of practice as being based on trust, shared values and knowledge, although they also change as shared activities and relationships change. They are complex mixtures of competition and cooperation, trust and suspicion, power and dependence. As a community develops and builds trust, it will often construct informal barriers to the external world. Importantly, participation in a community of practice allows individuals to renegotiate and strengthen their identities:

> We are always simultaneously dealing with specific situations, participating in the histories of certain practices, and involved in becoming certain persons. As trajectories, our identities incorporate the past and the future in the very process of negotiating the present (Wenger 1998: 155).

E-learning lends itself to the informal information-sharing that characterises communities of practice. Stuckey, Buening and Fraser have described one such online community of practice that was established in conjunction with *StageStruck*, an award-winning CD-ROM produced by Wollongong University and the National Institute for Dramatic Art (NIDA) and distributed to schools throughout Australia in 1999 (2002: 3–4). The StageStruck online community consists of teachers of performing and creative arts around Australia. It took two years in planning, web design, development and promotion to reach what Wenger describes as 'coalescing', the second phase of community development (1998). Establishing a critical mass of members for the network and connecting potential and existing members through the web site took much longer than anticipated. The experience of *StageStruck* suggests that it is difficult to establish virtual communities of practice when the main repository of learning resources and knowledge sharing (a CD-ROM) is not linked into an interactive network.

Mentis, Ryba and Annan (2001) suggest that individuals in an online community of practice can establish a strong sense of self-efficacy. The knowledge and skills gained through contributing to the community lead to positive self-perceptions and assist with the formation of identity. Through guided participation, individuals move from the periphery of the community towards the centre, where they can share knowledge and meaning.

Building shared meaning

Building communities with shared meaning results in a more enduring framework than just setting goals and objectives. Shared meaning involves constructing an agreed purpose or outcome underpinned by well-established values and beliefs. This can be particularly important in situations where differences of culture, experience and expectation within the projected learning community are such that they will jeopardise deployment of learning interventions. Under these conditions, the development of a shared sense of purpose becomes a precondition for effective management of an intervention. The building of shared meaning involves three components or steps: co-orientation; convergence; and creating shared futures (Bowles 1997: 68).

Co-orientation

Co-orientation involves individuals bringing their unique orientations together to co-ordinate their meanings. It is a learning process in which people watch others and develop responses that orient them towards the practices and procedures used in the workplace (Johnson 1977: 68).

Writing about how to build visions that create purpose and innovation, William Miller (1990: 165) identified two key processes:

- alignment, in which decision-makers agree on and affirm a basic direction and required actions; and
- attunement, involving collective action (teamwork) required to move in a particular direction or to achieve an agreed purpose.

Both alignment and attunement require management interaction and co-ordination towards an agreed vision and purpose. Without attunement, different realities exist: the management view of the organisation, and that held by employees.

Bormann contends that when members of an organisation share a common 'fantasy' — that is, a common conceptual and contextual framework — they experience similar emotions, develop similar attitudes and begin to interpret experiences in the same way. In other words, they achieve symbolic convergence (1983: 103). He suggests that much of what happens to employees in organisations is chaotic, and symbolic convergence is important in helping people to structure their experiences and understandings. Sharing fantasies makes uncertain futures clear by fitting them into narrative frames.

Convergence

Convergence occurs when individuals approach an agreed purpose without sacrificing their sense of identity in other networks, groups or contexts. For instance, a worker may become attuned to an agreed workplace purpose, but may also have a distinct identity as coach of the local football team, as a member of a trade union or as a participant in a school's parents and friends association.

In organisations with hierarchical structures, knowledge becomes compartmentalised and is hard to hold in a holistic way. Yet a holistic grasp of the organisation is needed to manage knowledge so that:

- those with complementary knowledge work together to achieve agreed outcomes;
- those holding different sets of knowledge cooperate as required, when required;
- operational efficiency is enhanced by sharing facilities or responsibilities between individuals and teams (Badaracco 1991: 84); and
- knowledge can be generated through the complex interaction of ideas, creative suggestions and innovations.

At the same time, organisations also need to manage the knowledge resident in groups to avoid the problems that arise when:

- a group uses its knowledge to the detriment of the overall strategic purpose;
- collective and tacit knowledge is lost, limiting a group's ability to work together to achieve enterprise outcomes;
- individuals conform to group thinking, alienating those who think differently and placing group cohesion above enterprise-wide strategic imperatives (Hellriegal & Slocum 1979: 298–302); and

- groups develop outcomes and frameworks that challenge or sideline the strategic goals or knowledge of the enterprise.

In this sense, the formation of groups or subcultures that hold knowledge but do not contribute to corporate outcomes may create barriers to information flow. For example, the formation of cliques and rhetorical communities may directly inhibit the transfer of knowledge and reduce the total organisation's access to information.

Cliques are groups of people who tend to work in close proximity and communicate mostly with each other. Clique members reinforce their beliefs and their differences from the organisation through their communications and language.

A rhetorical community consists of people who participate in a rhetorical vision (Bormann 1983: 115). This involves a common consciousness and aspirations, and a shared sense or feeling about what is good, bad, proper and improper. Rhetorical communities typically have agreed procedures for problem solving, build their own symbols, ensure that learning patterns reinforce behaviour within their community and question power that is structured to challenge their shared vision.

Attempts to break up rhetorical communities — for example, by job rotation or relocation of work units — eventually fail, because these communities exist across structural and functional divides. Often the task for management is to shake out the restrictive practices of rhetorical communities and get them to communicate holistically across the organisation. An early strategy for achieving this was the formation of quality circles (Deming 1986). In this strategy, members of a quality circle are drawn from across the corporation to co-exist as a team. Members have to co-orient towards a purpose that the quality circle team shares. In turn, the corporation has to attune the quality circle to the overall organisational goals and purpose.

A fundamental precondition for achieving a sense of strategic purpose is the development of shared meaning and the creation of an identity linking individual motivations with organisational goals. A community of individuals with shared meaning can meet multiple purposes. They need not reconvene continually to question why they are together or review the benefits of sharing a common purpose. They can spend more time engaged in work and learning. Identity is already established and continues to evolve as the group interacts and completes specified outcomes. This extends well beyond performance, creating commitment to adaptive practices that make it possible to seize future opportunities.

Creating shared futures

Learning needs to be promoted not just as the source of new organisational capabilities, but also as a strategic activity through which individuals' improved capability is translated into overall business success. The concept of shared futures brings together individual and organisational benefits.

To help develop relationships that capture knowledge, organisations need to look beyond their own boundaries. Many forms of knowledge capital will reside in external networks and relationships. If learning can help to encompass these relationships and networks, businesses can achieve a shared vision in which they can potentially draw on capabilities that contribute to competitive advantage while promoting wider social engagement.

Arie de Geus re-emphasised the role of learning as a source of innovation and the discovery of shared futures (1988: 74). He examined how strategic planning processes could involve individual staff members — and even people external to the organisation — and could thus help them learn about the business's purpose and roles. In this approach, the documents generated through a planning process become much more than a communication tool for an elite few. Plans can become a symbol of collective purpose, using a language shared by all involved. The better an organisation's management processes communicate information, the more effective they are as learning experiences, and the stronger the sense of a shared future they produce.

Group, organisational and community dynamics can be described as a web of interacting relationships, in which commitment is expressed by the desire to defend the group's beliefs from outsiders, share group experiences and gain rewards or acceptance from other members. A useful learning environment is created when the 'them and us' mentality is broken down by networking between groups attuned to a shared future. This in turn accelerates the learning process by ensuring that people share information and transfer knowledge through naturally occurring interactions (Robinson & Stern 1997: 104).

Convergence and divergence

Group membership is not the only basis for collective action or a shared vision. Some participants may take part in learning processes for other ends. Divergent learning partnerships can be constituted between people who share a system of shared meaning but have different reasons for being involved. A divergent community can be mutually supportive and facilitate knowledge transfer, but the ability to orient knowledge transfer to agreed outcomes is limited by the participants' different contexts and lack of shared identity. It is important to note that this divergence is not necessarily negative; for instance, it may be an asset in company boards of directors or stakeholder analysis groups. Without a clear focus, however, information in such networks can be subject to distortion and misinterpretation. Divergences that cause distortion of purpose can have severe consequences, in that they can lead to confusion and inhibit learning. See Figure 8.2.

Communication problems are at the heart of the most common reasons for symbolic divergence: inadequate consultation at the planning stage and employee confusion about expected roles. Consultation processes can take a great deal of time. Often management tires of waiting and impatiently imposes a plan from above, disregarding employee preferences. This is likely to create conflict if the plan embodies values that are inconsistent with the group's cultural value system. The implementation and communication of change should be considered early in the planning phase, not when the plan has been devised or the change enacted.

Figure 8.2   Divergent communities

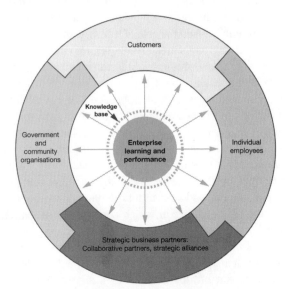

Symbolic divergence also arises when employees are not clear about their role in the planning process. Employee involvement is often limited to implementation strategies, not to deciding whether the plan is worthwhile in the first place. This can lead to symbolic divergence: if employees cannot see the purpose of the plan that is supposed to motivate them to collaborate, the collective goal will lack meaning to most of those involved. On the other hand, if shared objectives are deliberately worded to avoid conflict, they may devolve into 'motherhood' statements that similarly fail to articulate the required ends.

The consequences of divergence can be severe. Consider a situation where senior management sets unrealistic budgets for sales staff to meet. In many cases sales figures are then fudged, budgets are 'achieved' in creative ways, and the effort to meet targets does little for organisational performance. The dysfunctional basis for forming relationships is reinforced, and learning processes that enhance the utilisation of existing knowledge are impeded. Aware of the unrealistic expectations placed on them, staff may see managers as outsiders who are not contributing to the group's shared future.

A convergent learning community, by contrast, can bring many advantages to the organisation, adding value to all members. Figure 8.3 illustrates the relationships that form around a convergent learning community with strong linkages both inside and outside the organisation. Here, learning relationships establish shared meaning, which shapes individual and group interactions between all parties, both internal (individuals, teams and groups) and external (unions, suppliers, partners, customers, shareholders and so on).

Management commonly perceives two main drawbacks to building wider relationships that are not necessarily driven by immediate performance needs. The first is that corporate knowledge 'can walk out the door' with the employee. This is perceived not only as a waste, but also as a threat to competitive advantage. In a true learning community, however, the community of learners is widely dispersed through the organisation or across many organisations. The focus is also on building the network of relationships. As a result, knowledge is less codified and more tacit. It resides in the relationships, not the resulting products. Individuals who leave will not have all the knowledge; they will take only the sense of a relationship that may have little real value outside its operating context.

Figure 8.3   Convergent learning communities

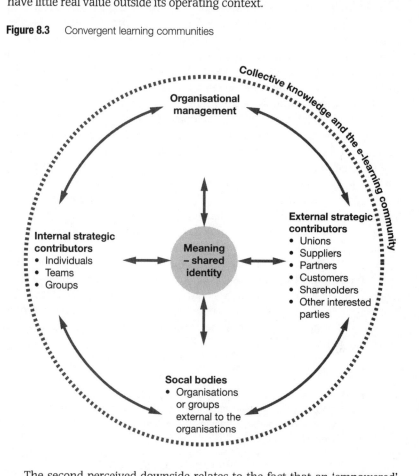

The second perceived downside relates to the fact that an 'empowered', 'enlightened' strategic learning community frees employees to integrate their lives as community members with their work in much more direct ways. Their lives are not nearly so compartmentalised, because they are encouraged to think and act across previously walled-in sectors.

These links and networks between the workplace and community are likely to create a new awareness of corporate responsibilities and ethics in relation to the physical site of their operation, the communities from which the organisations draw their labour and their wider client and stakeholder networks. The perceived downside in this scenario, then, is that there is pressure on firms to act more responsibly towards their communities. New ways of acting require a change in management's identity as well as in the organisation, and these changes often take a great deal of time to accept and implement.

Conclusion

Networks of shared meaning and mutual responsibility between an organisation's employees and stakeholders – including its geographic and virtual communities – are crucial to producing virtuous circles with the capacity to generate sustainable knowledge capital. The key is to identify the connections between human, infrastructural and social capital resources and the capabilities required to maximise potential productive capability. There are many positive results, not the least of which is that such networks can sustain improved knowledge and learning.

Two main perspectives can be adopted in relation to transformative learning, depending on how far it is contained by the organisational setting: learning as internal to organisational structures; and learning as extending beyond organisational structures. In the former, knowledge and learning are tied to strategic purpose and occur as part of the functioning of an organisation. Individual participants working in this community derive meaning through structures, systems and interactions occurring in the workplace. This is supported by the concept of learning organisations.

The latter perspective typically involves the belief that organisational learning and knowledge generation evolve out of individuals and communities that are not limited by organisational structures. Such an approach also suggests that individuals can choose paths to learning and source knowledge that may reside beyond workplace boundaries and systems. These different perspectives on the processes of generating and transferring knowledge are the crux of the next chapter.

Principle 8

E-learning can be intentionally designed to facilitate collaboration and build shared identity and meaning, thereby establishing a virtuous learning circle of knowledge transfer, innovation and adaptability to organisational change.

---

[7] See for example the case studies specifically commissioned by the Learning to E-learn project on developing a telehealth network (Bowles 2003b), and on Norway and New Zealand's national efforts to enable industries' and regions' development using e-learning (Wilson 2003a and 2003b).

Forces of Transformation

As the Information Age advances, organisations are placing greater emphasis on attributes such as agility, adaptability and responsiveness. People are valued not only for their skills but also for their ability to embrace change. From an organisation's point of view, developing agility is about much more than managing existing knowledge. It is about creating learning processes that enable the workforce to generate new knowledge and adapt old knowledge to new ends. Speed is a key element in this process.

There have been many changes in the operational environment for organisation leaders as a result of heightened competition, changing organisational structures and advances in technology. With rapid internationalisation and increased exposure to their external environment, businesses have become more market-driven and cost-conscious, with flatter, more decentralised structures. There has been a growing emphasis on 'horizontal' rather than 'vertical' management in order to address quality, service and technological imperatives. Business strategies are increasingly integrated with organisational cultures against the background of an unprecedented emphasis on people as an organisation's most vital resource (Barham, Fraser & Heath 1988: 37).

The duration of business and supply cycles is also decreasing. For example, at Woolworths, one of Australia's largest companies, the average shelf life of a non-perishable supermarket product (that is, the time elapsed before re-ordering and renewed production) plummeted from four years in 1950 to forty days in 1993. By 1999 it had dropped to a mere four days, and was predicted to be just four hours by 2005 (Bowles 1998b: ii). In fact, it reached this target in late 2002.

Under these conditions, corporate leaders can no longer afford to be inward-looking, but must constantly translate between the external world and the organisation's activities and future directions. As Table 9.1 outlines, every organisation is vulnerable to the global impact of major change. If an organisation can respond to such changes by deploying adaptive or generative learning, this can be a major source of competitive advantage. At present, e-learning has been propelled into this setting as both a harbinger of change and a vehicle of transformation, sometimes increasing the pressure on already strained business processes.

Table 9.1   Organisational imperatives in the Industrial and the Information Age

Industrial Age	Information Age
Industry-wide conformity	Organisation variance
Mass production	Mass customisation
Control of people	Control of process
Functional departmentalisation	Cross-functional integration
More of the same (vertical progression)	Continual change (process improvement)
Logical–deductive thinking	Logical–creative thinking
Lifelong employment	Contracted (self-)employment
National industrial awards	Local-enterprise agreements
Career progression	Career diversification
Paternalism	Self-determination
'Them' and 'us' (confrontation)	Partnership (co-operation)
New merchant class	New information class

Bowles & Graham 1994c: 6

Transformation and change continuums

Each organisation has a different mix of variables that influences its learning capacity, but the largest influence is the organisation itself, and its progress along what may be termed a change continuum. Change continuums provide a visual map of where a business is heading and allow us to plot its position so as to indicate when and how managers can deploy learning to achieve organisational goals.

A central issue here is organisational responsiveness. This is relevant to the question of how e-learning can assist a change process, and how it can be managed as a transformation in its own right. Where slow responsiveness leads to a loss of competitive advantage, it can have a negative impact on the entire organisation.

Figure 9.1 illustrates the impact of responsiveness on organisational dynamics. It depicts an organisation concentrating on a core goal and strategy, as represented by the A parabola. The aim, to advance to a competitive position, is marked as B. To respond to the need for change, the organisation must ensure that by the time it arrives at A2 it can transform its focus from A to B. The required responsiveness (time, expenses, resource commitment) to achieve the necessary change is represented by RR.

It is easy to see the impact of a lag between identifying the need for change and implementing a response. The time immediately following the identification of the need for change represents a window of opportunity or threat. If a company shifts focus soon after identifying the need for change at A1, it may shorten the lag before it reaches A2, the optimal point where the next 'wave' of transformation is beginning. Completing change before one's competitors involves some risks, but it also enables the organisation to move to the new operational state in a timely manner. In this case, the organisation is early to market and has the potential to become a market leader.

Figure 9.1   Change continuums

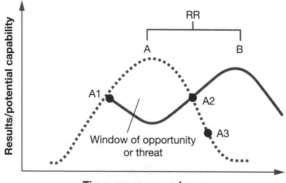

While some companies seek to optimise the window of opportunity by becoming early adopters or 'first entrants', others may not respond until the impact of change is evident, whether because they are unable to anticipate the change or because they wish to avoid risk. In Figure 9.1, A3 represents the point at which change is initiated so late that the organisation is already at a competitive disadvantage. In this scenario, the company will be trying to manage the change while its business revenue and competitive position are declining. While there are obvious risks in being an early adopter, a risk-avoidance strategy holds even more serious dangers if it involves changing too late.

The reduction of lag requires an understanding of the organisation's current competitive position and the likely changes in its competitive environment. This has to be managed across all the potential change scenarios – not just one – within the identified planning period.

Figure 9.2 expands on the late-response scenario. Here, change is initiated at A2 rather than A1; as a result, change will not be implemented until A3, late in the evolution of that change cycle. Meanwhile, early adopting competitors are already responding to another change cycle, depicted as C. By the point marked as B1, the late adopter is well behind the competition, struggling with a declining revenue base and facing yet another cycle of change. The situation is even worse if the C wave is based on a more sophisticated technology that is replacing B. Here, rather than developing a new market, the organisation is spending time, money and resources on a technology in market decline. The difference between B1 and C1 therefore represents a gap in responsiveness.

The required responsiveness (RR) to achieve the necessary change is not a simple move from one change continuum to another. As responsiveness is acquired or agility achieved, the organisation is better placed to improve its overall competitive position. In short, a virtuous circle is established. By contrast, failure to achieve the required responsiveness leads to a vicious circle of declining competitiveness, falling revenue and diminishing capacity for change. This becomes especially important when numerous cycles of change affect an organisation and cascade into further transformations, as shown in Figure 9.3.

Figure 9.2   Losing competitiveness through changing late

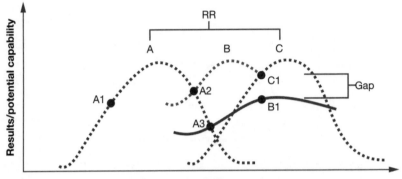

Figure 9.3 indicates the longer-term impact as the requirements for responsiveness accelerate. Assume that the first required responsiveness (RR), moving from A to B, occurs in one twelve-month period. During the next twelve months, however, the second RR interval experiences two cycles of change, from B to C and from C to D. In the last period, there are three RR intervals: D to E, E to F, and F to G. While the time and duration of the intervals can vary enormously, as change accelerates, the organisation's capacity to respond may decrease. Equally, the acceleration places pressure on the systems that manage responsiveness when they have to deliver three changes in the same time formerly taken to accomplish one.

Figure 9.3   Increased cycle of change

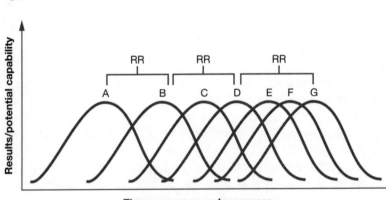

Figures 9.1, 9.2 and 9.3 highlight the fact that systems can no longer afford to lag behind for even one change imperative. Failure to respond rapidly to a change imperative in the first cycle (A) may mean a loss of competitiveness

at C. Two years later, the same lack of responsiveness could place the company three cycles behind. Assuming the same slow rate of response, the organisation would be moving from D to E while competitors have already arrived at G.

It is readily apparent why some companies have developed 'change fatigue'. Effort seems to be focused on managing change rather than on operational outcomes and core business. Organisations need to respond to change and develop the capabilities necessary to sustain this activity as the speed of change increases (Christensen 1997: 254–60).

Building learning initiatives can support the organisation's progress along a change continuum. To support change across all continuums, however, learning must be flexible. The organisation that embraces learning across all subsystems and accepts it as a builder of transformative capacity can also use learning to support accelerated responsiveness and organisational agility. This is imperative if organisations are to succeed in an aggressive marketplace.

The need for organisational agility

It is well over a decade since Stalk and Hout (1990) first advanced the notion that speed and responsiveness were crucial in competitive markets. In spite of this, the adoption of new systems and practices has itself been a slow process.

Organisational design, or the way roles are defined within organisations, has a significant impact on organisational agility. Rigid organisational structures and procedures emphasise certainty of outcomes for participants and efficiencies in processes, but they have shown poor capacity to produce innovation. Innovation and organisational agility are stifled by stratified organisational structures conceived in functional terms, where work is defined in terms of procedures and processes, and positions in terms of reporting roles. Such structures are increasingly inappropriate to workplaces where technology is used to perform routine tasks, while non-routine tasks are contracted out to knowledge workers.

Some organisational structures provide greater agility than others. Networks, which are the most dynamic and adaptable of organisational designs, have been gradually replacing traditional structures. At its extreme, the dynamic network consists of a number of market relationships brokered by a 'core' unit. Car manufacturers, for example, are no longer large, hierarchical factory-centred organisations. They now outsource component production, sales and marketing; the result is a network of partners, all centred on manufacturing and selling a vehicle. A more extreme example is online exchange companies, which maintain their virtual presence with a small cadre of administrative staff and mainly co-ordinate how partnering businesses sell products and services. In this case, conventional notions of organisational boundaries must be discarded.

Networks are more flexible and innovative than traditional structural relationships, and more responsive to changing conditions in products and markets. They are also less constrained in the way they source skills and take advantage of external opportunities.

The main concern in the development of network organisations is their comparative lack of stability and the difficulty of securing commitment from individual participants. Agile organisations not only compete on current strengths and competitive advantages but also nurture the capacity to respond to future opportunities. In network organisations, adaptability may be achieved either by enhancing staff capabilities or by sourcing knowledge outside the organisation. A network organisation may 'graft' on new capabilities by engaging contract employees or outsourcing critical functions. While these tactics can supply performance competencies, it still takes time to build collaboration and instil shared meaning, a sense of purpose and a culture that underpins the desired organisational identity. In this respect especially, e-learning has a lot to offer to network organisations.

Another alternative organisational model, as discussed in Chapter 8, is the workplace community. This is a more holistic approach in which community-based values formed within the organisation can change along with the organisation's needs. A third possibility is developing networks of knowledge, which value individual knowledge advancement both by employees and by people outside the organisation. All three of these approaches offer greater flexibility and more permeable organisational boundaries, which are of particular importance in assisting organisations to attune themselves to a changing environment.

Agility must be conceptualised as extending beyond the 'walls' of the organisation. This is not, however, a simple matter of separating out 'internal' and 'external' factors. Organisational knowledge and responsiveness are shaped by many and varied elements — business relationships, relationships with local communities, involvement with other business groups, and actions by government and other corporations (Rigby et al. 2001: 180–4).

The fit between the organisation and the environment is referred to as 'environmental attunement'. For an organisation to survive, it must be compatible with its environment. Increasing complexity and competition, combined with growing interdependence within and beyond the organisation, lead to a need for adaptation and change.

For organisations to achieve environmental fit, their values, norms, processes, reward systems and performance must recognise the importance of people. Agility is achieved above all through the development of capability in individuals, who are thus able to acquire new frames of reference while still achieving current performance outcomes.

Generative knowledge and strategic readiness

Transferring information into knowledge to improve productive outcomes is a critical organisational endeavour, and one that requires the integration of knowledge management with learning. The capacity to learn in order to address performance deficiencies or skills gaps is no longer sufficient to build unique competitive advantage. If strategic success depends on the speed with which companies translate learning into outcomes, then it must also be accepted that strategic solutions are best framed in terms of both current and future requirements. This perspective reinforces the need for a broader view of learning. Argyris and Schön (1978) encapsulated this view in their concept of 'double-loop' or generative learning, which translates individual learning into benefits for the whole organisation. See Figure 9.4.

Figure 9.4 Single-loop and double-loop learning

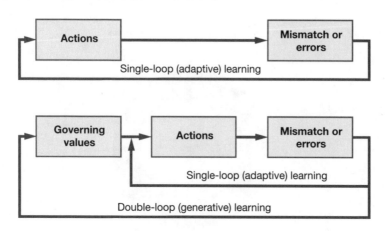

Based on Argyris 1990, cited in Morrison 1994: 26

Double-loop, or generative, learning moves beyond single-loop, or adaptive, learning — the benign absorption of information for applied purposes — by emphasising continuous experimentation and feedback. This is particularly relevant to the use of learning to solve problems by recognising and addressing root causes. The idea of generative learning requires a new mindset and the capacity to create new visions for future realities. Unlike adaptive learning, suggests Senge (1992), generative learning encompasses:
- systemic thinking;
- shared vision;
- personal mastery;
- team learning; and
- creative tension between the vision and the current reality.

Redding and Catalanello (1994) built on the view of learning as a cycle generating outcomes that vary with the individual, content and context. They were especially interested in how the learning cycle contributed to an organisation's strategic readiness and the construction of a learning organisation.[8] Redding in particular is noteworthy for suggesting that the organisational learning cycle has three core steps: planning, implementation and reflection. Each of these steps needs to be purposely managed to maximise the total impact of an individual's learning.

The three steps proposed by Redding and Catalanello (1994: 19, 23–6), as illustrated in Figure 9.5, are explained as follows:
- **Plan**: open, flexible learning plans, which are linked to strategic and organisational plans within a continuous process;
- **Implement**: execution of plans, including the nurturing of communication between all players involved; and

- **Reflect**: learning from reflection on individual interventions and overall success (adjusting and improving future planning and implementation as necessary).

All three steps form part of an individual's learning cycle, and are also 'how organisations learn to change' (Redding & Catalanello 1994: 17).

Figure 9.5   Redding and Catalanello's strategic learning cycle

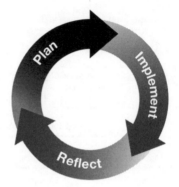

Redding & Catalanello 1994: 36

By contrast, the traditional management approach is single-loop, or adaptive, learning, which typically adopts a strategy of reinforcing learning in incremental steps in response to immediate triggers. It fails to deal with underlying questions about causation and change, and therefore limits management to a short-term focus. While adaptive learning can be used effectively to undertake a controlled change process or to fill skills gaps, it relies on periodic intervention rather than transformation. This may produce 'spurts of improvement', but cannot encompass rapid and sustained change.

McGill, Slocum & Lei (1992) highlight the difference between an organisation's ability to adapt and its ability to learn. They suggest the adaptive organisation is 'learning-disadvantaged': although it can transfer skills, it fails to do so in a manner that enhances *sustainable* capacity to change in response to environmental factors (1992: 5–17). In contrast, the ability to learn lends the generative organisation a competitive advantage by enhancing its capability, ultimately driven by its employees' competencies and identities. In this sense, generative learning addresses the business imperative to be competitive and responsive in the long term.

Figure 9.6 illustrates how the individual learning cycle can acquire added depth and breadth to promote organisational learning (Redding & Catalanello 1994: 36). Generative learning requires capabilities that relate to aspects of identity and tacit knowledge. These are key features supporting innovation, openness, creativity and responsiveness to new contingencies (McGill et al. 1992). Transformation is not achieved through reactive interventions; it is embedded in how people think, act and view their contribution to the organisation. How 'things are done' and the competence to 'do' are critical in terms of performance outcomes, but how people and systems adapt to change and improve their speed, depth and breadth of learning has even greater relevance in terms of *strategic* outcomes.

Figure 9.6   Managing learning to promote generative or adaptive change

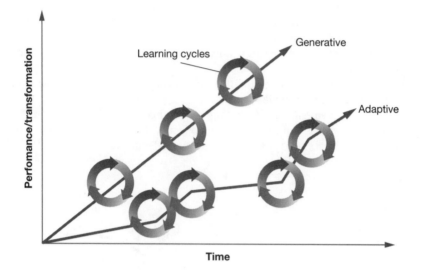

Based on Redding 1997: 485

The adoption of a strategy of generative learning also needs to take the organisation's *absorptive capacity* into account. Absorptive capacity is rather like the ability of the garden to take in water. In a strong downpour after a drought, much of the water will simply run off the soil. As the water seeps in, however, the soil loosens, changing its structure to enable further absorption and to allow plants to grow. Knowledge represents growth to organisations as water does to plants. A deluge of new knowledge poured onto unreceptive ground will have little positive effect.

Agility is the constant translation of knowledge into outcomes, but its influence on strategic direction is not necessarily linear and predictable. If an organisation is to generate new knowledge and maintain its responsiveness, learning has to be a continuous activity. This may require new understandings and frames of reference in relation to both learning and e-learning. Any discrepancy between expectations and readiness to adopt e-learning is likely to compromise the process of change.

Organisational e-learning readiness
The introduction of e-learning is an innovation and as such should be handled as an intervention that calls on all the knowledge generated in recent decades on how to implement change effectively. Some of the key questions for managers are:

- What are the risks in promoting this change?
- Is e-learning an appropriate response to the environmental pressures facing the organisation?
- To what extent does the organisational culture actively support e-learning and integrate it into its strategic planning and management?
- What structures are in place to facilitate e-learning, and what would need to be established?
- How far is the current training environment congruent with an effective e-learning environment?
- Are there processes to ensure that planning, implementing and evaluating e-learning address learners' needs?
- Will superiors and line staff, learning facilitators and learners answer these questions in similar ways?

In its engagement with e-learning, an organisation will move through a multi-stage process of implementation. Typically, this can be represented by the following four stages or levels, also shown in Figure 9.7.

Figure 9.7   S-curve of e-learning readiness

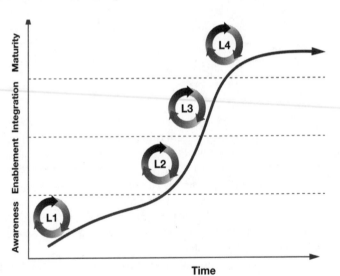

Level 1 — Awareness: The organisation is aware of the need for e-learning but has made only basic advances. Information is transferred electronically using static web pages, CD-ROMs or computer-based instruction on stand-alone platforms. There is little or no networking of individual learning, and data cannot be captured and analysed in real time. The relationship between learning and knowledge management is inadvertent at best. The main focus is on cost reduction and wider distribution and access.

Level 2 — Enablement: The organisation searches for interactivity and real-time data capture across networked electronic-learning media. Users can search and navigate stored content to access appropriate learning at the right time. Transfer of explicit knowledge between individuals increases as e-learning is used to enhance knowledge distribution, especially via self-paced content. At this stage, cost savings drive the advancement of the e-learning strategy.

Level 3 — Integration: The organisation or its suppliers generate personalised e-learning products and services with integrated architecture. Open architecture maximises the integration of front-end and back-end systems and permits learning to be translated into improved business processes and customer value. E-learning is integrated with knowledge management, performance management, personnel (human capital) management, and continuous improvement strategies. A conscious effort is made to enhance tacit knowledge in a way that promotes collaboration and further embeds knowledge within the unique context of the organisation.

Level 4 — Maturity: Innovation and extended deployment of e-learning are used to leverage core business interests and help redesign core services, supply chains and business processes to better meet customer needs and preferences. E-learning is an essential component for building the organisation's unique competitive advantage and enabling improved agility and responsiveness to future contingencies.

The process of transformation towards e-learning requires a long-term view of return on investment, impacts on business strategy and staff capacity to transfer knowledge. As we advance into the twenty-first century, the evolution of e-learning is entering a more mature and rapid growth stage. Not only has the transfer of knowledge between different fields of endeavour taken time to evolve, but organisations have also had to struggle to evolve e-learning as a productive factor integrated with existing business systems. Only when technology is integrated into known business processes is management likely to feel the interventions are 'under control'.

The gathering 'second wave' of e-learning development will augment the momentum for organisational and pedagogical change, spurred on by new Internet applications and increasingly powerful communications technology. This second major development is likely to increase the complexity and sophistication of e-learning. While earlier changes had a ripple effect, generating a series of breakthroughs affecting products, services and content, the new changes may take unexpected directions.

It is possible, however, to hazard some educated guesses about the likely directions of future change in the wider business environment:[9]

- Change will come from everywhere.
- Speed will matter: business will have to respond to market needs by rapidly moving new products and services from inspiration to sale.
- Systems will be customer-centred and personalised; customer-driven (pull) processes will dominate supplier-driven (push) processes.
- Business-to-consumer distribution will replace business-to-business systems, thereby empowering consumers, reducing distribution costs and increasing purchasing power.
- Product turnover will increase and convenience will be high value, with anywhere, anytime access — seven days, twenty-four hours will be the standard, not the exception.

- Process efficiencies will emerge through expert systems, leading to lower costs.
- Real breakthroughs will create new products and new expectations.
- Resources will shift rapidly to new opportunities across global markets.

These changes will produce powerful imperatives for existing businesses to change. While business-to-business dealings and improvement of existing processes will be the first profit opportunity, the real focus will be on success through transforming existing knowledge to new purposes. In the search for breakthrough innovations, failure will be tolerated as an opportunity to reflect, plan and implement change. And, as customer-led processes supplant supply-driven systems, businesses will increasingly be expected to convey visions that employees and others can understand, share and advance. Learning in general, and e-learning in particular, stands to play a key role in these transformations.

Conclusion

It has taken more than ten years for e-learning to reach a stage where we can fully appreciate the scope of the transformations it makes possible. As electronically mediated interactions stimulate collaboration, old institutional and organisational barriers are being bypassed, producing an unprecedentedly rapid movement of knowledge. This can extend to promoting the convergence of industries, communities and whole societies to encourage massive innovation and change.

To participate in this development, however, organisations need to view e-learning not as an isolated activity but as a catalyst and enabler of far wider change. There is an increasingly urgent requirement for organisations to develop their agility and responsiveness to changing market conditions and new technologies. In many cases, this has led to the adoption of less centralised organisational models, while at the same time it has placed a premium on human knowledge, skills and learning. E-learning offers unique possibilities for encouraging the exchange of ideas and skills across these complex organisational networks, facilitating the development of the new capabilities required for agility and continuous adaptation to change.

Principle 9

A holistic e-learning strategy can increase an organisation's responsiveness to change while also acting as an agent of continuous innovation and transformation.

[8] The cycle of learning is addressed by a number of authors. For the origins and variations of Redding and Catalanello, see Argyris and Schôn's double-loop learning (1978: 18–23), Kolb (1984), Garratt (1987), Revans (1982) and Dixon (1994).
[9] These follow other authors; for instance, Boulding (1964), Drucker (1969) and Gibson and Nolan (1974), as well as more recent insights from Newt Gingrich (2002: 48–52).

Organisational E-learning: Principles and Pressures

This chapter examines how e-learning can be advanced at an organisational level and surveys the historical precedents influencing the progress of this agenda. Two key approaches are examined: the drive to build learning organisations and the drive to enable organisational learning. The 'learning organisation' and 'organisational learning' approaches differ principally in whether they view learning as being internal to organisational structures or extending beyond the organisation's boundaries.

Internal to organisational structures – the learning organisation: In this scenario, learning is tied to the organisation's strategic purpose and occurs systematically as part of its functioning. Individual participants derive meaning through structures, systems and interactions occurring in the workplace. This leads to the concept of learning organisations where knowledge and learning are meaningful on an organisational level and e-learning is managed by the organisation to achieve specific performance outcomes.

Extending beyond organisational structures – organisational learning: This approach suggests that organisational learning is not limited by organisational structures but grows out of individuals and communities. In this view, knowledge and learning exist in social situations and in networks of individuals that have identified with a common purpose. These networks may well extend beyond the organisation. Individuals can contribute to the organisation's core purpose even when they choose learning paths outside the workplace's boundaries and systems.

The learning organisation revisited

Peter Senge's book *The Fifth Discipline: The Art and Practice of the Learning Organisation* (1992) spurred a surge of interest in the idea of the learning organisation. Yet Senge did not invent the concept, nor was his the only framework for analysing its principles. The concept of the learning organisation had been aired internationally for more than a decade before Senge's book appeared.

In early works on the subject, the learning organisation was presented as an ideal rather than as a basis for everyday practice. Alistair Crombie, writing in Australia in the late 1970s, was careful to present the learning organisation strictly as a utopian model, 'suggestive of a future ideal, rather than descriptive of present realities' (1978: 38). In Britain in the late 1980s, John Burgoyne consolidated a framework for creating what he termed a 'learning company'; he published his findings with Mike Pedler and Tom Boydell in *The Learning Company: Strategy for Sustainable Development* (1991). Pedler, Burgoyne and Boydell also presented the learning company as an ideal paradigm rather than a reality. They promoted the potential of the concept, but they explicitly rejected the idea that it could offer a 'quick fix' (1991: 3). Learning was advanced as a catalyst for improvement, not as a substitute for other management approaches.

Senge, by contrast, intended the learning organisation to provide a 'management solution' in the real world (Senge 1992: 37). His *Fifth Discipline* set out a new systems approach to management and presented a coherent and holistic framework for both study and practice (Senge 1992: 42). Senge summed up his approach as follows:

> Dividing an elephant in half does not produce two small elephants. Living systems have integrity. Their character depends on the whole. The same is true for organisations; to understand the most challenging managerial issues requires seeing the whole system that generates the issues (1992: 66).

The aim of a learning organisation is to create a compelling corporate vision that encourages employees to think about how they might improve the way they work. Senge depicts an organisational environment where individuals continually seek to expand their capacity to create desired results, where new patterns of thinking are nurtured and where people are continually 'learning how to learn' together. Such an environment has the potential to make work truly meaningful for employees and substantially increase the business's profitability and competitive advantage.

Senge drew on Chris Argyris's idea of 'double-loop learning', described in Chapter 9. Argyris suggested that organisations could rise above simply reacting to short-term problems by developing 'action strategies' to overcome their inhibitions against responding to changes in their external environment (Argyris 1993: 98–9). Such action strategies would make it possible to use learning to achieve improved outcomes by addressing problems in organisational cultures and structures, as well as leadership and decision-making styles (Argyris & Schön 1978: 143; Morrison 1994: 25).

Argyris's legacy was to imbue managers with the idea that they had to embrace the transfer of knowledge throughout the organisation. Senge promoted this vision to a strategic level where the enterprise's competitiveness and capacity to improve were underpinned by learning. He believed the success of a learning organisation would rest on its ability to recognise how learning shapes futures based on a shared understanding of the 'current reality' (Senge 1992: 250–1). Senge's writings also acknowledged that intellectual capacity resides in all employees, not just in management (Senge 1992: 350).

Under a learning organisation approach, there must be a commitment to learning both by the individual within the organisation and by the organisation as a whole. Learning is the means by which organisations can change existing practices and respond to sources of information that stimulate new knowledge and further learning (Sefton, Waterhouse & Cooney 1995: 56). Doron Gunzburg (1992: 29) outlined four defining characteristics of a learning organisation:

- a climate in which individual workers are encouraged to learn and to develop their full potential;
- a learning culture that includes customers and other significant stakeholders wherever possible;
- business policies that place human resource strategy at their centre; and
- a continuous process of organisational transformation based on individual learning and consequent learning assumptions, goals and norms.

These features alter some fundamental organisational relationships. Education, for example, is especially valued where it is contextualised to combine individual development and enterprise outcomes. This means that universities and other education providers need to recognise that lifelong learning is grounded in a relationship between the individual, the organisation and the education provider (Stern 1993: 3).

There is also greater emphasis on management communications. This may take the form of participative processes to produce corporate visions that are underpinned by shared, measurable objectives. Through these processes, management and staff can better understand the organisation's strategic goals and establish joint ownership of what they have created.

Peter Senge recognised that building a learning organisation required a substantial shift in prevailing mental models. In 1992 he expressed disappointment with the lack of implementation of learning organisation approaches, blaming this on the fact that 'new insights fail to get put into practice because they conflict with deeply held internal images of how the world works, images that limit us to familiar ways of thinking and acting' (1992: 7). Traditional training structures, for example, stress conformity as a source of cohesion and unity of purpose for participants. Training approaches are better at inculcating established belief systems than encompassing diversity. The idea is that if people all think and act like machines, they will interact efficiently and generate shared values, views and attitudes. In a predictable and unchanging environment, this approach facilitates process efficiencies and reduces the amount of co-ordination required of managers within a hierarchical structure.

When the environment is unstable and unpredictable, however, the lack of diversity limits organisational agility. Bureaucracy, which is the epitome of a cohesive organisational culture, experiences serious difficulties when presented with non-routine problems. This is the antithesis of a customer-responsive, service-oriented organisational approach. The development of a learning organisation is widely seen as requiring an organisational culture that balances functional efficiency with open systems — that is, the ability to take on and learn from diverse values, beliefs and experiences (McGill et al. 1992; Schrage 1990: ch. 5).

According to Redding and Catalanello (1994), there are five stages on the path to becoming a learning organisation. These five stages are outlined in Figure 10.1.

Figure 10.1 The five stages of the learning organization

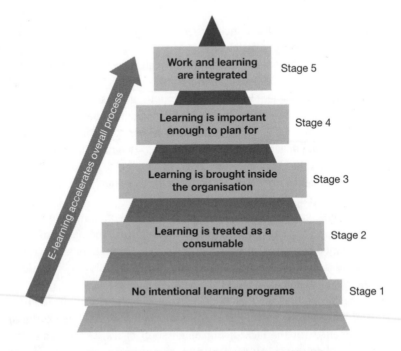

Based on Woolner and Lowey 1993, as depicted in Redding and Catalanello 1994: 135

The characteristics of each stage are as follows:

Stage 1: The start-up company is basically learning how to stay afloat. No effort is invested in deciding what people need to know to do their jobs better.

Stage 2: Training programs are made available through outside providers. Training is viewed as a consumable and is aimed at fixing short-term problems.

Stage 3: Some in-house training may be offered and there is a greater emphasis on gaining sustainable results, but training is not fully co-ordinated and may focus on 'flavour-of-the-month' subjects.

Stage 4: Senior managers realise that they need to develop the skills and knowledge of the workforce in order to remain competitive. Training is usually conducted offsite, and is targeted towards providing competitive advantage.

Stage 5: Learning is seen as vital to the success of the organisation, and there is a planned effort to make learning part of everyday work. The organisation encourages employees to learn by trying new things and experiencing different processes within the workplace itself.

In the fifth stage, which typifies the learning organisation, employees may work on projects outside their usual domain to promote reflective learning that can offer insights into the way they normally do things. A sales manager, for example, might join a production team to learn more about how the products work, or production staff might work with salespeople to develop a marketing strategy for a product that is in the pipeline. Employees are motivated to improve their existing skills by an organisation that makes it clear that their existing skills and knowledge are valued as part of day-to-day activities. In this scenario, e-learning can be deployed to encourage collaborative exchanges, to enable people in multiple locations to complete a common activity, or to integrate learning into the everyday work environment by making knowledge accessible on demand.

In spite of its attractions, the concept of the learning organisation is not above criticism. Some commentators have suggested that it is too much a 'systematic approach' that fails to take into account the vast array of processes that create and modify knowledge (Schulz 2001). The emphasis on creating systems that encompass the whole organisation risks overlooking the variations in how individuals interact, transact and learn.

Organisational learning

In contrast to the idea of the learning organisation, the concept of organisational learning is less evangelical and initially more modest in its aims. It starts from the insight that organisations are not primarily built to learn, but to engage in transactions both within and outside their structure. Therefore, organisational learning may be viewed as a means of enhancing an organisation's capacity to create a climate conducive to change and to realise competitive advantage through performance improvement. Organisational strategies for learning should not confine their emphasis to codifying or bureaucratising learning under a 'systems' model. Rather, learning exchanges and individual social interactions can be viewed as opportunities to stimulate relationships that can be strategically managed to encourage organisational learning through knowledge sharing. This process can be facilitated or inhibited by the ecological system in which transactions take place (Argyris cited in Malhotra 1996: 68).

Unlike advocates of the learning organisation approach, most organisational learning advocates believe the best approach is to accept that learning *will* occur, then set out to design, deploy and lead it towards agreed outcomes (Garvin 1993). The emphasis is on individuals within and outside the organisation. Ultimately, it is they who have to experience a desire to learn and adopt the requisite behaviours. The organisation's task is to harness this capability so as to generate the knowledge required to perform and adapt.

Furthermore, organisations may actually limit their learning capacity if they place an overriding emphasis on inculcating new ideas or perspectives into all their employees. Organisational agility is not simply about knowledge management; it is about the learning processes that enable information to be recalibrated into meaningful knowledge to meet redefined purposes. It thus depends on the 'absorptive capacity' of the workforce (Cohen & Levinthal 1990: 128–52). This involves not just the ability of individuals to absorb new knowledge but also how quickly this knowledge can be transferred and deployed to enhance strategic outcomes such as satisfying customer needs. Learning processes therefore have to enhance performance capabilities while also building individuals' capacity to transfer and generate knowledge in collective learning processes.

In their account of organisational learning, Crossan and Hulland present learning as a process very much like any other. They suggest that learning can be considered as a 'system of stocks and flows in the same way we think about a production management system', using concepts such as 'throughput, capacity utilisation, and bottlenecks' (1997: 3). In this view, intellectual capital and knowledge can be treated as 'stocks of product' (1997: 3). This linear, rational processing approach may not appeal to everyone, but it does lend itself to adoption by traditionally schooled managers looking to identify and then quantify the contribution of learning in a production process.

Crossan and Hulland identify six points of difference between an organisational learning approach and the concept of the learning organisation (1997: 4–14):

- **All organisations learn:** Patterns and processes of learning vary between and within enterprises, and no single theory can allow for all these differences.
- **Learning is not an end in itself:** The crucial question in assessing organisational learning is whether or not the organisation is skilled at developing new products, and is able to compete in a complex and changing world.
- **Organisational learning extends beyond dedicated 'learning' activities:** There is more to the translation of learning than managing individual acquisition of skills and knowledge. Learning is embedded in interaction and relationships within and outside the organisation.
- **There are learning processes that link organisational levels:** Learning is a meta-process; individuals absorb knowledge, integrate it at the level of the team and institutionalise it at the level of the corporation.
- **Organisational learning needs to consider the flow of learning among these levels:** Any learning process needs to integrate individual learning (competencies, capabilities and motivation) with processes affecting the group (group dynamics and development of shared understanding) and organisation (knowledge assets/capital, systems, structure, procedures and culture).
- **Individuals within the organisation are the ultimate arbiters of organisational learning:** Individual perceptions drive the system of building knowledge assets. To evaluate organisational learning success is not simply a matter of determining whether the organisation has achieved its overall goals; it is also necessary to measure individual employee perspectives and understanding.

The distinction between organisational learning and the learning organisation is a subtle but important one. The idea of the learning organisation, as advanced by Senge and others, is very much a systems-level approach in which learning becomes the focus of organisational design. Strategies to achieve organisational learning can underpin many of the same principles and practices, but they do not require learning to be viewed as the organisation's central purpose. In fact, many practitioners of organisational learning would not see any value in building a learning organisation. They would prefer to see learning managed as part of wider management systems.

The e-learning organisation: a note of caution

In the mid- to late 1990s, many companies claimed to be learning organisations without any real basis for their assertions. E-learning is in danger of being pulled into a similar quagmire. There are already calls to create 'e-learning organisations'. E-learning is seen as having a 'value-adding' role, strongly centred on the delivery of training to underpin the enterprise's search for quality improvement and competitiveness. The success of e-learning services can then be measured against the enterprise's existing goals and objectives.

E-learning may be able to provide an accelerated and perhaps more cost-effective means of facilitating individual and organisational learning. By itself, however, organisational learning does not make a learning organisation. Indeed, individual, team and organisational learning are not preconditions for a learning organisation (Lessem 1993: viii). Directing management efforts toward creating an e-learning organisation does not seem to be a constructive step.

One might suggest that what we are seeing here is the development of a supply-driven, learning-push model, in which suppliers of learning services attempt to influence users – in this case, other business units – to purchase their wares. The expectation is that if e-learning builds a strong strategic role, then organisational performance will follow and an e-learning organisation will be created.

There are several problems with this approach. Partnerships between corporate management and external learning providers are unlikely to support organisational goals if the goals themselves are poorly framed or focused on short-term profit. Managers, especially in small and medium-sized organisations, do not always give learning sufficient status or resources to respond to learning-driven initiatives. Given that the learning organisation approach is a totalising philosophy, to frame e-learning in terms of existing organisational goals may beg the larger question of whether the mindset of management is appropriate to a learning organisation.

At a more fundamental level, adopting the learning-push model goes against the grain of the contemporary emphasis on demand-driven business approaches. Thinking back to Redding and Catalanello's stages of development, the full development of a learning organisation relies on managers and staff driving the demand for learning, producing a learning-pull situation. In the absence of active demand within the organisation, the preconditions for a learning organisation will not necessarily be established by creating learning partnerships, focusing learning on the organisation's existing objectives and measuring e-learning's contribution against those objectives.

Learning in general, and e-learning in particular, has also been promoted as a critical component of continuous quality improvement systems. Garvin (1993) consolidates the view that the implementation of total quality management depends on continuous learning within a learning organisation model. Quality gurus such as Robert Galvin introduced the concept of a 'cycle of learning' built into quality systems, where organisations refine their processes to meet customer needs on the basis of feedback from service staff (Thompson 1992: 58). The principle here is that those in the chain already know their own parts well and can offer constructive suggestions, provided that they are imbued with a commitment to the whole.

The focus of quality improvement is on individuals and teams, with managers moving from a controlling role to one of empowering teams of individuals to achieve business outcomes. To achieve continuous quality improvement, organisations have to generate a shared vision of quality that transcends specific strategic goals and objectives. Individuals have to learn not only how to perform, but also how to *think*.

Yet there is nothing to suggest that quality improvement strategies depend on the adoption of learning organisation principles or create the preconditions for a learning organisation. While an organisation that has already adopted quality improvement may subsequently embrace a learning organisation approach, it may equally choose alternative approaches to learning. Continuous improvement necessitates learning, but it does not require the development of a learning organisation.

Establishing a learning culture

E-learning development requires both an inward focus on individual and group capacities and an outward focus on enhancing capabilities through the capture of knowledge residing in the complex relationships that make up an organisation and link it with its environment. These relationships are strongly influenced by an organisation's culture, encompassing shared beliefs, values, roles and patterns of behaviour. The organisational culture in turn contributes to the identity of individuals in the organisation and influences how it is viewed by both insiders and outsiders.

The relationship between the individual/team and the company is crucial to the dynamics of learning in a corporate setting. Efforts to build a learning environment must work at both levels simultaneously if they are to be successful. The following steps can be seen as characterising the evolution of a learning culture:

Awareness of training: A few people in the organisation are committed to learning, but they are probably scattered throughout the workplace or restricted to the training department. Internally, these people act as 'champions' of learning, but their efforts are not co-ordinated and often go unnoticed.

Promotion of training and development: The organisation becomes committed to the practice of training and retraining for job-related ends. At this stage, the individual/team values the acquisition of codified knowledge and will take the necessary steps to achieve organisational goals, while the organisation provides a vision that promotes guided individual development and rewards success. The organisation identifies the potential of individuals or groups, and is willing to change in order to maximise that potential.

Management of learning: Individuals' motivation is channelled towards achieving organisationally relevant goals, and employees are prepared to modify learning activities to ensure that they meet performance criteria. At an organisational level, standards for performance are clear and appropriate, so that all employees know what is required of them and how their input may benefit all.

Coaching and mentoring: At this level, corporate management recognises that learning often concentrates on tacit knowledge that is owned by individuals and resident in their interpersonal or social interactions (see Chapter 4). It is also recognised that learning exchanges can have individual as well as organisational benefits. Staff increasingly learn through on-site 'learning relationships', and the expertise of long-term employees is harnessed through coaching, mentoring and informal exchanges (based on Bowles & Graham 1994a).

The end point of this process of enculturation is a more informal and dispersed system of knowledge transmission than the learning organisation model would prescribe. A strategic approach to organisational learning acknowledges the value of integrating learning with management systems. At the same time, it differs from the learning organisation approach in placing greater emphasis on individuals and how they source knowledge from inside and outside the organisation. While Senge's later work sought to use a 'systems' model to link the learning organisation to change processes (Senge et al. 1996; Senge et al. 1999), the learning organisation as a systems model can still be criticised for its lack of a coherent mechanism to translate individual and organisational learning into organisational agility or renewal (Gilley & Maycunich 2000: 7).

At this point, it is useful to revisit the concept of learning communities (discussed in Chapter 8) to clarify how individuals can source knowledge from inside and outside the organisation without being in a formal structure of the kind that characterises the learning organisation model. Learning communities, or indeed communities of practice, may be based on informal, collaborative learning intended to stimulate interactions between employees or between employees and individuals from outside the organisation. These communities develop participants' capacity to learn and acquire different perspectives on knowledge. Knowledge related to performance outcomes may be secondary. It is not unusual for companies to establish learning communities that involve suppliers, customers and experts in order to stimulate knowledge exchange. In one case, an organisation sought to create a formal learning community it called 'cross-organisational brainstorming' on the direction of retail sales. The relationships forged between the players resulted in a network of interactions that not only generated useful knowledge, but also stimulated the desire to explore collaborative solutions to organisational problems. Over subsequent years, the same players continued to connect on shared concerns that did not necessarily centre on the 'founding' issue or needs (Bowles 1998b).

Using e-learning to build organisational capabilities

E-learning is not just a numbers game or a means of accelerating organisational learning. Once a virtuous circle is established, as discussed in Chapter 8, knowledge required for improved performance and agility can be captured, generated and circulated at individual, group or organisational levels. By continually building knowledge capital that underpins business outcomes, e-learning becomes a strategic activity that rewards everyone from employees to customers, suppliers and shareholders.

Capabilities, as outlined in Chapter 4, encompass all the competence and identity factors that learning can address while building human capital. Although a capabilities-based approach can be used within a learning organisation framework, it is more consistent with the principles of organisational learning, which focuses on how individuals learn.

The use of e-learning for training outcomes also needs to be differentiated from the wider process of e-learning. The outcomes of e-training are more limited, especially in relation to the capture and transfer of tacit knowledge. For e-learning to maximise individual performance, it must embrace the individual's capacity to learn, not just centre on specific competencies. Individuals' purposes and learning trajectories vary, but learning promotes collaboration, co-orientation of behaviours and alignment of personal capabilities to group and organisational outcomes. Within this frame of reference, e-learning can enhance performance and instil a sense of identity based on activities that hold meaning for each individual within the collective effort.

Essentially, e-learning can be deployed to stimulate organisational learning that combines an inward-looking focus on the individual with an outward-looking focus on interpersonal relationships and collaboration to collective ends. This collaboration and the 'network' of relationships between individuals can exist beyond organisational boundaries but still generate knowledge that directly contributes to organisational as well as individual outcomes. Well-designed e-learning lends itself to the formation of collaborative networks, offering the individuals involved superior access and greater flexibility in the exchange and transmission of knowledge.

A capability-based approach to e-learning

This section outlines how capabilities can be managed and mapped to build inventories of knowledge that contribute to productive outcomes. The analysis draws on systems implemented in companies across a range of Australian industries and locations, including major retailers, wholesalers and local governments.[10] Capabilities involve more than skills and knowledge. A capability profile may be generated for a person, position, class of occupation, community or organisation. Capabilities form a single currency that enables organisations to integrate the targeting, reporting and evaluation of e-learning with other activities, including knowledge management and performance assessment. Mapping or auditing capability inventories is a way of measuring existing capabilities and assessing their impact on current and future organisational performance requirements. While capability inventories can draw on existing information systems, they require a reappraisal of traditional approaches to profiling an organisation's human capital.

Profiling individuals within organisations

Capability profiling requires the identification of skills, knowledge and identity factors that enable the organisation, team or individual to attain required outcomes on a sustained basis. The outcomes indicate the standards required for responding to future customer and market demands. This is in sharp contrast with traditional management methods of profiling job functions and human capital.

Functional job profiling

Traditionally, jobs are treated as cogs in the machine; they are described in terms of functions or tasks without reference to the organisation's cultural or communications environment. This produces structural efficiencies, but it does not recognise individuals' truly productive qualities — that is, their ability to adapt to changing circumstances, to innovate and find solutions to problems. Fitting individuals into clearly defined roles inhibits innovation.

Profiling human capital

Human capital profiling as it is currently undertaken tends to focus on skills gaps for performing existing jobs within the organisation. Skills-based needs analyses, which identify the functions expected of staff in particular positions, are most successful where there are defined process outcomes. Skills-based profiling is of limited utility in identifying the knowledge components of jobs. It reflects a mechanistic approach to organisational design, and tends to lock in various forms of central authority and control.

The testing of knowledge or non-skills components of a job has been limited to benchmarking general traits against those of existing 'proficient' staff rather than assessing an individual's capability or capacity to perform. Traits are sometimes measured to determine whether an individual is behaviourally compatible with a role; these are retrospective judgments based on traits that have been seen to relate to performance.

Educational programs have contributed most to identifying and delivering the knowledge components of jobs, at least in management education. Here, universities have provided functional job-related vocational education through postgraduate study.

Framing capability inventories

Capabilities can be mapped by adapting existing measurement systems to produce a picture of possible individual contributions to organisational performance. A customised system maps individual traits and skills to organisational goals or key outcomes. Rather than relating an individual to a specific job, the capability inventory outlines the individual's capacity to contribute to wider organisational performance. See Table 10.1.

Building a capability inventory presupposes that management acknowledges learning as a strategic activity, and that the contribution of learning can be measured in terms of current performance and future organisational competitiveness. Where a capability approach has been adopted, it has been used to considerable effect in assessing how far training for individual development achieves immediate outcomes and rationales that relate to the overall effort of building human capital (Bowles 1999).

Table 10.1 Compiling capability data from traditional collection points

Capability field	Examples of information collection points
Competencies (skills and knowledge)	Productivity sheets, downtime records, checklists, procedure manuals, diagnostic ratings, training programs, job descriptions, job analysis forms, skills audits, occupational analysis data, industrial awards, occupational and industry classification data, competency profiles, performance improvement targets
Identity (culture, roles, behaviours, traits)	Cultural attributes: Cultural audits, climate audits, job satisfaction surveys Traits and values: Attitude surveys, value and climate audits, individual job satisfaction indices, behavioural descriptors, educational programs, job weighting scales Experience: Job selection frameworks, personnel records, job weighting scales, performance appraisal data Social interaction and communication: Organisational structures, span of control documentation, reporting relationship documents, workflow systems, quality system work procedures, job sampling, information system audits

Table 10.2 Comparison between skills-based audits and capability inventories

Skills-based approach	Capability approach
Tasks can be described using a single descriptor	It is recognised that tasks vary with time and situation
Information is based on current performance data and projections	People's perceptions are measured as well as their performance
Performance is concrete and can be quantified	Individuals can adapt to context to complete tasks
Evaluation is logic-based	Evaluation is value-based
Tasks define jobs	Tasks may define multiple purposes and futures
Job descriptions define current performance expectations	Job descriptions help to describe future expectations and career pathways
Focus is on portability of individual competencies between jobs	Focus is on capabilities for multiple futures
Audit defines current job roles within an organisation	Inventory identifies organisational current and future performance needs
Aim is to achieve efficiency	Aim is to provide adaptability
Focus is on job performance	Focus is on organisation-wide outcomes

Capability inventories are a dynamic business tool because they encompass the competencies, cognitive factors and experience required to achieve competitiveness. They also provide a framework for training, career development and organisational improvement.

Skills-based profiling focuses on functional processes, and as such produces task efficiencies that are one step removed from organisational outcomes. Capability profiling, on the other hand, is linked to strategic outcomes and the readiness to change and meet new challenges. Participants' roles are directly related to key result areas for the organisation. Functional efficiency may be reduced in the short term, but innovation and agility are increased resulting in long-term organisational advantage . See Table 10.2.

Linking individual and organisational capabilities

Individual and organisational performance must also be aligned to avoid wasted energy and effort. The key to aligning individual performance to collective outcomes lies in developing a shared mental model or frame of reference that orients particular groups and the organisation as a whole to focus on supporting individual efforts. Table 10.3 identifies the alignment required of organisational, group and individual capabilities.

Table 10.3   Applying capabilities at three levels of the organisation

Performance variables	Organisational level	Group/team/process level	Individual level
Strategic goals	Is the organisational purpose known, and are strategic goals attuned to the reality of economic, political and cultural forces?	Do the process goals enable people to work together to achieve both organisational and individual ends?	Are the professional and personal goals of individuals consistent with those of the organisation?
Performance	Do structure, policy and creative frameworks support improved performance?	Are processes designed to permit individuals and groups to modify systems to meet contingencies?	Are individual styles of learning and creative processes respected?
Expertise	Does the organisation select for capabilities (e.g. for cultural 'fit') as well as for 'skills'?	Are processes and teams developing expertise to respond to change and new customer demands?	Do individuals have the applied competencies to master both task performance and work in a specific context?
Future capacity	Does the enterprise manage human, infrastructure and social capital to achieve its goals?	Are management systems and processes designed to encourage learning that improves current and future capacity?	Does the individual want to perform, learn and respond to customer and market demands?
Cultural identity	Is there a sense of shared identity and convergence of values, beliefs and norms to support desired performance?	Are interrelationships identified and managed to encourage diversity, creativity and innovation while achieving team and process outcomes?	Is the individual committed to work and innovation while respecting divergent views and ideas?

Based on Ruona & Lyford-Nojima 1997: 791

Integrating capability reporting and management

Management information systems are the major tool in capability management. Data collection systems contain information about the development of relevant skills, educational qualifications, experience and expertise. A system of this type could be considered as an analytical framework for determining future capacity in terms of performance outcomes. At the same time, the system serves as a database for sourcing skills and building capability profiles.

A data bureau under the control of the enterprise, or managed on its behalf, can become the hub of a human resources system that underpins learning and individual performance outcomes by reporting and recording requirements. It can also streamline and integrate capability reporting for human capital at all levels (from individuals to business units or regions to partners such as suppliers, training providers and contractors). Figure 10.2 shows the inputs into a capability inventory of the kind implemented in Woolworths and other Australian organisations.

Figure 10.2 A capability inventory

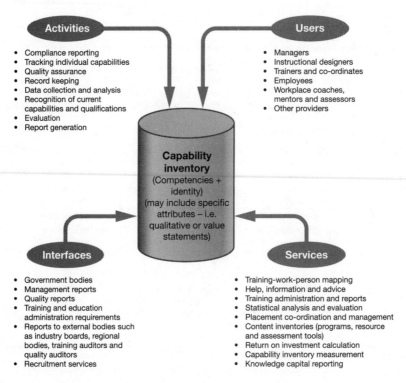

Activities
- Compliance reporting
- Tracking individual capabilities
- Quality assurance
- Record keeping
- Data collection and analysis
- Recognition of current capabilities and qualifications
- Evaluation
- Report generation

Users
- Managers
- Instructional designers
- Trainers and co-ordinates
- Employees
- Workplace coaches, mentors and assessors
- Other providers

Capability inventory
(Competencies + identity)
(may include specific attributes – i.e. qualitative or value statements)

Interfaces
- Government bodies
- Management reports
- Quality reports
- Training and education administration requirements
- Reports to external bodies such as industry boards, regional bodies, training auditors and quality auditors
- Recruitment services

Services
- Training-work-person mapping
- Help, information and advice
- Training administration and reports
- Statistical analysis and evaluation
- Placement co-ordination and management
- Content inventories (programs, resource and assessment tools)
- Return on investment calculation
- Capability inventory measurement
- Knowledge capital reporting

Based on Bowles 1999: 102–15, used with kind permission

The capability database acts as a central repository for data related to industry, occupational and organisational learning and performance. It can provide a quality-assured, accessible and consistent framework for the reporting and recognition of capability and competency. This permits the organisation to monitor its own capability acquisition and responsiveness, from the holistic level to that of particular teams, regions and individuals. The reporting system can also help employees to transfer their learning attainment into career pathways and further training.

As it applies specifically to e-learning, the system can manage qualified e-learning providers, assessors, coaches and mentors; report and analyse e-learning course completions; and stream learners between in-house learning, vendor courses and formal qualifications-based studies. It thus permits the enterprise to ensure that e-learning delivery and assessment will:

- relate to on-the-job outcomes wherever possible;
- recognise an individual's current capabilities;
- map learning requirements against potential work placements;
- map work placements to job performance requirements;
- generate cost profiles for workplace development activities;
- maintain a resource schedule (physical, human and time-based);
- generate capability profiles for any mix of individuals, groups, enterprises or strategic partners; and
- integrate e-learning with tools and procedures used in the workplace.

The database makes it possible to ensure that staff focus on training that meets their immediate job requirements or career development needs. Capability profiles thus provide an integrated human capital reporting system. See Table 10.4.

Table 10.4 Relationship between capability mapping and human resources development functions

Match	Profile		Useful for
Work match: Profiles capabilities required for perform-ance in a specific job, occupation, team or sector	Individual's profile: Matches individuals' abilities to work in a specific job and progress into a career area with their current capabilities to fill a vacant job	Learning profile: Maps learning required for a specific job or career progress	Functions: Recruitment, selection, succession planning, training needs analysis; profiling job seekers, promoting links with recruitment agencies
Person match: Enables an individual to be profiled through a database against learning completed, which may or may not be recognised through formal qualifications	Job profile: Allows an individual to choose future career moves and confirm competencies and learning required for a position	Learning profile: Records indi-vidual's existing qualification or current capacity	Functions: Coordination of where, when and how training should occur; maintenance of training records and current competency profiles; input into succession planning and skills audits and analysis
Learning match: Profiles learning required to provide an individual with the capabilities for a career path or a specific qualification	Individual's profile: Provides information so that training and educa-tion can be packaged for an individual seeking to fill capability gaps required for a job or career path	Job profile: Provides infor-mation so that training can be packaged for a job or for all applicants	Functions: Assurance that training programs deliver the required capabilities when, where and how the enter-prise specifies, while suiting the individual's job or career develop-ment: input into management planning of selection, recruitment and training

For example, a profile might show significant gaps between an individual's capabilities and those required for a position. This could indicate a need for a staffing change or for further e-learning on the part of the employee. Capability profiles also highlight areas where unrealistic expectations are placed on individuals' job performance. This can extend to all levels of the organisation and to all types of learning, not just traineeships and apprenticeships. At higher levels of the organisation, managers can be offered opportunities to augment vocational and trade qualifications, or replace them with university qualifications. Others might update their degrees or professional qualifications through refresher courses, short courses on new trends or research degrees. This kind of flexibility can benefit the individual, the organisation and the networks within which both operate. A capability approach to e-learning thus encompasses the growth of shared identity and human capital attributes that enhance the organisation's knowledge capital.

Conclusion

E-learning can play an important role in attracting knowledge by providing content, tools and an environment that encourages skills transfer as well as a converged sense of purpose that spans individuals and groups both inside and outside the organisational structure. E-learning solutions must maximise relationships across internal and external 'networks' that hold knowledge capital. All interactions represent opportunities for the organisation to learn and acquire valuable knowledge capital.

If e-learning is to add value in terms of sustainable performance capability, it must be embraced as an integral part of an organisation's learning, knowledge and performance framework, encompassing the company, its employees and others. Organisational learning offers a means to enhance learning activities and underpin the construction of knowledge capital. E-learning is part of the ongoing reinvention of organisational approaches to learning. Supported by a strong system of capability reporting, it can help to establish a learning culture that pervades the organisation.

Equally, e-learning embraces aspects of learning that extend beyond the organisation. Organisational learning can also occur through transactions between internal staff and external individuals (customers or suppliers), or from data captured during these transactions. This re-emphasises the need for data reporting across performance, knowledge, learning and service management systems. Chapter 11 will explore the implications of learning strategies that draw on the organisation's transactional relationships with its most significant others: its customers.

Principle 10

E-learning combined with capability reporting can strengthen organisational learning, help to establish a learning culture and facilitate the development of effective learning networks that extend beyond the boundaries of the organisation.

[10] See Bowles 1998b; Bowles & Baker 1998; and the tables and concepts included in Bowles 1999: ch. 6, used with kind permission.

Transactions and E-service

E-learning has similarities to and synergies with electronic service (e-service). E-learning strategies can be used to overcome barriers to providing services to customers in an electronic environment. At the same time, e-learning itself is a form of e-service, and its design and implementation can benefit from awareness of the commercial and communication strategies gaining currency in that arena.

The Internet is rapidly asserting itself as a marketing and sales medium. Typically, a business presents information and services on its web site, and potential customers access the information and services via the Internet. This process parallels the interactions involved in e-learning, and makes many of the same demands on those involved. Because online customers do not interact with the organisation face to face, it is crucial that they are provided with effective electronic information, services and feedback. A potential online customer can cancel a transaction with the click of a mouse, so a well-designed e-service strategy is a prerequisite rather than an option.

It is now widely recognised that businesses need to reconceptualise their strategies and processes to succeed in an e-service environment. Establishing brand loyalty is more difficult when customers are better informed about competing products and can source products and services from anywhere on the globe. Organisations can no longer afford to adopt a 'take-it-or-leave-it' approach. Electronic commerce (e-commerce) has introduced a new focus on responding to customer needs and preferences as part of a dynamic interaction aimed at building customer loyalty and increasing brand value.

An effective e-service strategy therefore needs to manage a learning strategy that will enable the business to:

- learn from its customers and respond to their needs and preferences;
- learn online about competitor businesses;
- provide staff and customers with accurate, up-to-date product and compliance information to increase sales and establish brand loyalty; and
- link training to experience to promote rapid skills transfer and adaptability to change.

Learning about customer needs and preferences

The e-service transaction provides an opportunity for service providers to capture a wide range of data about how well their products meet customer needs and preferences. Three broad strategies can be used:

- observing the behaviour of online customers;
- initiating interaction with online customers; and
- learning from online customers' experience and knowledge.

Observing the behaviour of customers

The behaviour of online customers can be observed and analysed in several ways:

Reviewing web site statistics reports: It is possible to generate web site statistics reports that detail what people do when they visit a business's web site. These reports, which are typically prepared monthly, can reveal how many visits a web site has had, when these occurred, how long visitors spent at the site, the typical paths they took through the site, where they came from – including which search engines and search terms they used – and from which pages they left the web site. All of this information can provide valuable insights. For example, if a large number of users are leaving the site after brief visits to the home page, it may indicate that the page needs to offer visitors more information of interest to them. Alternatively, if customers progress to the order page but seldom complete an order, this is likely to indicate a problem with the ordering process or the prices of products.

Designing web sites for accurate data analysis: Data about the behaviour of online customers can be analysed more accurately if information parameters are built into the web site design. For example, if products are separated into groups or assigned separate pages, it is possible to collect precise information on customers' preferences and to analyse their purchasing behaviour more accurately.

Similarly, information can be more closely targeted if customers are encouraged to supply information about themselves and their needs. For example, a visitor might be asked to select between products for 'primary school students' or 'high school students'. In this way, the paths that people take through a web site help to reveal their typical needs and preferences.

Many organisations also couple email marketing with an Internet presence. This may involve sending regular customers information about new products or directing customers to a section of the web site specifically designed to meet their needs. The web site statistics can then be used to gauge the effectiveness of the email campaign.

Initiating interaction with customers

Online customers often take their business elsewhere rather than reporting a problem with a web site or asking questions about a product that is inadequately described on the site. For this reason, it is essential to make the most of any direct contact from customers. Means of initiating interaction include:

- **Simple one-question surveys:** These surveys tend to focus on customers' opinions, with the results released only to those who respond. People will often respond just to see what other people think.
- **More detailed surveys:** If this is the route taken, it is important to keep it simple and look for a way to build a benefit into the process for the web site visitor. This may take the form of a general request to 'help us to help you', or include on offer of free information or other direct benefits as a pay-off to the respondent.
- **Free offers:** Many online businesses offer customers something of value in return for registering their names, contact details and interests. These offers typically include a question along the lines of 'Would you like us to email you about new products?'

Learning from customers' experience and knowledge

Online chat rooms and forums can encourage customer feedback and two-way communication, and also foster multi-directional interaction among customers. This kind of interaction can help the business to keep abreast of the market as a whole, and can also provide invaluable information on customers' post-sales experience. It should be noted, however, that online 'community' facilities need to be monitored, which requires an ongoing commitment of resources (Powazek 2002).

In e-learning as well, data and feedback from learners as customers can be used to improve programs to meet changing customer needs and preferences. If e-learning processes are designed to foster a high level of interaction, ongoing feedback for evaluation purposes can be built into the program. This is in line with the broader emphasis on developing organisational processes that can constantly adapt to change.

Learning about competitor services

The Internet offers businesses an opportunity to learn by benchmarking competitor activities. It is possible to visit dozens of businesses in an hour, see what they offer and learn about their electronic sales strategies. Spending time on the Internet 'researching' other businesses can be extremely valuable.

Researchers often talk about an 'Internet year' as being six months or less, implying that business activities on the Internet change much more quickly than in the traditional business world. Spending time on the Internet is the most effective way to get a sense of what other businesses are doing right now. The research should include:

- **Learning from competitors:** By viewing competitors' e-service strategies, businesses can learn about the customers these businesses are targeting and prepare strategies to match or surpass their efforts and differentiate their own site from that of the competition.
- **Learning from similar businesses:** By looking at the web sites of companies that deal with slightly different products or operate in other countries, businesses can find out what a new entrant needs to do. Other companies' sites may also have developed features that make them better

than their competitors. These provide a 'baseline' point of entry into the online marketplace.

- **Learning how target customers are likely to behave online:** A business can adopt the perspective of a potential customer and try to find out where customers could go to buy a product the business is selling. Product reviews, testimonials, media reviews, newsgroups and special interest web sites can provide insights into customer behaviour and expectations, including insights into how potential customers are likely to find out about the types of products the business sells.
- **Learning from being the customer:** When visiting competitors' sites, a business can shop for comparisons to find the 'cheapest' or 'best' product on offer.
- **Learning from technology/sales process issues:** As electronic sales strategies become more refined, a business may try searching for sites that use the types of electronic processes it is planning to deploy. By investigating how these processes work (or don't work), the business can incorporate improvements into its own electronic strategy.

Keeping staff and customers informed

In his book *Information Space*, Max H. Boisot describes information as the common currency of social transactions, which are integral to the acquisition of knowledge:

> The largest part of an individual's stock of concrete and abstract knowledge . . . is acquired, more often than not, off the shelf through a process of social interaction, internalised by force or repetition, and gradually embedded into an individual's world view (1995: 179).

Interactions involve individuals in a constant process of elaborating and testing their understanding. This is nowhere more evident than on the Web, where the sheer novelty of the medium and the diversity of information it carries require continuous learning from all who interact and transact.

Here, organisations can energise their e-service provision by using e-learning processes to support learning by external customers as well as staff. A consumer's decision to buy online is influenced by a wide range of factors. The customer's first impression may be influenced by the design of the site, its speed of loading and its ease of use, while the existence of a secure mechanism for online transactions is an essential prerequisite for customers to part with their credit-card details. But the factors that build repeat visits and customer loyalty tend to revolve around the provision of useful information and efficient services. As summarised by Bowles and Wilson (2003: 37), these include:

- availability of information to enable informed buying decisions;
- reliability of site functionality and on-demand access to computer help and sales support;
- efficient post-sales and service support; and
- offers of catalogues and information updates.

E-commerce providers have an important role to play in assisting customers to make effective use of their web sites and the services they offer. The mental models customers bring to electronic transactions are strongly influenced by the style of the web interface (Hong, Tam & Yim 2002: 108–10). The usability of web sites is strongly dependent on the sites being designed in such a way that their structure enables intuitive navigation, while offering specialist support (either in electronic form or by way of one-on-one communication) when technical problems arise.

The adequacy of human–computer interface (HCI) design is a determining factor in the success of e-commerce. The dominant force in Internet-based communication is no longer the specialist computer programmer or designer but the vast number of self-taught users who inhabit the World Wide Web. In the words of Tesler, as computer technology has developed, the early 'priesthood of programmers . . . [has] vanished to be replaced by a single user . . . for whom the computer [is] a tool, not a calling' (1991: 86). This requires HCI design to address users' learning and information needs.

From an e-learning perspective, a usable web site can be seen as engaging customers in a virtuous circle through a twofold e-learning process: while the customers' search for codified information drives their interaction with the site, the interaction simultaneously builds their tacit knowledge of how the site works and what it has to offer. Contemplating the future of computer technology, Weiser observes:

> The most profound technologies are those that disappear. They weave themselves into the fabric of everyday life until they are indistinguishable from it . . . Whenever people learn something sufficiently well, they cease to be aware of it . .. only when things disappear in this way are we freed to use them without thinking and so focus beyond them on new goals (1991: 94).

In essence, the purpose of HCI design is to facilitate this 'disappearance' or invisibility by unobtrusively assisting users to acquire familiarity with the technological interface.

Linking training to experience

For companies competing in a global connected economy, speed and adaptability are touted as key sources of competitive advantage (Davis & Meyer 1998). Against this backdrop, learning is essential to develop staff capabilities to deliver businesses's core value propositions in markets that are subject to constant change. This emphasis has placed people at the heart of modern service organisations. As Charles Fred puts it, the cycle time to achieve proficiency has become an important indicator of an organisation's performance (2002: 36).

Speed and competitiveness are achieved by advancing individuals rapidly along the learning curve to the point of proficiency (Fred 2002: 95), but the learning curve does not stop there. Once proficiency is achieved, individuals continue to learn, acquiring new skills, information and knowledge (including knowledge of how to transfer knowledge), and accumulating the hands-on experience necessary to deal with unexpected contingencies (2002: 67).

To speed the development of proficiency, Fred suggests (2002: 34) that businesses have to:

- establish the proficiency threshold;
- accelerate the accumulation of experience; and
- measure the cycle time to threshold proficiency.

To use learning as a process that sustains rapid change, it is necessary to maximise both current learning and the retention of learning in a way that promotes the accumulation of experience and the transfer of knowledge. This requires that skills transfer be balanced with work-based experience, and emphasises the importance of learning that promotes interactivity and high levels of cognitive development.

As Figure 11.1 depicts, individuals' progress towards service excellence does not stop when they become proficient. As well as learning how to serve the customer, learners need to build identity attributes (culture, behaviours and values) that enable them to keep meeting customer needs. The motivation to achieve this outcome has to shape electronic and physical learning and service strategies.

E-learning offers obvious advantages in reducing the total time to reach threshold proficiency. Permitting learning to occur in an electronic mode removes the scheduling restrictions imposed by classroom-based training. As Fred points out, e-learning is particularly attractive to younger staff and those familiar with online service in other contexts (2002: 125). This 'digitally literate' generation accepts lifelong learning and online transactions as part of everyday existence.

The principles of e-learning are particularly useful in learning from customers and rapidly responding to their needs. Data on customer preferences can be conveyed to staff in real time as packages of online 'educative' information. Up-to-date information on products and service procedures can also be supplied to staff electronically, and online experts

Figure 11.1 S-curve of learning and implementation of e-service

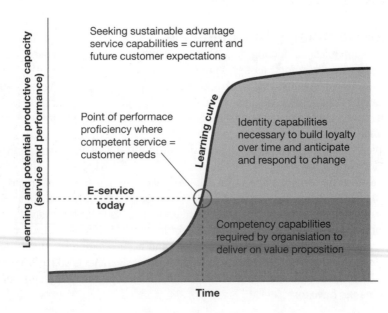

and mentors can be made available to support less experienced staff. Such strategies help build the organisation's stock of experience and assist staff to transfer both explicit and tacit knowledge.

By thus embedding e-learning as an integral part of an e-service environment, businesses can:

- reduce the time taken to raise an individual's performance to the point of proficiency;
- facilitate the transfer of mental models that make possible the assimilation of new information, the transfer of knowledge and the accumulation of experience;
- allow individuals to control when, where and how they acquire learning relevant to immediate work performance;
- provide 'episodes' of concise information on new products or changing customer expectations;
- enable collaboration, interaction and knowledge transfer; and
- support rapid, customer-focused adaptation and change.

E-service and e-learning transactions

There are six parallel lessons that are common to e-service and e-learning transactions.

Customers' needs and wants should drive the transaction

Individuals today are exposed to a vast amount of information. Some business strategists talk in terms of competition for customer 'mindshare' in an 'attention economy'. At the heart of any successful e-service, including e-learning, is the need to change behaviours originally shaped by transactions in physical environments. Attracting customers to a web presence and encouraging them to complete an electronic transaction requires effective textual and visual communication. The following factors are critical to the success of an e-commerce venture (Singh 2002; Bowles & Wilson 2003: 77–8):

- **Analysis and planning:** All communication requires strategic planning – what shall we communicate, to whom, when and how?
- **Ease of access:** When interacting online, individuals expect to access relevant information swiftly, but the supply of information has to be balanced against the 'capture' of customers' business.
- **Competitive differentiation:** Communication should lead to a relationship that results in sales, or preferably in brand identification and customer loyalty. Considerable effort needs to be put into differentiating one's online offerings from those of competitors, especially when online customers can so easily compare offerings and move to another supplier.
- **Customer preferences versus business outcomes:** Customers' needs and preferences should be given priority over the business's short-term goals. Online strategies should be demand-led, not supply-driven.
- **Help and directions:** First-time visitors should have access to directions on how to find and sort the information they need and engage in the exchange.

- **Provision of information:** Choice abounds in the online world. Potential customers can compare products, prices and features at unprecedented speed. E-service providers have to acknowledge that consumers are better informed than ever before.
- **Personalisation:** Online information should be tailored to identifiable market segments and customer groups. To encourage repeat visits, customers should be able to customise their interaction with the web site.

Electronic transactions vs traditional business processes

Businesses that expect improved customer acquisition and retention from an online strategy are often confronted with a new set of realities. Some of the common problems are outlined by Bowles & Wilson (2003: 58):

- It often costs more to acquire an online customer than a physical customer.
- What appear to be fixed costs that will scale to meet any number of customers become less 'fixed' as customer numbers increase.
- Margins on e-services vary by service categories, customer segments and market areas.
- Attracting customer visits is less important than inducing customers to make purchases.
- Offering certain products and services online can create real problems for inventory management, supply and distribution; order fulfilment is a critical determinant of success.
- While technology is at the core of online sales, e-service providers still have to provide access to 'real' people to advise customers.

'Build the site and they will come' is the catch-cry of e-service providers who have not understood all the dimensions of satisfying online customers. Many businesses underestimate the costs and overestimate how many customers will be acquired.

Many providers of e-learning services too are under the illusion that the investment is a one-off fixed cost. This ignores the rules of investment in technology and business processes. The increased complexity of the electronic supply chain produces new problems. Online strategies require rapid responses, which tend to bring to the fore any weaknesses in content delivery and difficulties in managing the technological interface. Costs tend to escalate as businesses find they have to improve inferior processes and systems.

The technical limitations of electronic transactions

Infrastructure limits the types of e-services available. The infrastructure and bandwidth available to Australian and Asian customers are less sophisticated than those available to North American and European customers. Bandwidth influences the range of services and products that can be offered, and thus influences the customer's decision to purchase.

Bandwidth has a greater effect on some services than others. Interactive computer games and videos on demand require greater bandwidth, for example, but an increase in bandwidth may have only a marginal impact on products such as books and hardware items, which can be sold through static web pages with a minimum of visual content. Similarly, a real-estate site may be more effective if it can offer virtual tours and on-demand video. Figure 11.2 indicates how interactive features and increased bandwidth affect the customer appeal and saleability of a range of products and services.

Figure 11.2   Bandwidth and the resulting influence on e-services

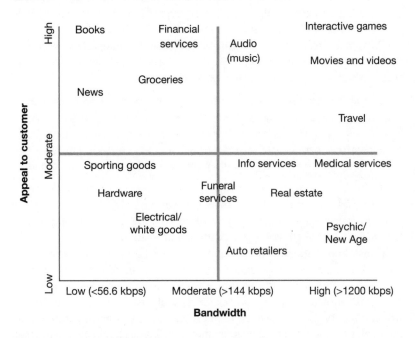

Based on Kierzkiwski et al. 1996: 12; Bowles & Wilson 2003: 49

The focus should be on customer retention

Retaining online customers is the key to successful e-commerce. The cost of acquiring new customers is much higher than that of retaining loyal customers. Furthermore, businesses that get to know their current customers can develop more profitable acquisition strategies. Customers who are dissatisfied with a site rarely return, while those who are satisfied return more frequently and are less inclined to shop around.

Just like the physical marketplace, the online marketplace may have too many stores in a location or have market segments that are saturated by companies all vying for dominance. To win and retain market share, businesses must offer value propositions that appeal to the customer. This often requires them to anticipate and respond to shifting customer needs and preferences.

Seybold (2001) highlights three principles of the 'service' or 'customer economy' that provide an additional rationale for satisfying customers online:

- **Customers are in control:** Customers are reshaping businesses and transforming industries.

- **Customer relationships count:** The value of current customer relationships determines the value of the business.
- **Customer experience matters:** The feeling that customers have when they interact with the brand and business determines their loyalty.

In these circumstances, businesses need to use electronic systems to help customers to derive satisfaction via the Internet, while also deploying customer feedback and data on customer behaviour to refine the capabilities of the business's online presence.

Customer relationship management (CRM) integrates processes, people and technology to improve how an organisation can build service relationships with customers. Thompson describes CRM as:

> a business strategy to select and manage the most valuable customer relationships. CRM requires a customer-centric business philosophy and culture to support effective marketing, sales, and service processes. CRM applications can enable effective customer relationship management, provided that an enterprise has the right leadership, strategy, and culture (2002: 1).

In CRM, information about customers is used to reinforce relationships and thus gain competitive advantage. Birch, Gerbert and Schneider (2000) identify four steps to building relationships with online customers.

Know and understand the customer: Businesses need to collect data on the customer as an individual and as a member of a specific segment and market. The strongest advantage that bricks-and-mortar organisations have when moving online is their existing list of customers and a strong (one would hope) basis for collecting data on the customers and their needs and preferences. Established businesses may also have relationships with mail-order companies that have distribution databases.

Often a service provider learns details about customers only when they begin a purchase. This is too late. On average, only 3 per cent of visits to a site result in sales. To get to know customers better requires some smart ways of managing the relationship.

A business needs to ensure that it is attracting and serving the customer base it wants, whether those customers are high-value purchasers or fit profiles and priorities that match the design of the online environment or transaction process.

Personalise all service: The ability to adapt e-service transactions to customers' needs and preferences is a major strength of the Internet. Various techniques can be adopted to personalise the service. Customers may be encouraged to select their preferred language and visual layout when they first log on. They can also be encouraged to register so that on repeat visits their name will appear on the web page and the presentation of information will be tailored to their preferences and needs. Personalised emails may be sent offering services that reflect a customer's previous purchase preferences or nominated areas of interest.

Personalised strategies also permit tighter control of costs by avoiding expenses associated with marketing and business activities that fail to convert into sales. For example, personalised services can reduce the cost of maintaining a help desk (Birch et al. 2000: 179).

It is now possible for businesses to 'personalise' automated services. Some of these practices are ethically questionable. For example, a computer can generate automated emails that appear to come from a 'staff member' to give the illusion of one-to-one interaction. The customer may then interact with staff who all pose as the person named on the original email.

Give the customers control: Surveys of Australian online consumers continue to highlight the consumer's desire to be in control. Among the most common reasons customers give for leaving sites are reluctance to disclose personal details (more than 4 per cent) and scepticism about the security of payments (20 per cent) (Budde 2002: 60). To overcome these obstacles, a business must establish a sense of reciprocity and customer control. For example, customers who register may be given the opportunity to nominate what products they wish to see, what recommendations they receive, how they wish to pay, and whether or not they wish to see specials and 'discounted' options.

Promote customer communities: Many suppliers of CRM packages now provide applications that promote the formation of customer communities (e-CRM). E-learning application providers are building CRM interfaces in the form of user evaluation into content and learning management systems (Chapman 2002). Studies of web site metrics consistently show improvements when online communities promote relationships between customers (Wang, Head & Archer 2000: 374).

Another reason to create virtual communities is to increase the customer's connection with the site, the brand and the organisation. This is more than just promoting loyalty. It is building online behaviours to a point where the organisation can shape expectations and satisfy them in a manner others cannot match.

E-services must adapt to changing customer expectations

What is required to satisfy each market segment or individual customer varies over time? To adapt to changing customer expectations, the e-service provider has one major advantage: data capture. Gianforte (2002) presents the following checklist for organisations seeking to determine how well their e-service is meeting customer expectations:

- **Capture customer feedback:** As with all communication, listening is a crucial factor.
- **Respond rapidly:** Speed is everything in the online world. Does the online presence make it easy for the customer to find what they want using their own hardware and connection, which may be far less sophisticated than the service provider's? Does the company streamline routine tasks to provide rapid electronic processing?
- **Anticipate needs:** Can customers access resources, find answers to queries or locate other information quickly?
- **Manage the channels:** How do customers get to the site? Where do they go after leaving the site? This information may suggest ways to improve

channels to market and make the web site a cornerstone of customers' online activity.

- **Measure individual satisfaction:** The Web permits businesses to capture data on how individuals rate their experience. Does a site permit customers to provide feedback and rate the site?
- **Value the knowledge of customers:** In the global information economy, knowledge of customers' needs and preferences is often as valuable as a business's existing products and services. Intelligence on customer expectations, present and future, has a knowledge value that can be reported on the bottom line. Many e-service providers find that the sale of information is becoming their primary source of income.
- **Forge partnerships:** E-service providers do not have to do everything themselves. They may outsource functions to other companies expert in the provision of services, or work with affiliates to improve cross-selling and supply.

All the above issues need to be considered together, not in isolation. For example, businesses should avoid the situation where visitors who need assistance have to phone a help line or download a form and fax it to the help desk. If done online in real time the customer interaction can be recorded and the capacity to learn from this experience captured.

A major theme in customer-focused business strategies is establishing relationships with customers that extend beyond fulfilment of an immediate need and actually fulfil future needs. As Wood suggests:

> Customer relationships are not developed through upsell or cross-sell campaigns, but by offering new services that anticipate customers' needs and create a unique bond. This allows the engaged business to provide exceptional levels of personalized service . . . necessary to strengthen these relationships and ultimately maximise return on relationships (2002: 3).

E-service and e-learning must build brand value

Building staff competency and identity capabilities can also help customers to learn within an e-service exchange, establishing a virtuous circle in which all individuals continuously learn and benefit from the relationship. By taking such an approach, e-learning can target identity attributes that directly influence brand value or brand propositions.[11] The brand represents distinctive qualities with which a customer can identify, differentiating one product from another and building customer loyalty. Brand value can be immediately enhanced when a business builds effective online learning and service transactions.

Attracting customers, particularly in low-spending but high-volume market segments, requires a strong brand recognition and value proposition. This is especially important for businesses that are moving from traditional transactions to an online strategy. Customers' attitudes in a physical environment may not necessarily translate into the brand value they seek in an electronic environment.

If an organisation can track customers' attitudes, it can shape its brand to be congruent with their values and beliefs. This requires the organisation to establish a sense of trust and alleviate customers' anxieties. Organisations can consciously use e-learning processes that reinforce brand strategies linked to customers' attitudes and expectations by:

- stimulating changes in behaviour;
- building a value proposition that has utility;
- demonstrating an authentic and reliable return for the customer's loyalty; and
- building a relationship that holds meaning and value.

To become a learning process that reinforces brand loyalty, the online experience needs to offer the following features:

- a strong focus on the distinctive features of the core product or service;
- a functional Web presence, including ease of access, navigation and payment;
- a personalised experience that rapidly translates content and services into meaningful knowledge or outcomes (Hackos 2002: 17);
- collaborative exchanges that reflect the social and cultural needs of particular demographics or groups with common interests (Duyne, Landay & Hong 2003: 41); and
- a strong sense of credibility to reassure customers that the transaction is secure and supported by competent staff.

Using the online presence to reinforce brand attributes can extend the market reach of a brand or enable e-service providers to extend their sustainable competitive advantage.

The process of communicating a brand promise to online customers involves learning, which occurs predominantly in an electronic environment. Ultimately, the online service provider must also learn about the customer's level of satisfaction. Building brand equity, therefore, involves e-learning to capture and evaluate customer satisfaction with the brand value proposition. Communication and learning strategies that build brand position and brand value are tightly interwoven, as shown in Figure 11.3.

Conclusion

Any online service should communicate clearly how the organisation intends to meet a customer's needs. Failure to do so can only result in high levels of customer dissatisfaction, no matter how many customers visit the online site. This focus on what customers want has produced a rethinking of how organisations provide e-services. E-commerce has forced a review of business-to-business transactions and supply chain management. Internal processes and business-to-business transactions have been streamlined through better systems integration, the use of computers to undertake routine tasks, and improved co-ordination and packaging of information and data flow. Finally, there is a new emphasis on the value of accurate knowledge: knowledge not just as codified information, but as insight into customer needs and preferences provided by experienced service personnel. Customers also have to learn how to transact in an electronic environment. This involves not only the explicit knowledge associated with transacting online but also tacit knowledge of why they should transact with a given online provider.

While e-learning can accelerate individuals' and organisations' achievement of performance proficiency, it has a role beyond supporting service delivery. E-learning is embedded in the capacities of the business and the online customer. E-learning is chartered not only with building performance proficiency, but also with ensuring that the service provider can continually adapt to meet customer needs and preferences.

Figure 11.3 Embedding e-learning in the e-service transaction

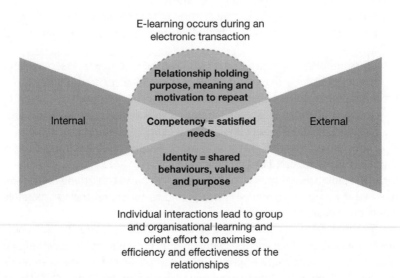

Shaping expectations and being able to meet them influences service provision in both the physical and electronic environment. To be satisfied, customers need to be confident that their personal expectations will be met. Similarly, organisations do not want to have to continually re-engage online customers' attention. They want to develop a degree of comfort and brand identification that will encourage customers to return. This makes for loyal customers, the ultimate target of any service excellence strategy. E-learning can thus enable individuals both inside and outside the organisation to provide an environment for communication, collaboration and commercial exchange.

Principle 11

By enhancing the e-learning component of electronic service exchanges, businesses can build staff and customer capabilities and improve their own responsiveness to customers' current and future needs.

---

[11] The Learning to E-learn project is continuing its research on the relationship between e-service and e-learning. For updates, see the project site at http://www.portal.unitas.com.au.

Building Effective and Efficient E-learning

As previous chapters have suggested, many corporate e-learning initiatives have been compromised by a lack of attention to issues of design, implementation and evaluation. Managers who have been sold on the idea of e-learning as a 'quick fix' have ultimately been disappointed. This chapter begins by drawing together some of the key design and implementation issues canvassed in earlier chapters. It then considers the important issue of how e-learning should be evaluated, and closes by mapping out the elements of an implementation process for efficient and effective e-learning.

Structuring e-learning interventions

There is an emerging consensus that the process involved in developing the e-learning environment constitutes a social intervention, which in turn involves processes of deliberately planned human interaction. In this context, investigating how and why the intervention is undertaken can help uncover what an efficient and effective e-learning process requires of those involved at each stage of the process, from planning to delivery to evaluation and redesign.

Who decides on e-learning interventions?

E-learning in any organisation begins as a concept. People endeavour to give this concept life within the context and activities of their organisation. This presents some interesting challenges, mainly because inducing the organisation to invest in an e-learning initiative often depends more on the nature of organisational processes than on the nature of e-learning itself.

In a competitive business environment, a key task of management is to evaluate a range of investment options. The sheer diversity of options can make it difficult to find a common basis for evaluation. The challenge tends to be resolved by using fiscal approaches, such as return on investment (ROI), or by evaluating options against outcomes and strategies already identified by organisation decision makers. Shelton describes the characteristics that define an effective 'internal marketplace for innovation':

Inside the company, innovators actually 'sell' management their creative ideas — embodied in R&D projects, product-development collaborations, or strategic alliances. If management likes what it sees, the management team funds projects based on the perceived commercial value to the company. Otherwise, management holds back on funding. And across the organization, everyone knows that no amount of cheerleading will make an innovation successful in the external market if the company's internal marketplace does not value it for both its creative and commercial promise (2001: 15).

Proponents of e-learning participate in this internal marketplace of ideas. To secure organisational investment, they must promote the value of e-learning over alternative strategies. In doing so, however, they frequently face significant obstacles.

Often the e-learning initiative will come from human-resources (HR) and training professionals who are not familiar with the usual processes of proposing organisation-wide strategic projects. This can pose a challenge in forming e-learning initiatives, because such initiatives involve decision makers in finance, technology and senior management, as well as internal clients. Compared with pre-existing levels of HR investment, e-learning involves substantial investment in an unfamiliar field where there is uncertainty over the long-term pay-offs.

Problems arise from the sheer newness of the concept of e-learning. Many organisations are even uncertain whether its most appropriate managerial and functional 'home' is in HR, IT or elsewhere. On the one hand, the technologies for e-learning are new, sometimes complex and mostly beyond the day-to-day experience of HR professionals; on the other, the issues involved in its deployment tend to be beyond the experience of decision makers and IT professionals. Related initiatives such as knowledge management and customer relationship management can also cloud efforts to develop e-learning.

Despite the prospect of significant benefits, e-learning can represent a minefield of risks and complexities for an organisation. There are two main areas of risk: innovations may be confronted by institutional inertia and an 'if-it-ain't-broke-don't-fix-it' mentality; and, conversely, given the prospective cost savings, e-learning can be almost too easy to 'sell' to decision makers on a short-term basis, without the necessary awareness of its impact on existing organisational processes and modes of learning.

There are thus significant knowledge gaps within many organisations, and these gaps need to be bridged before an organisation can embark on effective e-learning strategies. Peter Drucker (1994) points out that 'every organisation, whether a business or not, has a theory of the business', which is made up of assumptions that shape the organisation's behaviours and what it considers meaningful outcomes. The need for theory and logic equally applies to e-learning. Its development, however, can be a slow process; often new concepts are accepted only after they have proved themselves. It is not until the results of new approaches can be measured that progressively higher degrees of implementation become achievable and the full benefit of the strategy begins to flow.

Framing e-learning proposals

As mentioned earlier, e-learning can require significant upfront investment in technology, time and development. As a result, e-learning proposals need to reach the senior and strategic decision makers of an organisation. Whether an e-learning initiative emerges from the bottom up (from HR and training) or from the top down (as a management decision), training and HR staff can quickly find themselves in new territory.

For bottom-up e-learning initiatives, proponents need to frame their proposals in terms of financial and strategic benefits. Top-down initiatives are likely to result in involvement from training and HR staff. In either case, there is a need to establish a common basis of understanding between senior managers and training and HR professionals. As Brandon Hall suggests, there is a real art in making a successful presentation to those executives responsible for deciding whether the organisation will or will not learn to e-learn (2001: 2). Learning practitioners must be able to talk to executives in a language they understand. At the same time, e-learning proposals often stretch the limits of the criteria senior managers adopt for evaluating strategic initiatives. Principal among those criteria is return on investment.

ROI and beyond

Most organisational investments are evaluated using a financial paradigm. Other business concepts have also migrated towards this paradigm. Greenagel suggests that the need to justify infrastructure investments for intangible outcomes has hastened this emulation of financial language and approaches (2002: 1).

For proponents of e-learning, there are obvious advantages in aligning oneself with the financial paradigm, because it enables their proposals to compete with other existing and emerging business strategies. In effect, the financial paradigm serves as a gatekeeper to the types of strategies that an organisation might consider. Unless its proponents address this gatekeeper, the emerging business strategy is unlikely to get the decision makers' attention. Furthermore, their chances of attracting investment in e-learning will be better if they can use the decision makers' existing worldview as a starting point. Concept recognition is of paramount importance here.

A standard way for new organisational initiatives to gain attention is by presenting a business case, including ROI and related measures framed in terms of reducing costs, increasing revenues, or both. E-learning proposals have tended to focus on cost reduction as an initial justification. Thus, classroom costs minus e-learning costs should produce a positive equation that represents cost savings and immediate ROI advantage. A typical set of e-learning ROI calculations is shown in Table 12.1.

In this example, e-learning would save $191,100 over existing classroom-based methods. Many e-learning providers' web sites demonstrate how to calculate traditional ROI for training and e-learning. The literature and online tools seem to be obsessed with cost-reduction aspects of ROI. To quote a leading e-learning information web site: 'E-learning is too new to have produced hard evidence of learning gains. E-learning's top-line upside is speculative; its bottom-line savings are on more solid ground' (Cross 2002; also attributed to the American Society for Training & Development [ASTD] cited in Baker 2002: 10).

Table 12.1 Calculating ROI

Costs	Classroom training	E-learning
Wages of trainees ($20 per hour, burdened)	$400,000	$240,000
Travel costs (50% of people travelling)	$250,000	$ ———
Trainer wages	$47,500	$11,400
Trainer travel	$20,000	$ ———
Development costs (custom training)	$160,000	$400,000
Delivery systems (first year amortised)	$ ———	$35,000
Total	$877,500	$686,400

Kurtus 2002: 1

Making the initial case for an ROI from e-learning does not appear particularly challenging. As Urdan and Weggen point out, traditional training models involve heavy costs in travel and accommodation expenses, and time spent away from the job travelling or sitting in a classroom dramatically reduces employee productivity and revenue (2000: 4). Hum and Ladouceur also emphasise the cost-saving potential of e-learning but, significantly, point to the prospect of additional intangible benefits that should be included in an evaluation of ROI. These include increased employee productivity and autonomy in career development (2001: 19). The question that remains, however, is whether a cost-reduction rationale for e-learning captures its nature and potential.

Does cost reduction make sense?

An approach that favours cost reduction to justify e-learning investment is in danger of compromising the quality of the learning experience and outcomes delivered. As Grant observes:

> It is easier and cheaper to produce pages of scrolling text than to produce highly interactive and engaging educational material. It is easier and cheaper to produce trivial tests and interactions than complex and challenging ones. So, while the demo is often so impressive, you'll often find that by module 4 of an 8 module course, the viewer is nearly paralysed with boredom and looking for a noose — or at least a career change (cited in Baker 2002: 40).

Yet e-learning can offer complex educational experiences. Medical students, for example, can be offered the experience of simulated surgery; business management students can be confronted with simulated scenarios in which they gather information, make decisions and deal with unexpected changes in the business environment (Blurton 1999 cited in Bell et al. 2002: 28).

Unfortunately, as is so often the case with industries migrating towards new technologies, the message of opportunity has been interpreted in terms of adapting existing practices rather than transforming them. As a result, the main advantages of new technologies are sometimes missed, ignored or forgotten. As Hammer and Champy have observed, 'the real power of technology . . . is not that it can make old processes work better, but that it enables organisations to break old rules and create new ways of working' (1994: 7). A commitment to this kind of change is the missing ingredient in many organisations' approaches to e-learning.

It seems worth restating that e-learning is not simply traditional learning delivered electronically. Beyond the issues of justifying investment and developing technologies, it is essential to come to terms with both the advantages and the limitations of e-learning. Any assessment of ROI needs to consider the potential differences between the observable outcomes of electronic and non-electronic modes of learning. The essential raison d'être for e-learning is learning, not technology.

Where this principle does not prevail, the risk is that both the outcomes of learning and the potential for strategic advantage are compromised. ROI estimates are just one dimension of an e-learning plan, and they cannot capture the overall benefit to the company. Justifying e-learning as an economy measure risks developing a cost-cutting mindset among project sponsors and participants.

Those who promote e-learning primarily as a cost-reduction measure often suggest that increasing the 'economies of scale' will achieve further cost efficiencies. Yet the idea of increasing the scale runs counter to the logic of designing programs for a unique mix of individual needs, in a particular context and at a given point in time. In such cases, the costs of development and design may actually rise as the number of students increases and learner populations become more diverse (Greenagel 2002: 1).

In the longer term, promoting e-learning as a cost-reduction measure may undermine subsequent attempts to promote investment in human skills and capabilities. Reducing costs has immediate bottom-line visibility, and is often a major selling point as far as project sponsors are concerned. It is a different story when a new e-learning system has failed to fulfil expectations and further expenditure is requested. Such follow-up requests are unlikely to receive a favourable hearing. It is far better to portray e-learning from the start as a wise investment, with any anticipated cost savings reinvested in more and better staff training. This approach also offers more budgetary room in the development stage, and therefore increases the chances of demonstrating the real value of e-learning.

In spite of providers' emphasis on ROI, their faith does not appear warranted or widely shared. Even some senior executives are sceptical of its usefulness as a measure. One of the most scathing critics of the 'hype' surrounding the ROI 'bandwagon' is Kruse (2003), who suggests that ROI calculations are often based at best on educated guesses at potential savings and gains, because the formula omits so many real-world variables. Furthermore, the 'guesstimates' ignore actual results, such as employee engagement scores before and after management training. Given the vagaries of calculating and using ROI, reports of e-learning successes and ROI benefits need to be viewed with caution.

E-learning is unlikely to have useful outcomes if an organisation simply yields to pressure to jump on a bandwagon and does not formulate a clear rationale for e-learning adoption. At the very least, the following qualifications should always be taken into account:

- The validity of an ROI evaluation depends on the assumptions on which it is based.
- Because some potential impacts of e-learning require qualitative evaluation, projections and evaluations based on ROI can only be estimates.
- A positive ROI result should not be allowed to pre-empt broader consideration of the possibilities of e-learning.
- The results of e-learning are not exactly comparable with those of conventional learning programs, and ROI must take this into account.

ROI calculations must also reflect the outcomes that can be attained given the organisation's readiness at any given time. As outlined in Chapter 3, it is possible to devise a dynamic model for organisational e-learning readiness that can link e-learning ROI with realistic business outcomes. All too often, however, proponents of e-learning set the e-learning ROI calculation too narrowly (i.e. they understate it), or claim ROI benefits that are not attainable in the proposed timeframe given the organisation's current e-learning readiness (i.e. they overstate it and raise false expectations).[12]

Many businesses are beginning to witness dramatic cost savings from the shift to e-learning, and a few forward-thinking companies have already started developing systems to measure e-learning's positive impact on customer service, productivity and sales. In 2000, Gartner Group estimated that 30 per cent of its e-learning clients were using qualitative and quantitative metrics to chart the impact on the company's performance. The use of metrics to justify e-learning seemed likely to increase as more companies used e-learning to support high-priority business goals, rather than to provide training for training's sake (Berry 2000: 1). Table 12.2 summarises some of the factors that can be assessed as part of a qualitative and quantitative evaluation of e-learning.

E-learning is no panacea. It is a transformation process that requires organisations to take a long-term view of ROI, impact on business strategy and staff capacity to transfer knowledge using the medium. This is best achieved through a wide-ranging and continuous process of evaluation, review and further innovation, as the following section outlines.

Evaluating e-learning

The following discussion starts from the assumption that evaluation should be an intrinsic part of e-learning implementation. Effective evaluation provides tangible proof to participants, organisations and communities that their investment of time or money has generated a result. This may simply take the form of reporting whether a known skill deficiency has been met. The larger challenge for the instructional designer, learning manager or provider is to demonstrate that this result has occurred within an efficient and effective e-learning strategy that continuously builds sustainable advantage.

Table 12.2   E-learning metrics

Field of evaluation	Metrics
Overall company performance	Return on investment Skill levels and profiles Matching of skills to job performance requirements Performance and productivity standards Achievement of business strategic outcomes Process quality measures Product quality measures Incidence of training performance problems Accident statistics Incidence of customer complaints
The development of a learning culture	Staff willingness to learn Integration of training as a strategic function Differentiation of education and training Use of action learning to rectify operational problems Team cohesiveness Staff willingness to apprise management of training needs
Individual learning and satisfaction	Satisfaction with learning program Motivation to learn Confidence in capabilities Access to further career and learning pathways

Evaluations of education and training usually concentrate on measuring individual reactions, quantitative learning outcomes or the effect on specific performance. This often comes down to asking participants to fill in 'happy sheets', and perhaps asking managers about their satisfaction with the cost and targeting of the initiative. These forms of evaluation do little to assure market responsiveness and competitiveness. The evaluation of a company's learning systems should encompass its total ongoing contribution to business performance and individual development (Bowles 1995: 3).

There is no point in evaluating e-learning unless the evaluation itself adds value. In the case of informal e-learning activities, for example, the expense and effort of devising rigorous evaluation frameworks may outweigh the benefits. Information on such activities may be better captured and measured through wider reporting and evaluation regimes. The aim should not be to measure for the sake of measurement. Certainly e-learning technologies make it possible to capture a wide range of data, but this does not mean that the information they provide will have strategic value. There seems to be a notable lack of analytical investigation into how learning can be assessed in terms of its capacity to add value, at both the individual and the organisational level. There is a similar dearth of investigation into evaluating the management of knowledge and the growth of human capital as a component of knowledge capital assets.

What emerges from our research is a worrying dichotomy between the evaluation practices of educational institutions and businesses: educational institutions are preoccupied with evaluating learner satisfaction, while businesses are equally preoccupied with ROI and job performance. Educators mostly use traditional methods to elicit student feedback. A US study found that 90 per cent of teachers still use 'pen and paper' questionnaires for this purpose, although many believe web-based evaluation would be useful (Bonk 2002: 7, 49). Businesses, however, evaluate courses in terms of cost, time savings and skills transfer related to job performance (Kruse 2003; Berry 2000: 2). In neither case is measuring organisational performance seen as a priority.

Achieving a balance in e-learning evaluation

If e-learning is to become more effective, it must first be evaluated effectively. If it is to be truly strategic in its impact, its outcomes must be evaluated at individual, group, community and organisational levels.

Clearly this kind of evaluation requires a broad approach that can address a range of longer-term impacts. One influential approach has been the four-level model advanced by Donald Kirkpatrick, which was popularised by its success with early adopters of e-learning such as AT&T (Welber 2002; Kruse 2002a; Horton 2000; Bonk & Wisher 2000). Kirkpatrick's model for summative evaluation (1988) aims at an integrated approach across the four levels.

Level 1 – Students' reactions: Students are asked to evaluate the training after completing the program. The aim is to assess learners' satisfaction with the session or program of learning. While often narrowed down to simplistic surveys completed at the end of a session, this type of evaluation can survey individual responses on matters that can be compared across the student population. Kruse (2002a) proposes that evaluation should address the following areas:

- the relevance of the objectives;
- the ability of the course to maintain interest;
- the amount and appropriateness of interactive exercises;
- the ease of navigation; and
- the perceived value of the course and its transferability to the workplace.

With the available technologies and simple configuration of existing learning content, educators operating in networked e-learning environments have found this type of evaluation useful and easy to adopt (Bonk 2002: 7).

Level 2 – Learning results: Evaluation at this level measures what participants have actually learnt. It seeks to quantify the extent to which participants' knowledge, skills and other attributes have changed. It may involve comparison of test scores before and after a course, or across different classes (learning teams) and demographic groups. This type of evaluation is not as widely conducted as Level 1, but is still very common.

Level 3 – Behaviour in the workplace: Capability retention is an important attribute for knowledge-based workers. Learners may score well on post-tests, but it is more important to determine whether they can apply their new knowledge and skills in the workplace (Kruse 2002a; Horton 2000). Level 3 involves follow-up evaluation between three and twelve months after the learning programs have been completed, to determine whether students' behaviours actually change as a result of new learning. Examples might include collecting data on changes in customer satisfaction and customer behaviour, or compliance with government requirements. These kinds of data are harder to collect and analyse, but they have real value in terms of planning future e-learning strategies and investments.

Level 4 — Business results: The focus at Level 4 is on how learning affects the business. The results may be organisation-wide, or across specific populations of learners. This level requires evaluation metrics to examine how an organisation's investment in learning has contributed to its overall success.

There are significant limitations in Kirkpatrick's approach, however. The model seems to assume a linear progression from Level 1 (learner reactions) to Level 4 (business outcomes), but there is no research to indicate that this actually occurs (Dixon 1990). It takes too long to reach Level 4 evaluation, which is the most important level for managers making investment decisions. Critics have also suggested that the available electronic environments and requirements for knowledge work in the New Economy are so dynamic that the original four levels bear little relevance to measurement of the transfer of knowledge in its many diverse forms (e.g. Dixon 2000; Weiss 1998).

The Kirkpatrick model has also been criticised for ignoring the learning situation and focusing too much on outcomes and immediate knowledge transfer (Holton 1995). It has been suggested that the evaluation of e-learning environments needs to be extended to include learning objects and technology design (Wiley 2000). Perhaps the most serious criticism is that the model is too linear and insufficiently adaptive to accommodate the broader cultural and environmental factors affecting learning capacity and knowledge transfer within organisations and communities (Cohen & Levinthal 1990; Crossan & Hulland 1997; Ruona & Lyford-Nojima 1997; Song 2002).

Surveys consistently show that 80 to 90 per cent of training managers use Level 1 forms of evaluation and up to 30 per cent employ Level 2 approaches, but the 'higher' levels of evaluation are rare. Less than 20 per cent of training managers use Level 3 approaches, and fewer than 5 per cent deploy Level 4. There does not seem to be a verified framework for collecting and analysing Level 4 data in a way that separates the effectiveness of learning from broader situational changes.

Kirkpatrick's model is at best indicative. Its virtue is that it emphasises the need to evaluate how well e-learning operates at different organisational levels. This can help businesses to evaluate their e-learning readiness and assess their current investments in e-learning, including vendor selection (Welber 2002). Such evaluation not only determines current progress, but also analyses progress towards improved business results.

Many different methods have been used to evaluate organisational effectiveness at Kirkpatrick's Level 4. Kirkpatrick himself suggested a cost-benefit ratio (calculated by dividing program benefits by program costs); others argue for adding an ROI step (Phillips 1997). Phillips identified ten strategies that develop monetary values for an intervention and that can vary with the type of data and the particular situation. This has proved very useful for those seeking to justify e-learning in terms of its business outcomes (Wentling et al. 2000a: 20). His strategies are as follows:

- Output data is converted to profit contribution or cost savings.
- Cost of quality is calculated.
- Wages and benefits are used as value for time.
- Historical costs are examined.
- Internal and external experts are sourced.
- External databases are used.
- Participants provide estimates.
- Participants' supervisors provide estimates.
- Senior management provides estimates.
- HR provides estimates.

Evaluation should always balance qualitative and quantitative data, especially where e-learning is linked with business outcomes. Qualitative data can be obtained by assessing the output or outcome of learning, including learners' performance, progression and cultural change. It can include graphs and charts of outcomes and their spread, and information on how problems are removed or resolved over time. Quantitative data can be drawn from analysis of learners' assessment results, feedback sheets and specific learning outcomes; this data may include calculating pass rates, average and median marks, the range and standard deviation, and summary data from feedback sheets.

Questions to elicit qualitative data might include:

- **Content:** Was it relevant, up-to-date?
- **Method of delivery:** Was it appropriate for the subject, mix of methods, context?
- **Method of assessment:** Was it appropriate for the subject, mix of methods, context?
- **Scope:** Was it appropriate for the learner and the workplace? Should the mix be modified to promote earlier or later coverage of some materials? Did it confirm or revise earlier learning?
- **Amount of material supporting learning:** Was all the material necessary? Was there too little or too much for the allocated time?
- **Facilitator's skills:** Did the facilitator possess the skills to present the materials and transfer the learning?
- **Learning style and pace:** Was it appropriate to the e-learning outcomes and the trainee?
- **Learning sequence:** Was the learning program sequenced correctly? Were some aspects given too much or too little emphasis?
- **Omissions:** Were any essential aspects of the e-learning omitted or not given enough emphasis?
- **Facilities and location:** Was the environment conducive to e-learning? Were all the facilities provided and suitable for the topic?

- **Administration:** Was the training appropriate for critical administrative/ business measures such as time, cost and service support?
- **Relevance and timing:** Was the e-learning delivered when it was required? Did the timing fit work commitments?
- **Application in workplace:** Did the e-learning transfer into practices appropriate to the workplace?

The following list indicates some of the quantitative data that can be collected to evaluate the benefits of e-learning:

- **Performance:** increased productivity, higher sales revenue, reduced waste and error rate, lower ratio of labour cost to total production or service cost, better fit of job incumbent's current competency profile to job competency profile (by job, occupation, team, site etc.);
- **Commitment:** improved job satisfaction, lower absenteeism, reduced staff turnover, improved attitude of workers and teams, greater value of intellectual capital;
- **Reduced cost and better integration of learning tools:** integration of, or reduced completion costs for training, skills audits, training needs analysis, performance appraisals, recruitment and succession planning;
- **Workforce responsiveness:** improved customer satisfaction, reduction in complaints, greater adaptability of workforce to market opportunities, more rapid adoption of innovations in work practices and technology, improved teamwork;
- **Reduced staff replacement costs:** increased mobility of existing staff to vacancies within the organisation, reduced costs of retraining and recruitment, increased number of potential recruits, staff retention, promotion and term of employment, movement of part-time or casual staff into full-time jobs; and
- **Reduced costs of recruitment, selection and succession planning:** selection targeted to 'match' an individual to a job, better match between training and individual career needs, higher retention rates, improved relationship between completion of learning and subsequent promotion.

E-learning can also be targeted to improve compliance with various legislative requirements, such as occupational health and safety, food handling, financial advice, security and privacy.

E-learning evaluation thus involves more than reporting on capability attainment and individual assessment results, or giving workers credit for performance so that they can receive recognition and eventually a qualification. Capturing, analysing and reporting data is an essential part of any business improvement process. The effectiveness and efficiency of e-learning evaluation depends on the quality of the data and its relevance to organisational decision makers. The financial paradigm is a fundamental part of this process, but ROI calculations need to be supplemented by the measurement of broader, non-financial aspects.

Such aspects extend well beyond finding a cost-benefit or human value of training. If agility and productive capacity are the two key components in an organisation's development of knowledge capital, then the evaluation and implementation of e-learning must be based on a realistic match between the organisation's readiness and the progress of e-learning technology. It will be impossible to achieve high-level business benefits if the business is not ready to implement e-learning or has exaggerated expectations of its short-term benefits.

E-learning standards and compliance

International developments in e-learning standards affect the selection of technology, the design of content and the processes used for delivery, assessment and reporting. The importance of standards cannot be overstated. At a global level, there is a push for compatibility between different technologies. This will affect how solutions are integrated within e-learning systems, and how they relate to organisations' existing processes and technologies. Equally, access to content will depend upon technology variables (different vendor systems, computer hardware, operating systems or databases) and infrastructure variables (single platforms, Internet-enabled platforms and bandwidth).

The formation of standards has thus become crucial in shaping the evolution of e-learning, just as it has been in shaping the evolution of other technologies. Hodgins argues that electricity, railroads and the Internet have become ubiquitous precisely because of their common standards. Equally, common standards in relation to learning objects, metadata and learning architecture are essential for e-learning's success in the knowledge economy (2001: 15).

As major market sectors in the e-learning ecosystem, providers of e-learning services, content and technology effectively act as intermediaries between organisations and individuals implementing e-learning. Over time, the providers' understanding of the differing needs of organisations, as well as their efforts to match and differentiate their own offerings from competitors, should help create industry- and market-wide conceptual convergence on e-learning technologies, functions and services.

This convergence can be accelerated by the formation of 'cooperative technology organisations' (Rosenkopf & Tushman 1998: 315) that participate 'in technological information exchange, decision-making or standard setting for a community'. Such organisations can promote the ongoing improvement of technologies (Rosenkopf 2001). Various organisations are currently fulfilling this role in the e-learning market (e.g. EdNA, SCORM, Cetis, IEEE, EduSpecs and OASIS).[13] The relationship of these organisations to e-learning practice, however, needs to be clearly understood. Lichstein engages a metaphor of community to argue that standards develop from practice in an organic but controlled fashion:

> standards follow practice, they don't lead . . . A community grows up around a practice, and the community influences and then controls its evolution. Some form of committee process is created, within certain boundaries. It is a process fraught with peril: defined too tight, a standard cannot grow;

defined too loose, a standard does not yield sufficient benefit. A standard will survive and evolve over time only if it attracts adherents and offers them value (Lichstein 2002: 1–2).

The main focus of e-learning standards at present is on technology, but the emphasis is likely to shift back to learning-centred issues and to language as the importance of broader organisational outcomes is recognised. Thor Anderson comments:

> unless all e-learning specifications turn the focus from infrastructure to pedagogical soundness, they are in danger of becoming instructionally irrelevant (Thor Anderson, cited in Welsch 2003).

Standards that are focused on technology and 'interoperability' are based on how technology and content are currently used. This 'known-purpose' approach suggests a strong orientation towards enhancing codified and explicit knowledge. The potential for transmitting tacit knowledge is, then, far from the fore of the standards debate. Time will determine the importance of this broader focus, and in the meantime it is hoped that the standards do not limit the flow of all forms of knowledge and the forms of pedagogy that generate competitive advantage and maximise learning in specific situations.

An e-learning implementation and design process

As discussed in the introduction to this book, e-learning is a journey by different individuals and organisations, with very few elements in common to allow comparative positioning. Instructional design (ID) therefore has special importance, because it needs to provide markers, guides and signposts that will allow individual learners, communities and organisations to navigate towards their goals.

Instructional design is to e-learning what architectural planning is to building; it is at once the blueprint and the vision of the process, providing a unifying structure for what might otherwise be discrete and unstructured experiences. More specifically, ID needs to accommodate learning transfer, customer needs and preferences (usability), and information systems design and architecture.

Implementing an e-learning strategy requires a focus on continuously improving processes and outcomes. This involves more than just performing a set of tasks. The process of e-learning needs to be systematic and replicable and form part of the organisation's knowledge assets (Rothwell & Kazanas 1997: 10). It must focus on building a culture and a 'way individuals think' to ensure that processes, people and strategic frameworks are integrated within a continuous search for the means to improve customer satisfaction.

Implementation models for e-learning are based on models from traditional fields of learning. ID has been the most widely used methodology for systematic development of educational content and supporting technologies. This involves a systematic process of translating general principles of learning and instruction into plans that ensure quality instruction, and thus improve learners' performance and close learning gaps.

Most ID approaches commence with analysis of learning needs and goals, and end with the development of a delivery system to meet those needs and goals. Within this, there are different instruction and learning theories, or philosophies, about what the learning process involves.

The ADDIE model

One widely used model for instructional systems design is ADDIE, which stands for analysis, design, development, implementation and evaluation.[14] Each step in the process has an outcome that feeds into the subsequent step: that is, analysis reports are based on needs, content and technical data; these inform the design and development phase; the system implemented evolves out of a developed and trialled prototype; evaluation of system and learning effectiveness follows implementation and feeds back into the system through recommendations.

For many years, professionals and experts in the information systems field have argued that instructional design processes should be more sensitive to end users' needs.[15] The application of the ADDIE approach to e-learning has also been widely criticised, but the criticisms are often hard to separate from general criticisms of e-learning. For instance, Elliott Masie (2001) blames ADDIE for the fact that most e-learning content used in corporate environments is modelled on textbook or classroom metaphors. It is unfair, however, to blame this entirely on ADDIE. As we have already shown, there are far deeper problems in the current implementation of e-learning.

The attack on ADDIE came to a head in April 2000, when the journal Training featured six major online training experts criticising the approach (Gordon & Zemke 2000:43-53). Among the criticisms were:

- It is too slow and clumsy to meet today's training challenges.
- It is more a project management system than an instructional development algorithm, with inviolable steps that assure the development of successful training programs.
- It produces bad solutions because it is too rigid. It is tied to specifiable, observable outcomes that make the process and outcomes conform to a homogeneous model. This model lacks the flexibility and creativity required in the modern workforce.
- It clings to a misguided or outmoded worldview, in that it does not focus on users' needs and preferences. It assumes that learners are stupid and experts are smart.
- It ignores how adults learn from unstructured events, from their own actions (action learning), context (situational learning) and investigation (experiential learning and self-directed learning). Such learning processes are often the most rewarding for individuals and organisations.

The criticisms of highly structured, systematic approaches to ID/ISD suggest a need to investigate alternatives, or at least integrate solutions that improve user focus, speed and flexibility.

The EID model

Using an ethnographic methodology, Dorothy Leonard and Jeffrey Rayport (1997) have developed a user-centred approach known as empathetic design. Clients or customers are observed in their everyday environments so that a clear understanding of their needs and desires can be developed, and so that innovation is sparked in the quest for a design solution.

Maish Nichani (2002) applied this approach to e-learning and developed a five-step empathic instructional design (EID) process. The five steps comprise observation, data capture, reflection and analysis, brainstorming for solutions and prototype development. While EID pursues quality outcomes, it embraces a systems-level (systemic) rather than a process-level approach to e-learning.

The focus on user needs has strong appeal to many emerging markets. For instance, EID has been popular with some instructional designers and many corporate and community clients because of frustration over the failure of e-learning content to evolve beyond the approaches used in print- or classroom-based materials.

The RID model

Sivasailam Thiagarajan (Thiagi) has, quite possibly, been the person most responsible for promoting a rapid instructional design (RID) process for learning design. From the early to mid-1990s Thiagi promoted the RID approach as a means to ensure that some forms of learning, particularly electronic simulations, could evolve rapidly, all the while delivering user needs 'just in time'. He was especially critical of the ADDIE approach, which was considered both bureaucratic and unable to respond to the rapid evolution of new and improved technologies. Technology change, he argued, necessitated more rapid change to prevailing pedagogies and instructional design mindsets. Thiagi's RID strategy advocates partial roll-out of the system while continuously reviewing and improving it; combining appropriate design phases and skipping others deemed unnecessary; and using existing materials, templates and generic instructional materials to reduce the time required for documentation. The rapid roll-out was nonetheless linked to an integrated approach to the management of resources, including team members, and the overall instructional design process.

Responsive instructional design

A review of these approaches suggests that each has advantages. The advantage of an ADDIE approach is its ability to control resources, timelines and progress. Weighed against this decision-making certainty is a lack of responsiveness. Flexibility and responsiveness give rapid prototyping and empathic instructional design substantial advantages over an ADDIE approach.

E-learning has taken an evolutionary path similar to that of other technologies, and the same can be said of e-learning design. Whatever the approach adopted, management is more likely to promote e-learning where control systems are in place and the needs and preferences of the end user are being met (Lambe 2001: 2–3). This argues for a rapid-design approach.

It is possible to accommodate this within a modified ADDIE model (Kruse 2002b: 1) by treating the process as one of continuous improvement and responsiveness.

Equally, rapid prototyping and empathic design can be included in the design stage. This obviates the need for a separate, subsequent stage of applied testing and validation. Customer acceptance can be tested as an integral part of design and development. By integrating these activities, feedback on the design can be collected and the prototype improved. This iterative process can continue until the e-learning content, technology or service is ready for a wider audience. The final product or service is therefore delivered in a more complete form, based on user needs, and final programming and technical configuration begin only after its efficiency and effectiveness have been demonstrated.

Although terms differ, companies such as PricewaterhouseCoopers, Cisco and Woolworths Australia are using processes variously featuring the following four steps:

- assess/analyse/research;
- build/design and develop;
- implement/deliver/operate; and
- improve/review/evaluate.

Figure 12.1 illustrates how a four-step process can be implemented to generate a 'responsive' instructional design process (ABII).

The revised framework for systematically completing the design of e-learning is summarised in Table 12.3. A manual has been devised to translate the principles advanced here into a detailed approach to the proposed ABII design and implementation process.[16]

Figure 12.1   The responsive instructional design process

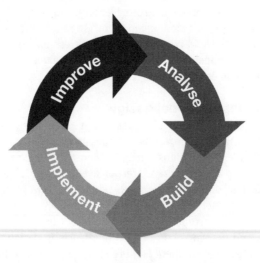

Table 12.3   The ABII strategic e-learning design process

Phase	Typical activity	Deliverables
Analyse	Establish project plan and timetable	E-learning readiness (organisation)
	Analyse capabilities to be targeted and learning, performance and individual outcomes (skills and knowledge competencies and cultural roles and behavioural identity attributes)	Capability target and e-learning delivery plan
	Allocate capability outcomes to learning process (learning outcomes/ goals/competency standards/ performance indicators)	Content audit (existing and required digital content to be converted)
	Confirm change context and transformational impact on the organisation (sponsor)	
	Identify audience and individual learning and capability profiles	Metrics and reporting frameworks
	Analyse type of learning required	
	Establish architecture required to deliver outcomes (tools and technology requirements), i.e. authoring/ media tools selection	Individual learning 'trajectory' profiles
	Complete a content audit on existing content and support resources	
	Establish storage and infrastructure requirements for hosting and distributing content	
	Develop metrics to assess, report and evaluate impact on business and process changes (i.e. framework to measure success or program/content on areas such as customer, financial, systems and processes, and performance outcomes)	
Build (design, develop and test)	Test learning components and objectives against individual/group learning profiles ('fit')	Individual learning plans
	Confirm mode of learning/delivery options to satisfy outcomes (including performance and compliance standards)	Requirements specification
	Write instructional strategies and lesson designs	Repurposed existing content and learning support resources
	Determine assessment and reporting systems (administration and delivery)	
	Confirm interaction design and media treatments	Tested (instructionally and technically valid) courseware ready for implementation
	Configure architecture, i.e. authoring/media tools selection	
	Set data reporting (evaluation design)	
	Modify or renew existing programs (content and services)	Integrated and functional architecture (technologies and tools)
	Apply standards to learning content and technology	
	Write content	
	Develop learning support resources (tests, assessment tools, case studies etc.)	Best technology for mode of learning appropriate to outcomes to be achieved by individual learners
	Build and test pilot content and delivery architecture (i.e. media production/sourcing, programming/coding, authoring and integration of media elements)	
	Test interactivity and integration of architecture	

Table 12.3 continues over the page.

Phase	Typical activity	Deliverables
Implement	Provide access to content (upload, duplicate, distribute) Provide ongoing maintenance and logistical support for program/content Complete ongoing reporting and tracking	Implemented learning program Report on student learning Qualification or mapped capabilities for all individuals, groups or entities
Improve (evaluate)	Apply metrics to measure capabilities (skills, knowledge, behaviours, roles, culture etc. across individual, group or organisation) Compare actual against planned capability outcomes (effectiveness) Collect formative and summative evaluation data Calculate ROI Confirm overall knowledge capital asset improvement Report and suggest improvements	Evaluation report and recommendations for continuous improvement Report on ROI and knowledge capital including human capital growth and overall business impact (productivity capacity increase) Valid, reliable and authentic content and learning support resources

Conclusion

Central to the deployment of efficient and effective e-learning is the need to appreciate e-learning's role not just in transferring existing knowledge but also as a value-adding process that can generate new knowledge: a process whereby analysing, building, implementing and improving e-learning will hold and generate knowledge. This knowledge, as much as the outcomes resulting from e-learning, will raise potential productive capabilities (performance and agility) and therefore build knowledge capital.

E-learning can achieve this by providing content, tools and an environment that encourage skills transfer as well as a converged sense of purpose that links individuals and groups inside and outside an organisational structure. Any e-learning solution must maximise relationships across internal and external 'networks' that hold knowledge capital. All interactions represent opportunities for the organisation to learn and acquire valuable knowledge capital.

E-learning is also a critical strategy to leverage the creation of a learning culture. It can build competencies to perform while reinforcing the behaviours and processes of interaction that generate identity capabilities.

The processes or e-learning must not become overlays built in isolation from existing business systems. E-learning has not evolved to a point where a stable set of concepts and technologies has gained ascendancy. Common standards are now setting the scene for a convergence of technologies, but we are still far from a convergence of views on the nature and importance of e-learning and its contribution to the generation of all forms of knowledge within an organisation.

E-learning is born of the coupling of learning and technology. If the initial focus was on technology, attention is now turning to the crucial issue of learning. The perceived potential for both technological and pedagogical advances has led to a great enthusiasm for exploring and investing in new applications and approaches. The task that remains is to establish more effective techniques for evaluating these divergent approaches and establishing a cycle of improvement — indeed a virtuous circle — that will enhance learning outcomes and add value to organisations' human capital.

Principle 12

To implement e-learning efficiently and effectively, a quality instructional design process (e.g. ABBI) must ensure a continuous cycle based on rigorous evaluation at all levels.

[12] A number of different ROI calculators exist; each can be viewed not just as a single method, but also as methods appropriate to different stages of an organisation's readiness to implement e-learning. For examples and web links go to http://www.portal.unitas.com.au.

[13] For a list of standards organisations affecting e-learning go to http://www.mup.unimelb.edu.au/ebooks/0-522-85130-4/standards.html.

[14] See ADDIE Instructional Design Model 2002, Californian State University: Fullerton, available at http://distance-ed.fullerton.edu/pages/faculty_staff/online_guide/guide24.htm

[15] For example, see Hirschheim & Klein (1989), Seels & Glasgow (1990), Hirschheim & Newman (1991), Orlikowski & Baroudi (1991), Hirschheim, Iivari & Klein (1997) and Fitzgerald (2000).

[16] The manual was completed by the Learning to E-learn project and is available at http://www.portal.unitas.com.au.

References

Abraham, R 2000, 'The Role of Job Control as a Moderator of Emotional Dissonance and Emotional Intelligence-outcome Relationships', *The Journal of Psychology*, vol. 1342, pp. 169–84.

ABS – see Australian Bureau of Statistics.

Adkins, S 2002, *The 2002 U.S. Market for E-learning Simulation*, Brandon-Hall.com: Sunnyvale, CA.

Aldrich, C 2001, 'Can LMSs Survive the Sophisticated Buyer?' *ASTD Learning Circuits Online Magazine*, November, viewed 5 February 2003, <http://www.learningcircuits.com/2001/nov2001/ttools.html>.

Allee, V 1997, *The Knowledge Evolution: Expanding Organisational Intelligence*, Butterworth-Heinemann: Boston.

Allen, M 2002, *Michael Allen's Guide to E-learning*, John Wiley & Sons: New York.

Argyris, C 1962, *Interpersonal Competence and Organisational Effectiveness*, Irwin-Dorsey: Homewood.

——1993, *Knowledge for Action: A Guide to Overcoming Barriers to Organizational Change*, Jossey-Bass: San Francisco.

Argyris, C & Schön 1978, *Organizational Learning: A Theory of Action Perspective*, Addison-Wesley: Reading, MA.

Ashforth, BE & Mael, FA 1989, 'Social Identity Theory and the Organization', *Academy of Management Review*, vol. 14, pp. 20–39.

Australian Bureau of Statistics 2001, *'Internet Activity in Australia'*, cat. no. 8153.0, AGPS: Canberra.Avolio, BJ & Bass, BM 1995, 'Individualized Consideration is more than Consideration for the Individual when Viewed at Multiple Levels of Analysis', *Leadership Quarterly*, vol. 6 [2], pp. 199–218.

Badaracco, J 1991, *The Knowledge Link: How Firms Compete through Strategic Alliances*, Boston: Harvard Business School Press.

Baker, K 2002, 'E-learning Myths and Realities for the IT Professional: Hands on Technology Transfer', viewed 17 December 2002, <http://www.traininghott.com/E-learning-Myths-and-Realities-for-IT-Professional.pdf>

Bandura, A 1986, *Social Foundations of Thought and Action*, Prentice Hall: Englewood Cliffs, NJ.

——2001, 'Social Cognitive Theory: An Agentic Perspective', *Annual Review of Psychology*, vol. 52, pp. 1–28.

Barham, K, Fraser J, & Heath, L 1988, *Management for the Future*, Ashridge Management Research Group: Berkhamsted, Hampshire.

Barrett, E & Lally, V 1999, 'Gender Differences in an On-line Learning Environment', *Journal of Computer Assisted Learning*, vol. 15 [1], pp. 49–61.

Barron, T 2000, 'The LMS Guess', *ASTD Learning Circuits Online* Magazine, viewed 5 February 2003, <http://www.learningcircuits.com/apr2000/barron.html>.

Bass, BM 1985, *Leadership and Performance Beyond Expectations*, The Free Press: New York.

Bass, BM 1997, 'Does the Transactional/Transformational Leadership Paradigm Transcend Organizational and National Boundaries?', *American Psychologist*, vol. 52, pp. 130-139.

Beardsley, SC & Evans, AL 1998, 'Who will connect you?' *McKinsey Quarterly*, [4], pp. 18-31.

Beer, V 2000, *The Web Learning Fieldbook: Using the World Wide Web to Build Workplace Learning* Environments, Jossey-Bass Pfeiffer: San Francisco.

Bell, M, Bush, D, Nicholson, P, O'Brien, D & Tran, T 2002, *Universities Online: A Survey of Online Education and Services in Australia*, Occasional Paper Series, Higher Education Group: Commonwealth Department of Education, Science and Training, viewed 15 June 2002, <http://www.detya.gov.au/highered/occpaper/02a/02_a.pdf>.

Bennis, WG 1989, *On Becoming a Leader*, Addison-Wesley: Reading, MA.

——& Thomas, RJ 2002, *Geeks and Geezers: How Era, Values, and Defining Moments Shape Leaders*, Harvard Business School Press: Mass.

Berry, J 2000, 'The E-learning Factor: Companies are using Metrics to Justify E-learning's Impact on Strategic Business Goals', *InternetWeek*, 1 November, viewed 17 December 2002, <http://www.cultureworx.com/cultureworxarticles/e-learning.pdf>.

Bielawski, L & Metcalf, D 2003, *Blended E-learning: Integrating Knowledge, Performance, Support, and Online Learning*, HRD Press: Amherst, MA.

Birch, A, Gerbert, P & Schneider, D 2000, *The Age of E-tail: Conquering the New World of Electronic Shopping*, Capstone Publishing: Oxford, UK.

Blake, RR & Mouton, JS 1984, *The Managerial Grid II1*, Gulf Publishing: Houston, TX.

Block, H & Dobell, B 1999, 'The E-bang Theory', *Education Industry Overview*, vol. 2, September, USA Banc of America Securities, Equity Research.

Bloom, B 1956, *Taxonomy of Education Objectives — Cognitive Domain*, London: Longmans.

Boisot, MH (ed.) 1995, *Information Space: A Framework for Learning in Organizations, Institutions and Culture*, Routledge: London.

Bonk, CJ 2002, *Online Teaching in an Online World*, May, Bloomington, Jones Knowledge & CourseShare.com: Illinois, viewed 10 November 2002, <http://courseshare.com/Reports.php> and <http://www.publicationshare.com>.

——& Cummings, JA 1998, 'A Dozen Recommendations for Placing the Student at the Centre of Web-based Learning', *Educational Media International*, vol. 35 [2], pp. 82–9.

Bonk, CJ & Wisher, RA 2000, 'Applying Collaborative and E-learning Tools to Military Distance Learning: A Research Framework', Technical Report #1107, U.S. Army Research Institute for the Behavioral and Social Sciences: Alexandria, VA.

Bontis, N (ed.) 2002, 'Managing Organizational Knowledge by Diagnosing Intellectual Capital', *World Congress on Intellectual Capital — Readings*, Butterworth Heinemann: Boston, pp. 13–56.

Bormann, E 1983, 'Symbolic Convergence: Organizational Communication and Culture', in LI Putman & ME Pacanowsky (eds), *Communication and Organizations*, 10 November 2002, Sage: California.

Boulding, KE 1964, *The Meaning of the Twentieth Century: The Great Transition*, Harper & Row: New York.

Boulton, P 2002, 'Summary of Data on the Survey on Organisational Use of E-learning', November, Monash University: Melbourne.

Bowles, M 1995, *National Scoping Project: Evaluating Gaps between Learning Needs and Current Learning Systems and Resources*, Woolworths Australia: Sydney.

——1997, *Building Strategic Learning Communities at The Don College*, Vols 1–4, Australian Student Traineeship Foundation: Sydney.

——1998, *The Woolworths Service Standards: An Overview of the Implementation of Standards-Based Performance and Learning Systems*, August, Woolworths Australia: Sydney.

——1999, *Learning the True Value of Strategic Knowledge: Valuing capabilities and knowledge assets in the Knowledge Based Economy*, Major White Paper, Huon Institute: Melbourne.

——2002a, *Final Scoping Report – E-business Standards in the Australian Retail Industry*, National Wholesale Retail and Personal Services ITAB: Sydney.

——2002b, *IT Training Package ICA99 Review – Stage 1 Final Report*, Australian National Training Authority and the Information Technology and Telecommunications Industry Training Advisory Board Australia: Melbourne.

——2002c, *Electronic Commerce Training Audit – Final Report*, Multimedia, Department of Innovation, Industry and Regional Development: Melbourne, Victoria.

——2002d, '*Community of Practice on Flexible & Responsive Vocational Education & Training*', background research paper, Australian National Training Authority and TAFE Tasmania: Launceston.

——July 2003a, *Byzedium: Building Emotional Capital: Learning to E-learn Case Study 10*, Unitas Company Ltd: Hobart, Australia.

——July 2003b, *Telehealth Tasmania Network: Learning to E-learn Case Study 12*, Unitas Company Ltd: Hobart, Australia.

Bowles, M & Baker, T 1998, *Training Reform @Purity: Implementation of Capability-based Performance and Learning Systems in Woolworths 1994–1997*, Woolworths Australia: Sydney.

Bowles, M & Graham, C 1994a, *Corporate Planning – From Learning to Action Handbook*, The Centre for Working Futures Sydney.

——1994b, *A National Qualifications Framework*, Paper for Consultation to the National Working Party, Vocational Employment, Education and Training Working Party on Recognition Frameworks: Melbourne.

——1994c, 'Service Quality Implementation', Sydney: NSW Government.

Bowles, M & Wilson, PT 2003, 'Acquire and Retain Online Customers', *National Retail Training Package WRRO15 Learner's Guide*, National Wholesale, Retail & Personal Services Training Council and Australian National Training Authority: Sydney.

Boyatzis, R 1982, *The Competent Manager: A Mode for Effective Performance*, John Wiley & Sons: New York.

Boyer, E 1995, *The Basic School: A Community for Learning*, 2nd printing, Princeton Fulfillment Services Ewing: NJ, California.

Brandon Hall 2001, 'Building the Business Case for E-learning', Executive Summary, viewed 17 December 2002, <http://www.brandonhall.com/public/execsums/execsum_bbc.pdf>.

Brennan, M, Funke, S & Anderson, C 2001, 'The Learning Content Management System: A New E-learning Market Segment Emerges', IDC Whitepaper, viewed 11 March 2002, <http://www.idc.com>.

Brennan, R, McFadden, M & Law, E 2001, *All that Glitters is not Gold: Online Delivery of Education and Training*, National Centre for Vocation, Education and Research: Adelaide.

Brooking, A 1999, *Corporate Memory: Strategies for Knowledge Management*, International Thompson Business Press: London.

Brown, JB 2000, 'Growing up Digital: How the Web changes Work, Education, and the Ways People Learn', *Change*, March–April, pp. 11–20, viewed 12 October 2002, <http://www.aahe.org/change/digital.pdf>.

Brown, JB, Collins A & Duguid, P 1989a, 'Situated Cognition and the Culture of Learning', *Educational Researcher*, vol. 18 [1], Jan–Feb, pp. 32–42, viewed 3 July 2002, <http://www.ilt.columbia.edu/ilt/papers/JohnBrown.html>.

——1989b, 'Situated Cognition and the Culture of Learning', *Educational Researcher*, vol. 18 [1], Jan–Feb, pp. 32–42, viewed 18 October 2002, <http://www.ilt.columbia.edu/ilt/papers/JohnBrown.html>.

Brown, JB & Duguid, P 1991, 'Organizational Learning and Communities of Practice: Towards a Unified View of Working, Learning, and Innovation', *Organization Science*, vol. 2 [1], February, pp. 40–57.

——1992, 'Stolen Knowledge', Education Technology Publications: New Jersey, viewed 12 October 2002, <http://www2.parc.com/ops/members/brown/papers/stolenknow.html>.

Budde, P 2002, *2002/2003 Content & E-Services Market Australia*, Paul Budde Communication: Sydney.

Burns, W, Williams, H & Barnett, K 1997, *Flexible Delivery and Women in TAFE*, Department of Employment, Education, Training and Youth Affairs: Adelaide.

Californian State University: Fullerton 2002, 'ADDIE Instructional Design Model', viewed 12 December 2002, <http://distance-ed.fullerton.edu/pages/faculty_staff/online_guide/guide24.htm>.

Carnegie, D 1936, *How to Win Friends and Influence People*, Pocket Books: New York.

Carpenter-Smith, T 1999, *Technology-Based Training: Global Strategies for Learning*, American Productivity & Quality Centre: Houston.

Carrier, C & Sales, G 1987, 'Pair versus Individual Work on the Acquisition of Concepts in a Computer-based Instructional Lesson', *Journal of Computer-Based Instruction*, vol. 14, pp. 11–17.

Castells, M 1997, *The Information Age: Economy, Society and Culture, Volume II – The Power of Identity*, 2002 reprint, Blackwell Publishing: Massachusetts.

Castleman, T & Cavill, M 2002, *Facilitating Victorian Business Use of eCommerce for Export – Project Report*, CollECTeR@Deakin, School of Management Information Systems, Department of Innovation, Industry & Regional Development Victoria: Melbourne.

Cerri, SA, Loia, V, Maffioletti, S, Fontanesi, P & Bettinelli, A 1999, 'Serendipitous Acquisition of Web Knowledge by Agents in the Context of Human Learning', 21 June, THAI-ETIS: Varese, Italy, pp. 1–25, viewed 20 February 2003, <http://citeseer.nj.nec.com/cerri99serendipitous.html>.

Chapman, B (ed.) 2002, *LCMS Report: Comparative Analysis of Enterprise Learning Content Management Systems*, Brandon-hall.com: CA: Sunnyvale.

Chapman, B & Hall, B 2001, *Authoring Tool Strategies: Choosing Tools that Match your Company's E-learning Initiative*, Brandon-Hall: CA: Sunnyvale.

Chappell, C 1996, 'Quality & Competency Based Education and Training', in *The Literacy Equation*, Queensland Council for Adult Literacy: Red Hill, Australia, pp. 71-9.

Choo, C & Bontis, N (eds) 2002, 'Knowledge, Intellectual Capital, and Strategy: Themes and Tensions', in *The Strategic Management of Intellectual Capital and Organizational Knowledge*, Oxford University Press: New York, pp. 3–19.

Choy, S, McNickle, C & Clayton, B 2002, *Learner Expectations and Experiences – An Examination of Student Views of Support in Online Learning*, Australian National Training Authority, National Centre for Vocation, Education and Research: Adelaide.

Christensen, CM 1997, *The Innovator's Dilemma*, Harvard Business School Press: Boston, MA.

Chung, J & Reigeluth, C 1992, 'Instructional Prescriptions for Learner Control', *Educational Technology*, vol. 32, pp. 14–20.

CIA Factbook, viewed 4 September 2003, <http://www.cia.gov/cia/publications/factbook/index.html>.

Clancey, WJ 1995, 'A Tutorial on Situated Learning', in J Self (ed.) *Proceedings of the International Conference on Computers and Education*, Taiwan, Association for the Advancement of Computing in Education: Charlottesville,VA, pp. 49–70.

Close, RC, Humphrey, R & Ruttenbur, BW March 2000, *E-learning & Knowledge Technology: Technology & the Internet are Changing the Way We Learn*, SunTrust Equitable Securities: USA.

Cohen, V 2001, 'Learning Styles and Technology in a Ninth-Grade High School Population', *Journal of Research on Computing in Education*, vol. 33 [4], pp. 355–66.

Cohen, W & Levinthal, D 1990, 'Absorptive Capacity: A New Perspective on Learning and Innovation', *Administrative Science Quarterly*, vol. 35, pp. 128–52.

Cole, M, John-Steiner, V, Scribner, S & Souberman, E 1978, *Mind in Society: The Development of Higher Psychological Processes*, Harvard University Press: Cambridge.

Collins, H 1997, 'Humans, Machines, and the Structure of Knowledge', in R Ruggles, III (ed.) *Knowledge Management Tools*, Butterworth-Heinemann: Boston, pp. 145–63.

Commission on Technology and Adult Learning 2001, *A Vision of E-learning for America's Workforce*, CTAL: USA.

Compeau, DR, Higgins, CA & Huff, S June 1999, 'Social Cognitive Theory and Individual Reactions to Computing Technology: A Longitudinal Study', *MIS Quarterly*, vol. 23 [2], pp. 145–60.

Connell, R 2001, *Educommerce: Online Learning Migrates to the E-commerce Arena*, Eduventures.com Inc, viewed July 2002, <http://www.eduventures.com/pdf/educommerce.pdf>.

Cooke, J & Veach, I 1997, 'Enhancing the Learning Outcome of University Distance Education: An Australian Perspective', *International Journal of Educational Management*, vol. 11 [5], pp. 203–8.

Covey, S 1992, *Principle-Centred Leadership*, Fireside edn, Simon & Schuster: New York.

Crawford, C 2001, 'Developing Webs of Significance through Communications: Appropriate Interactive Activities for Distributed Learning Environments', Campus-Wide Information Systems, vol. 18 [2], pp. 68–72.

Crombie, A 1978, 'The Concept of the 'Learning Organisation' , in A Crombie, C Duke, F Emery & N Haines (eds), Lifelong Learning and Recurrent Education and The Australian Public Service, Occasional Papers in Continuing Education Number 9, Australian National University: Canberra, pp. 38–48.

Cross, J 2002, 'E-learning Source Information', Internet Time Group, viewed 8 February 2003, <www.internettime.com/itimegroup/forum/faq.htm>.

Crossan, M & Hulland, J 1997, 'Measuring Organisational Learning', draft, Academy of Management, Richard Ivey School of Business: London, Canada, September , pp. 1–43.

Crowley, R 2002, 'Blueprint for an Enterprise E-learning Architecture', October, viewed 13 February 2003, <www.esalesandservice.com>.

CTAL — see Commission on Technology and Adult Learning.

Damon, W & Phelps, E 1989, 'Critical Distinctions among Three Approaches to Peer Education', International Journal of Educational Research, vol. 13, pp. 9–19.

Davenport, T & Prusak, L 1998, Working Knowledge: How Organizations Manage What They Know, Harvard Business School Press: Boston, MA.

Davis, S & Meyer, C 1998, Blur: The Speed of Change in the Connected Economy, Addison-Wesley: Reading, Mass.

de Geus, A 1988, 'Planning as Learning', Harvard Business Review, March–April, pp. 70–4.

Deming, W 1986, Out of the Crisis, MIT Centre for Advanced Engineering Study: Cambridge.

Department for Education and Skills 2003, Towards a Unified E-learning Strategy, consultative document, July, United Kingdom.

Dieng-Kuntz, R & Matta, N (eds) 2002, Knowledge Management and Organizational Memories, Kluwer Academic Publishers: London.

Dierickx, I & Cool, K 1989, 'Asset Stock Accumulation and Sustainable Competitive Advantage', Management Science, vol. 35, pp. 1504–11.

Dilworth, RL 1998, 'Setting the Stage: Special Edition on Action Learning', Performance Improvement Quarterly, vol. 11 [1], pp. 5–8.

Dixon, N 1990, 'The Relationship between Trainee Responses on Participation Reaction Forms and Post Test Scores', Human Resource Development Quarterly, vol. 1, pp. 129–37.

——1994, Organizational Learning Cycle: How We Learn Collectively, McGraw-Hill: New York.

——2000, Common Knowledge: How Companies Thrive by Sharing What They Know, Harvard Business School Press: Cambridge, MA.

Dreyfus, H & Dreyfus, S 1997, 'Why Computers may never Think like People', in R Ruggles (ed.), Knowledge Management Tools, Butterworth-Heinemann: Boston, pp. 31–50.

Drucker, P 1969, The Age of Discontinuity — Guidelines for a Changing Society, Pan Books: London.

Drucker, PF 1994, 'The Theory of the Business', Harvard Business Review, September–October, pp. 95–104.

Dunphy, D & Griffiths, A 1998, *The Sustainable Corporation*, Allen & Unwin: St Leonards, Australia.

Dutton, JE & Dukerich, JM 1991, 'Keeping an Eye on the Mirror: Image and Identity in Organizational Adaptation', *Academy of Management Journal*, vol. 34, pp. 517–54.

——& Harquail, CV 1994, 'Organizational Images and Member Identification', *Administrative Science Quarterly*, vol. 39, pp. 239–63.

Duyne. D, Landay, J & Hong, J 2003, *The Design of Sites: Patterns, Principles, and Processes for Crafting a Customer-centred Web Experience*, Addison-Wesley Pub. Co: Boston.

Eastmond, D 1998, 'Adult Learners and Internet-based Distance Education', in B Cahoon (ed.), *Adult Learning and the Internet*, Jossey-Bass: San Francisco.

Education Lifelong Learning Group 2001, E-*learning for the Workplace: Creating Canada's Lifelong Learners*, Canadian Conference Board: Canada.

Eduworks 2003, 'Table of Standards Organizations', viewed 18 February 2003, <http://www.eduworks.com/web/new.cfm?page=organizations.cfm>.

Edvinsson, L & Malone, MS 1997, *Intellectual Capital: The Proven Way to Establish your Company's Real Value by Measuring its Hidden Brainpower*, Piatkus: London.

Edvinsson, L & Sullivan, P 1996, 'Developing a Model for Managing Intellectual Capital', *European Management Journal*, vol. 14 [4], pp. 356–64.

Egan, D 2002, 'Top 10 LMS Purchasing Mistakes (and how to avoid them)', *ASTD Learning Circuits Online Magazine*, March, viewed 5 February 2003, <http://www.learningcircuits.org/2002/mar2002/egan.html>.

Entwistle, N 1992, *The Impact of Teaching Learning Outcomes in Higher Education*, Committee of Vice Chancellors – UK, Staff Development Unit, Sheffield.

Ericsson Australia 2001, 'Future of Wireless', Mobile Applications Workshop, Tasmanian Electronic Commerce Centre: Launceston.

Falk, I, Grady, N, Ruscoe, J & Wallace, R 2003, *Designing Effective E-learning Interventions, Learning to E-learn Research Paper 1*, Centre for Teaching and Learning in Diverse Educational Contexts at the Northern Territory University and Unitas Company Ltd: Hobart.

Falk, I & Kilpatrick, S 2000, 'What is Social Capital? A Study of Interaction in a Rural Community', *Sociologia Ruralis*, vol. 40, pp. 87-110.

Felder, RM & Solomon, BA 1999, 'Index of Learning Styles Questionnaire', June, North Carolina State University, viewed November 2002, <http://www.engr.ncsu.edu/learningstyles/ilsweb.html>.

Fitzgerald, B 2000, 'Systems Development Methodologies: The Problem of Tenses', *Information Technology & People*, vol. 13 [3], pp. 13–22, viewed 18 February 2003, <http://www.csis.ul.ie/staff/bf/tense1.doc>.

Flavell, JH 1979, 'Metacognition and Cognitive Monitoring: A New Area of Cognitive-Development Inquiry', *American Psychologist*, vol. 34, pp. 906–11.

——1987, 'Speculations about the Nature and Development of Metacognition', in FE Weinert & RH Kluwe (eds), *Metacognition, Motivation and Understanding*, Lawrence Erlbaum: Hillside, New Jersey, pp. 21–9.

Fox, R & Herrmann, A 2000, 'Changing Media, Changing Times: Coping with Adopting New Educational Technologies', in T Evans & D Nation (eds), *Changing University Teaching: Reflections on Creating Educational Technologies*, Kogan Page: London, pp. 73–84.

Fred, CL 2002, *Breakaway: Deliver Value to Your Customer – FAST*, Jossey-Bass: New York.

Frenkel, S & Donoghue, L 1996, *Call Centres and Service Excellence: A Knowledge Worker Case Study, Paper No. 66*, Centre for Corporate Change, University of New South Wales: Sydney.

Gale, R 2003, *The Virtual Facilitator — A Personal Journey of Teaching and Learning: Case Experience at Royal Roads University: Learning to E-learn Case Study 2*, Unitas Company Ltd: Hobart, Australia.

Galvin, T 2001, 'Industry Report 2001', *Training Magazine*, October, pp. 1–12.

Garratt, B 1987, *The Learning Organisation*, Fontana: New York.

Gardner, H 2002, 'Multiple Intelligences: An Overview', *Theory into Practice Database*, viewed 2 December 2002, <http://tip.psychology.org/gardner.htm>.

——& Hatch, T 1993, 'Multiple Intelligences go to School — Educational Implications of the Theory of Multiple Intelligences', in A Woolfolk (ed.), *Readings and Cases in Educational Psychology*, Allyn and Bacon: Needham Heights, MA.

Garvin, D 1993, 'Building the Learning Organization', *Harvard Business Review*, vol. 71 [4], pp. 78–91.

Gianforte, G 2002, 'The Insider's Guide to Customer Service on the Web: Ten Secrets for Successful E-service', *CRM Project*, vol. 3, October, viewed 10 January 2003, <http://www.crmproject.com>.

Gibson, C & Nolan, RL 1974, 'Managing the Four Stages of EDP Growth', *Harvard Business Review*, January/February, pp. 76–88.

Giddens, A 1991, *Modernity and Self-identity: Self and Society in the Late Modern Age*, Polity Press: Cambridge.

Gilley, J & Maycunich, A 2000, Beyond *the Learning Organisation: Creating Cultures of Continuous Growth and Development through State-of-the-Art Human Resource Practices*, Perseus Books: Cambridge, Mass.

Gingrich, N 2002, 'Vision for the Converging Technologies', in M Roco & W Bainbridge (eds), *Converging Technologies for Improving Human Performance*, Nanotechnology, Biotechnology, Information Technology and Cognitive Science of the National Science Foundation: Arlington, VA, pp. 36–55.

Gioia, D 1998, 'From Individual to Organizational Identity', in DA Whetten & PC Godfrey (eds), *Identity in Organizations*, Sage Publications: Thousand Oaks, pp. 17–32.

Global Reach 2003, 'Global Internet Statistics', viewed 30 January 2003, <http://www.glreach.com/globstats/index.php3>.

Goldman Sachs 2000, *Internet: E-learning*, United States, Goldman Sachs: New York.

Goleman, D 1995, *Emotional Intelligence: Why Can it Matter More than IQ?* Bantam Books: New York.

——1998, *Working with Emotional Intelligence*, Bloomsbury: London.

Goodfellow, R, Lea, M Gonzalez, F & Mason, R 2001, 'Opportunity and E-quality: Intercultural and Linguistic Issues in Global Online Learning', *Distance Education*, vol. 22 [6], pp. 65–84.

Gordon, J & Zemke, R. 2000, 'The Attack on ISD: Have we got Instructional Design all Wrong?' *Training*, April. pp. 43-53.

Goss, H, Cochrane, T & Hart, G 2002, 'Communities of Practice — the QUT Approach to Online Learning', The Global Summit of Online Knowledge Networks, viewed December 2002, <http://www.educationau.edu.au/globalsummit/papers/hgoss.htm>.

Greenagel, FL 2002, *The Illusion of E-learning: Why We're Missing Out on the Promise of Technology*, 4 May, viewed 17 December 2002, <http://www.guidedlearning.com/illusions.pdf>.

Gregorc, A 1982, *An Adult's Guide to Style*, Gregorc Associates: Columbia, CT.

Gunawardena, C, Nolla, A, Wilson, P, Lopez-Islas, J, Ramirez-Angel, N & Megchun-Alpizar, R 2001, 'A Cross-Cultural Study of Group Process and Development in Online Conferences', *Distance Education*, vol. 22, 1, pp. 85–121.

Gunzburg, D 1992, *Identifying and Developing Management Skills: Towards the Learning Organisation, Public Service Commission Occasional Paper No. 14*, Australian Government Publishing Service: Canberra.

Hackos, J 2002, *Content Management for Dynamic Web Delivery*, John Wiley & Sons: New York.

Hall, R, Buchanan, J & Considine, G 2002, *You Value What You Pay For — Enhancing Employers Contributions to Skills Formation and Use*, Australian Centre for Industrial Relations Research and Training, University of Sydney for Dusseldorp Skills Forum: Sydney.

Hammer, M & Champy, J 1994, Reengineering *the Corporation: Manifesto for Business Revolution*, Allen & Unwin: New York.

Hara, N & Kling, R 2000, 'Students' Distress with a Web-based Distance Education Course: An Ethnographic Study of Participants' Experiences', *Information, Communication & Society*, vol. 3 [4], Spring, pp. 557–79.

Harper, B, Hedburg, J, Bennett, S, & Lockyer, L 2000, 'Review of Research. *The On-line Experience: The State of Australian On-line Education and Training Practices'*, National Centre for Vocation, Education and Research: Adelaide.

Hellriegal, D & Slocum, JW 1979, *Organisational Behaviour*, West Publishing: Minnesota.

Hill, J 2001, 'Building Community in Web-based Learning Environments: Strategies and Techniques', AUSWEB 01, viewed November 2002, <http://ausweb.scu.edu.au/aw01/papers/refereed/hill>.

Hill, R, Malone, P, Markham, S, Sharma, R, Sheard J & Young, G 2003, *Researching the Size and Scope of Online Usage in the Vocational Education and Training Sector*, National Centre for Education, Vocation and Research: Adelaide.

Hill, T, Smith, ND & Mann, MF 1987, 'Role of Efficacy Expectations in Predicting the Decision to Use Advanced Technologies: The Case of Computers', *Journal of Applied Psychology*, vol. 72 [2], pp. 309–13.

Hirschheim, R & Klein, HK 1989, 'Four Paradigms of Information Systems Development', *Communications of the ACM*, vol. 32 [10], pp. 1199–1216.

Hirschheim, R & Newman, M 1991, 'Symbolism and Information Systems Development: Myth, Metaphor and Magic', *Information Systems Research*, vol. 2 [1], March, pp. 1–34.

Hirschheim, R, Iivari, J & Klein, HK 1997, 'A Comparison of Five Alternative Approaches to Information Systems Development', *Australian Journal of Information Systems*, September, vol. 5 [1], viewed 18 February 2003, <http://www.cba.uh.edu/~parks/fis/sad5.htm>.

Hodgins, WH 2001, 'The Future of Learning Objects', online chapter in DA Wiley (ed.), *The Instructional Use of Learning Objects*, viewed 17 February 2003, <http://reusability.org/read/>.

Hollander, EP 1964, *Leaders, Groups, and Influence*, Oxford University Press: New York.

—1978, *Leadership Dynamics — A Practical Guide to Effective Relationships*, The Free Press (Macmillan Publishers): New York.

Holt, M, Kleiber, P, Swenson J, Rees, E, & Milton, J 1998, 'Facilitating Group Learning on the Internet', in B Cahoon, *Adult Learning and the Internet*, Jossey-Bass: San Francisco.

Holton, EF 1995, 'In Search of an Integrative Model for HRD Evaluation', *Proceedings of the 1995 Academy of Human Resource Development Annual Conference*, Academy of HRD: Baton Rouge, LA, pp. 4–2.

—& Naquin, SS 1999, 'Personality Traits, Affect, and Values: A Model of Dispositional Effects on Motivation to Learn', *Proceedings of the 1999 Association for HRD Conference*, March, Arlington, pp. 649-656.

Honey, P & Mumford, A 1986, *The Manual of Learning Styles*, Printique: Maidenhead, Berkshire.

Hong, W, Tam, KY & Yim, CK 2002, 'E-service Environment: Impacts of Web Interface Characteristics on Consumers' Online Shopping Behavior', in RT Rust & PK Kannan (eds), *E-Service: New Directions in Theory and Practice*, ME Sharpe: Armonk, New York, pp. 108–30.

Hooper, S 1992, 'The Effects of Peer Interaction on Learning During Computer-based Mathematics Instruction', *Journal of Educational Research*, vol. 85, pp. 108–19.

Horton, W 2000, *Designing Web-based Training: How to Teach Anyone Anything Anywhere Anytime*, John Wiley: New York.

HRD Canada 1999, *The Impact of Technology on Learning in the Workplace*, March, Ekos Research Assoc. & Lyndsay Green: Canada.

Hum, D & Ladouceur, A 2001, *E-learning The New Frontier*, Special Surveys Division at Statistics Canada: Canada, <http://www.cata.ca/china/documents/e-learning.pdf>.

IDC — see International Data Corporation.

IDP Education Australia 2001, '*International Education Markets for Vocation Education and Training Online Products and Services: A Research Audit*', FLAG & Department of Education, Training and Employment, South Australia: Adelaide.

IDP Education Australia 2003, 'International Student Demand', Media release, viewed 17 September 2003, <http://www.idp.edu.au>.

International Data Corporation 2000, Corporate E-learning Market Forecast, IDC: New York.

—2001, *E-learning in the Asia/Pacific: Barriers and Accelerators*, IDC: Singapore.

—2002, *The U.S. Corporate E-learning Market Forecast and Analysis*, 2000-2005, IDC: New York.

—2002, 'Revised data', viewed 12 June 2002, <http://www.idc.com>.

—2003, 'India Spearheads Growth', report, 6 January 2003, viewed 6 January 2003, <http://www.news.com>.

International Telecommunication Union 2002, *World Telecommunication Development Report 2002 — Reinventing Telecoms*, ITU: UK.

—2003, 'Free Statistics', viewed June 2003, <http://www.itu.int/ITU-D/ict/statistics>.

ITU — see International Telecommunication Union.

Jefferies, P & Hussain, F 1998, 'Using the Internet as a Teaching Resource', *Education & Training*, vol. 40 [8], pp. 359–65.

Johnson, B 1977, *Communication: The Process of Organizing*, Allyn & Bacon: Boston.

Johnson, SD, Aragon, S, Palma-Riva, N, Shaik, N & Bilsbury, N 1999, 'Comparative Analysis of Online vs. Face-to-face Instruction', *Proceedings of the 1999 AHRD Conference*, March, Arlington, pp. 68–76.

Jonassen, D & Hernandez-Serrano, J 2002, 'Case-based Reasoning and Instructional Design: Using Stories to Support Problem Solving', *Educational Technology, Research and Development*, vol. 502, pp. 65–9.

Jonassen, D & Hyug, I 2001, 'Communication Patterns in Computer Mediated versus Face-to-face Group Problem Solving', *Educational Technology, Research and Development*, vol. 491, pp. 35–52.

Kaplan, S 2002, 'Building Communities – Strategies for Collaborative E-learning, Learning Circuits', viewed August 2002, <http://www.learningcircuits.org/2002/aug2002/kaplan.html>.

Katezenbach, J & Smith, D 1993, *The Wisdom of Teams*, Harvard Business School Press: Boston, MA.

Kathawala, Y, Abdou, K & Elmuti, D 2002, 'The Global MBA: A Comparative Assessment for its Future', *Journal of European Industrial Training*, vol. 26 [1], pp. 14–23.

Kearns, O, McDonald, R, Candy, P, Knights, S & Papadopoulos, G 1999, *VET in the Learning Age: The Challenge of Lifelong Learning for All*, National Centre for Vocational Education & Research: Adelaide.

Keefe, JW 1979, 'Learning Style: An Overview', in JW Keefe (ed.), *Student Learning Styles: Diagnosing and Prescribing Program*, National Association of Secondary School Principals: Reston, VA, pp. 1–17.

Khan, B 1997, 'Web-based Instruction (WBI): What is it and Why is it?' in B Khan (Ed.), *Web-based Instruction*, Educational Technology Publication: Englewood Cliffs, NJ.

Khan, B (ed.) 1997, *Web-based Instruction*, Educational Technology Publications: Englewood Cliffs, NJ.

Kierzkiwski, A, McQuade, S, Waitman, R, & Zeisser, M 1996, 'Marketing to the Digital Consumer', McKinsey Quarterly, no. 1.

Kilpatrick, S & Bound, H 2003, *Learning Online: Benefits and Barriers in Regional Australia*, vol. 1, Adelaide: National Centre for Vocation, Education and Training.

Kim, AJ 2000, *Community Building on the Web*, Peachpit Press: Berkeley, CA.

Kirkpatrick, D L 1988, *Evaluating Training Programs: The Four Levels*, 2nd edn, Berret-Koehler: San Francisco.

Kitchen, P 2002, *The Outlook for mCommerce: Technologies and Applications to 2005*, Reuters Business Insight: USA.

Kolb, D 1981, 'Learning Styles and Disciplinary Differences', in *The Modern American College*, Jossey-Bass, Chickering & Associates: San Francisco.

——1984, *Experiential Learning: Experience as the Source of Learning and Development*, New York: Prentice Hall.

Koolen, R 2001, *Learning Content Management Systems: The Second Wave of E-learning*, A Knowledge Mechanics Whitepaper, July, viewed 5 February 2003, <http://www.internettime.com/itimegroup/lcms/IDCLCMSWhitePaper.pdf>.

Kotter, JP 1990, *A Force for Change: How Leadership Differs from Management*, Free Press: New York.

Kouzes, JM & Posner, BZ 1987, *The Leadership Challenge*, Jossey-Bass: San Francisco.

——2002, T*he Leadership Challenge*, 3rd edn, Jossey-Bass: San Francisco.

Kruse, K 2002a, 'Evaluating E-learning: Introduction to the Kirkpatrick Model', viewed 12 December 2002, <http://www.e-learningguru.com/articles/art2_8.htm>.

—2002b, 'Introduction to Instructional Design and the ADDIE Model', viewed 12 December 2002, <http://www.e-learningguru.com/articles/art2_1.htm>.

—2003, 'The ROI Debate', *The E-learningGuru E-zine*, 30 January, viewed 1 February 2003, <http://www.e-learningGuru.com/articles/ezine/guru2_2.htm>.

Kurtus, R 2002, 'Return-on-Investment (ROI) from E-learning, CBT and WBT', 12 October, viewed 12 December 2002, <http://www.school-for-champions.com/e-learning/roi.htm>.

Lally, V & Barrett, E 1999, 'Building a Learning Community On-line: Towards Socio-academic Interaction', *Research Papers in Education*, vol. 142, pp. 147–63.

Lambe, P 2001, 'How Not to Implement an E-learning Programme', *Business Times Online*, 12 January, viewed 10 December 2002, <http://business-times.asia1.com.sg/supplement/story/0,2276,354,00.html>.

Lave, J & Wenger, E 1991, *Situated Learning: Legitimate Peripheral Participation*, Cambridge University Press: Cambridge, UK.

Lawyer, Gail 2001, 'Learning from Each Other: Symbiosis Seen Between E-learning Vendors, Telecom Service Providers', viewed 10 December 2002, <http://www.xchangemag.com/articles/131sec4a.html>.

Learnframe 2000, *Facts, Figures and Forces Behind E-learning*, Learnframe Research Report: USA.

Leonard, D & Rayport, JF 1997, 'Spark Innovation through Empathic Design', *Harvard Business Review*, 1 November, pp. 102–13.

Lessem, R 1993, *Business as a Learning Community*, London: McGraw-Hill.

Leu, D 2001, 'New Literacies for New Times: The Convergence of the Internet and Literacy Instruction', Keynote Speech to International Adult Literacy Conference, 30 March, Adult Literacy Conference: Normandy Hotel, Renfrew, Scotland.

Lichstein, H 2002, 'Standards Follow Practice, They Don't Lead', *Viewpointz*, February, viewed 22 June 2002, <http://www.taskz.com/ucd_standards_indepth.php>.

Likert, R 1961, *New Patterns of Management*, McGraw-Hill: New York.

Lindsley, DH, Brass, DJ & Thomas, JB 1995, 'Efficacy-performance Spirals: A Multilevel Perspective', *Academy of Management Review*, vol. 20 [3], pp. 645–78.

Livingston, JA, 1997, 'Metacognition: An Overview', New York: University of Buffalo, viewed 11 November 2002, <http://www.gse.buffalo.edu/fas/shuell/cep564/Metacog.htm>.

Luthans, F, Hodgetts, R & Rosencrantz, S 1988, *Real Managers*, Ballinger Publishing: Mass.

Maki, RH 2000, 'Evaluation of a Web-based Introductory Psychology Course: Learning and Satisfaction in On-line versus Lecture Courses', *Behavior Research Methods, Instruments and Computers*, vol. 32 [2], pp. 322; 230–9.

Malcolm, I 1998, 'You gotta talk the proper way', in G Partington (ed.), *Perspectives on Aboriginal and Torres Strait Islander Education*, Social Science Press: Katoomba, Australia.

Malhotra, Y 1996, 'Organisational Learning and Learning Organisations: An Overview', viewed 2 January 2002, <http://www.brint.com/papers/orglrng.htm>.

Manz, CC & Sims, HP 1987, 'Leading Workers to Lead Themselves: An Investigation of the External Leadership of Self-managing Work Teams', *Administrative Science Quarterly*, vol. 32, 106–29.

Martinez, M 2001, 'Designing Learning Objects to Personalize Learning', online chapter in DA Wiley (ed.), *The Instructional Use of Learning Objects*, viewed 17 February 2003, <http://reusability.org/read/>.

Masie, E 1997, *The Computer Training Handbook*, Lakewood Books: Minneapolis.

——2001, 'No More Digital Page-Turning', *E-learning Magazine*, 1 November, viewed 12 June 2002, <http://www.e-learningmag.com/e-learning/article/articleDetail.jsp?id=5054>.

McFadzean, E 2001, 'Supporting Virtual Learning Groups. Part 1: A Pedagogical Perspective', *Team Performance Management*, vol. 7 [3], pp. 53–62.

——& McKenzie, J 2002, 'Facilitating Virtual Learning Groups: A Practical Approach', *The Journal of Management Development*, vol. 20 [6], pp. 470–94.

McGill, M, Slocum, J & Lei, D 1992, *Management Practices in Learning Organisations*, Organisational Dynamics, vol. 42, Summer, pp. 5–17.

McGregor, D 1960, *The Human Side of Enterprise*, McGraw-Hill: New York.

McInerney, M & McInerney, V 2002, 'Educational Psychology', *Constructing Learning*, Prentice Hall: Frenchs Forest, NSW.

McLaughlin, C 2001, 'Inclusivity and Alignment: Principles of Pedagogy, Task and Assessment Design for Cross-cultural Online Learning', *Distance Education*, vol. 22 [1], pp. 7–29.

McNicol Williams 2001, 'E-barriers, E-benefits and E-business: Bridging the Digital Divide for Small and Medium Enterprises', vols 1 & 2 (attachments), SkillsNet Association Cooperative Limited: Victoria.

McRea, F, Gay, RK & Bacon, R 2000, *Riding the Big Waves: A White Paper on the E-learning Industry*, Thomas Weisel Partners: USA, viewed 11 May 2001, <http://www.e-weisel.com/client/public/white/mccrea.pdf>.

Mentis, M, Ryba, K & Annan, J 2001, 'Creating Authentic On-line Communities of Professional Practice', Australian Association for Research in Education Conference, Australian Association for Research in Education Conference: Fremantle.

Miller, W 1990, *The Creative Edge*, Addison-Wesley: Massachusetts.

Mintzberg, H 1973, *The Nature of Managerial Work*, Harper & Row: New York.

Mitchell, JG 2000a, *International E-VET Market Research Report: A Report on International Market Research for Australian VET Online Products and Services*, John Mitchell & Associates, Education Image & Adskill: Sydney.

——2000b, 'Market-driven E-VET: A Study for a National VET Consortium to Market, Distribute and Support Online Products and Services Overseas', Flexible Learning Advisory Group: Adelaide.

——2000c, 'E-competent Australia: Report on the Impact of E-commerce on the National Training Framework', Australian National Training Authority: Melbourne.

——2001, 'Marketing Tools and Models for VET Online', Flexible Learning Advisory Group & Australian National Training Authority: Melbourne.

Mitchell, JG & Wood, S 2001a, 'E-VET National Market Research Project — Scan of the Literature', Flexible Learning Advisory Group & Australian National Training Authority: .

——2001b, 'E-VET National Market Research Project — Summary of Existing Market Research', Flexible Learning Advisory Group & Australian National Training Authority: Adelaide.

Moe, Michael, et al. 1999, 'The Book of Knowledge: Investing in the Growing Education and Training Market', Merrill Lynch & Co. <http://www.ml.com/>.

Morrison, M 1994, 'Learning about the Learning Organization, Management, October, pp. 25–7.

Myer Briggs, I 1975, *Introduction to Type*, Consulting Psychology Press: USA.

National Centre for Vocational Education & Research 2000, Australian Adult and Community Education – An Overview, Statistics 2000, National Centre for Vocation, Education and Research. Adelaide.

——2002, FlexibilityThrough Online Learning, viewed 18 November 2002, <http://www.ncver.edu.au/research/proj/nr1F12.pdf>.

National Office for the Information Economy 2002, eBusiness in Education: Case Studies on the Effective Use of Electronic Business in the Education Sector, Department of Communication, Information and Arts: Canberra.

NCVER – see National Centre for Vocational Education & Research.

Nichani, M 2001, 'Serendipitous Learning', *E-learningpost*, viewed 23 September 2002, <http://www.e-learningpost.com/elthemes/serendip.asp>.

——2002, 'Empathic Instructional Design', *E-learningpost*, viewed 17 February 2003, <http://www.e-learningpost.com/features/archives/001003.asp>.

Nightingale, N, Te Wiata, I, Toohey, S, Ryan, G, Hughes, C & Magin, D 1996, 'Assessing Learning in Universities', Committee for the Advancement of University Teaching, University of NSW: Sydney.

NOIE – see National Office for the Information Economy.

Nonaka, I & Takeuchi, H 1995, *The Knowledge Creating Company: How Japanese Companies Create the Dynamics of Innovation*, Oxford University Press: New York.

Nua.com 2003, 'How Many Online', January, viewed 25 September 2003, <http://www.nua.ie/surveys/how_many_online/index.html>.

OECD – see Organisation for Economic Cooperation and Development.

Oliver, M & Dempster, J 2002, 'Strategic Staff Development for Embedding E-learning Practices in Higher Education', *Interactions*, vol. 6 [3], Autumn, viewed 12 December 2002, <http://www.warwick.ac.uk/ETS/interactions/vol6no3/oliver.htm>.

Oliver, R & Omari, A 2001, 'Student Responses to Collaborating and Learning in a Web-based Environment', *Journal of Computer Assisted Learning*, vol. 171, pp. 34–47.

Oliver, R & Towers, S 2000, *Uptime: Students, Learning and Computers*, Department of Employment, Education, Training and Youth Affairs: Canberra.

Organisation for Economic Cooperation and Development 2001, *Education at a Glance: OECD Indicators Education & Training*, Centre for Educational Research & Innovation: Geneva.

Orlikowski, W & Baroudi, J 1991, 'Studying Information Technology in Organizations: Research Approaches and Assumptions', *Information Systems Research*, vol. 2 [1], pp. 1–28.

Pedler, M, Burgoyne, J & Boydell, T 1991, *The Learning Company: Strategy for Sustainable Development*, McGraw-Hill: London.

Peterson, RW, Marostica, MA & Callahan, LM 1999, *E-learning: Helping Investors Climb the E-learning Curve*, November, US Bancorp Piper Jaffray Equity Research: USA.

Polanyi, M 1948, *Personal Knowledge*, University of Chicago Press: Chicago.

——1966, *The Tacit Dimension*, Routledge & Keegan Paul: London.

Porter, M 1990, *Competitive Strategy and Competitive Advantage*, Macmillan Press Ltd: London.

Portes, A 1998, 'Social Capital: Its Origins and Application in Modern Sociology', *Annual Review of Sociology*, vol. 24, pp. 1–24.

——& Landolt, P 1996, 'The Downside of Social Capital', *American Prospect*, vol. 26, pp. 18–22.

Powazek, D 2002, *Design for Community: The Art of Connecting Real People in Virtual Places*, New Riders: USA.

Prahalad, C & Hamel, G 1990, 'The Core Competencies of the Corporation', *Harvard Business Review*, vol. 68 [3], pp. 79–93.

Pratt, MG 1998, 'To Be or not to Be', in DA Whetten & PC Godfrey (eds), *Identity in Organizations*, Sage Publications: Thousand Oaks, pp. 171–208.

Putnam, R 1992, *Making Democracy Work*, Princeton University Press: Princeton.

Redding, J 1997, 'Fast Cycle Development: Analysis and Assessment from an Organisational Learning Perspective', *Academy of Human Resource Development – Conference Proceedings*, Atlanta, pp. 478–85.

——& Catalanello, RF 1994, Strategic Readiness: The Making of the Learning Organization, Jossey-Bass: San Francisco.

Reuters 2002, 'IBM eyes $43-B E-learning Market', IT Matters, viewed 12 July 2002, <http://itmatters.com.ph/news/news_05232002b.html>.

Revans, R 1982, *The Origins and Growth of Action Learning*, Chatwell-Bratt: London.

Rieber, LP 2002, *Supporting Discovery-based Learning within Simulations, Department of Instructional Technology*, University of Georgia: Georgia, USA, viewed 10 October 2002, <http://www.iwm-kmrc.de/workshops/visualization/rieber.pdf>.

Rigby, C, Day, M, Forrester, P & Burnett, J 2001, 'Agile Supply: Rethinking Systems Thinking, Systems Practice', *International Journal of Agile Management Systems*, vol. 2 [3], pp. 178–86.

Robinson, A & Stern, S 1997, Corporate Creativity, Business and Professional Publishing: Australia.

Rosenberg, M 2001, *E-learning: Strategies for Delivering Knowledge in the Digital Age*, McGraw-Hill: New York.

Rosenkopf, L 2001, *Cooperative Technical Organizations (CTOs): Windows into Technological Communities*, viewed 6 February 2003, <http://www.management.wharton.upenn.uedu/rosenkopf/documents/CTOreview paper.pdf>.

——& Tushman, ML 1998, 'The Coevolution of Community Networks and Technology: Lessons from the Flight Simulation Industry', *Industrial and Corporate Change*, vol. 7, pp. 311–46.

Ross, J & Schulz, R 1999, 'Can Computer-aided Instruction Accommodate all Learners Equally?' *British Journal of Educational Technology*, vol. 31, pp. 5–24.

Ross, MR, Powell, SR & Elias, MJ 2002, 'New Roles for School Psychologists: Addressing the Social and Emotional Learning Needs of Students', *School Psychology Review*, vol. 311, pp. 43–53.

Rothwell, WJ & Kazanas, HC 1997, *Mastering the Instructional Design Process: A Systematic Approach*, 2nd edn, Jossey-Bass/Pfeiffer: USA.

Rumelhart, D & Norman, D 1978, 'Accretion, Tuning and Restructuring: Three Modes of Learning', in J W Cotton & R Klatzky (eds), *Semantic Factors in Cognition*, Erlbaum: Hillsdale, NJ.

Ruona, W & Lyford-Nojima, E 1997, 'Performance Diagnosis Matrix: A Discussion of HRD Scholarships', *Futures of HRD: Academy of Human Resource Development Conference Proceedings*, AHRD: Atlanta, March, pp. 791–98.

Ruttenbur, B, Spickler, GC & Lurie, S 2000, 'E-learning: The Engine of the Knowledge Economy', New York: Morgan Keegan.

Sabnani, K 2002, 'Future of Mobile Internet Presentation', Lucent Technologies, Bell Laboratories: New Jersey.

Salovey, P & Mayer, J 1990, 'Emotional Intelligence', *Imagination, Cognition and Personality*, vol. 9, pp. 185–211.

Sanchez, R & Heene, A 1997, 'A Competency Perspective on Strategic Learning and Knowledge Management', in R Sanchez & A Heene (eds), *Strategic Learning and Knowledge Management*, John Wiley & Sons: Chichester, pp. 3–18.

Savage, C 1996, 'Knowledge Management: A New Era Beckons', *HRMonthly*, November , pp. 12–15.

Schank, R 1997, *Virtual Learning: A Revolutionary Approach to Building a Highly Skilled Workforce*, McGraw-Hill: New York.

Schrage, M 1990, *Shared Minds*, Random House Australia: Sydney.

Schrum, L 1998, 'On-line Education: A Study of Emerging Pedagogy', in B Cahoon (ed.), *Adult Learning and the Internet*, Jossey-Bass: San Francisco.

Schulz, M 2001, 'The Uncertain Relevance of Newness: Organisational Learning and Knowledge Flows', *Academy of Management Journal*, vol. 44 [4], pp. 661-81.

Schunk, DH 1981, 'Modelling and Attributional Effects on Children's Achievement: A Self-efficacy Analysis', *Journal of Educational Psychology*, vol. 73, pp. 93–105.

Seels, B & Glasgow, Z 1990, *Exercises in Instructional Design*, Prentice Hall: New Jersey.

Sefton, R, Waterhouse, P & Cooney, R December 1995, *Workplace Learning and Change: The Workplace as a Learning Environment*, Australian National Training Authority Research Advisory Council: Melbourne.

Senge, P 1992, *The Fifth Discipline: The Art and Practice of the learning Organisation*, reprint of 1990 original, Random House Australia: Sydney.

Senge, P, Kleiner, A, Roberts, C, Ross, R & Smith, B 1994, *The Fifth Discipline Fieldbook: Strategies and Tools for Building a Learning Organisation*, Nicholas Brealey Publishing: London.

Senge, P, Kleiner, A, Roberts, C, Ross, R, Roth, G & Smith, B 1999, *The Dance of Change: The Challenge of Sustaining Momentum in Learning Oganisations*, Nicholas Brealey Publishing: London.

Seybold, P 2001, *Customers.com Handbook: An Executive Guide and Technology Roadmap*, viewed 10 January 2003, <http://www.psgroup.com>.

Shelton, RD 2001, Developing an Internal Marketplace for Innovation: Balancing Creativity and Commercialization, [1], *Prism*, viewed 15 February 2001, <http://www.adlittle.com>.

Simmons, DE 2000, 'E-learning: Adoption Rates and Barriers', *The Forum Report*, vol. 1 [1], October, pp. 1–4.

Singh, M 2002, 'E-services and their Role in B2B E-commerce', *Managing Service Quality*, vol. 12 [6], pp. 434–46.

Slaski, M & Cartwright, S 2002, 'Health, Performance and Emotional Intelligence: An Exploratory Study of Retail Managers', *Stress and Health*, vol. 18, pp. 63–8.

Smircich, L 1983, 'Concepts of Culture and Organizational Analysis', *Administrative Science Quarterly*, vol. 28, pp. 339–58.

Snewin, D 1999, 'Internet Delivery for VET Sector Students at UniSA', Quality and Diversity in VET Research Second National Conference of AVETRA, Australian Vocational Education and Training Research Association: Melbourne.

Song, Y 2002, 'Creation and Utilization of Evaluative Information for Organizational Learning', *Proceedings AHRD 2002 Conference, Honolulu, Hawaii Symposium*, AHRD, February–March , pp. 1–7.

Stajkovic, AD. & Luthans, F 1998, 'Self-efficacy and Work-related Task Performance: A Meta-analysis', *Psychological Bulletin*, vol. 124, pp. 240–61.

Stalk, G & Hout, TM 1990, *Competing Against Time: How Time-Based Competition Is Reshaping Global Markets*, Free Press: New York.

Stern, D 1993, 'How Educational Institutions and Industry can Help Each Other', *Learning Partnerships: Working for Australia Conference*, Sydney, November, pp. 1–12.

Stewart, T 1997, *Intellectual Capital: The New Wealth of Organisations*, Nicholas Brealey Publishing: London.

Stieva, Ginni 2003, *Pan-Canadian Health Informatics Collaboratory (University of Victoria, British Colombia, Canada): Learning to E-learn Case Study 5*, Unitas Company Ltd: Hobart, Australia.

Straw, BM & Sutton, RI 1993, 'Macro Organizational Psychology', in JK Murnighan (ed.), *Social Psychology in Organizations: Advances in Theory and Research*, Prentice Hall: Englewood Cliffs, NJ, pp. 350–84.

Stuckey, B, Buening, A & Fraser, S 2002, 'The Rationale for Growing Communities of Practice as On-line Support for Dissemination and Implementation of Innovation', draft, February, viewed 10 December 2002, <http://rite.ed.qut.edu.au/oz-teachernet/profiles/e-learn_draft.doc>.

Sveiby, K 1997, *The New Organisational Wealth: Managing and Measuring Knowledge-based Assets*, Berrett-Koehler: San Francisco.

TAFE Frontiers 2001, *The Current Status of Online Learning in Australia*, TAFE Frontiers: Victoria.

Tesler, LG 1991, 'Networked Computing in the 1990s', *Scientific American*, September, special issue, pp. 86–93.

Thi Lam, L & Kirby, S 2002, 'Is Emotional Intelligence an Advantage? An Exploration of the Impact of Emotional and General Intelligence on Individual Performance', *The Journal of Social Psychology*, vol. 1421, pp. 133–43.

Thiagarajan (Thiagi), S 1993, 'Rapid Instructional Design', in GM Piskurich (ed.), *ASTD Handbook of Instructional Technology*, McGraw-Hill: New York, viewed 17 February 2003, <http://www.thiagi.com/article-rid.html>.

Thompson, B 2002, 'The Customer Relationship Primer: What you need to Know to get Started', *CRM Guru*, viewed 4 January 2003, <http://www.crmguru.com>.

Thompson, K 1992, 'A Conversation with Robert W. Galvin', *Organisational Dynamics*, Spring, pp. 56–69.

Tough, A 1999, 'Reflections on the Study of Adult Learning', 3rd New Approaches to Lifelong Learning (NALL) Conference, University of Toronto: Ontario Institute for Studies in Education, Canada, viewed 12 December 2002, <http://www.oise.utoronto.ca/depts/sese/csew/nall/res/toughtalk.htm>.

Tu, C & Corry M 2001, 'A Paradigm Shift for Online Community Research', *Distance Education*, vol. 22 [2], pp. 245–63.

——2002, 'Research in Online Learning Community', *Journal of Instructional Science and Technology*, vol. 51, viewed January 2003, <http://www.usq.edu.au/electpub/e-jist/docs/html2002/chtu.html>.

UNCTAD: see United Nations Conference on Trade and Development.

United Nations Conference on Trade and Development 2002, 'E-commerce and Development Report – Executive Summary', UNCTAD: Geneva.

Urdan, TA & Weggen, CC 2000, 'Corporate E-learning: Exploring a New Frontier', Research Report, W R Hambrecht & Co: USA.

Van Dyne, L, Graham, JW & Dienesch, RM 1994, 'Organizational Citizenship Behavior: Construct Redefinition, Measurement, and Validation', *Academy of Management Journal*, vol. 37, pp. 765–802.

Vincent, A & Ross, D 2001, 'Personalize Training: Determine Learning Styles, Personality Types and Multiple Intelligences Online', *The Learning Organization*, vol. 81, pp. 36–43.

Voci, E & Young, K 2001, 'Blended Learning Working in a Leadership Program', *Industrial and Commercial Training*, vol. 37 [55], pp. 157–61.

Volery, T & Lord, D 2000, 'Critical Success Factors in Online Education', *The International Journal of Educational Management*, vol. 14 [5], pp. 216–23.

Wallace, R, Grady, Dr. Neville & Falk, Ian 2003, *Understanding and Celebrating the Cultural Aspects of E-learning: Learning to E-learn Case Study 11*, Unitas Company Ltd: Hobart, Australia.

Wang, F, Head, M & Archer, N 2000, 'A Relationship-building Model for the Web Retail Marketplace', *Internet Research: Electronic Networking Applications and Policy*, vol. 10 [5], pp. 374–84.

Wang, C, Hinn, M & Kanfer, A 2001, 'Potential of Computer-supported Collaborative Learning for Learners with Different Learning Styles', *Journal of Research on Technology*, vol. 341, pp. 75–85.

Weik, K 1995, *Sensemaking in Organisations*, Sage Publications:Thousand Oaks, CA..

Weiser, M 1991, 'The Computer for the 21st century', *Scientific American*, vol. 265 [3], pp. 94–104, viewed 12 June 2002, <http://www.ubiq.com/hypertext/weiser/SciAmDraft3.html>.

Weiss, CH 1998, 'Have we Learned Anything New about the Use of Evaluation?' *American Journal of Evaluation*, vol. 19 [1], pp. 21–33.

Welber, M 2002, 'How AT&T Adapted Kirkpatrick's Evaluation Tools to E-learning then Applied the same Rigor to Selecting Vendors', *E-learning*, vol. 3[6], June, viewed 24 February 2003, <http://www.e-learning.nl/publicaties/artikelen/XHLP_ATT_Article.pdf>.

Weller, M 2000, 'Implementing a CMC Tutor Group for an Existing Distance Education Course', *Journal of Computer Assisted Learning*, vol. 163, pp. 178–183.

——2002, *Delivering Learning on the Net: The Why, What and How of Online Education*, Kogan Page: United Kingdom.

Welsch, E 2003, 'SCORM: Clarity or Calamity?' viewed 10 February 2003, <http://www.online-learningmag.com/online-learning/magazine/article_display.jsp?vnu_content_id=1526769>.

Wenger, E 1998, *Communities of Practice: Learning, Meaning and Identity*, rev. edn 2002, Cambridge University Press: Cambridge.

——, McDermott & Snyder, W 2002, *Cultivating Communities of Practice*, Harvard Business School Press: Boston.

Wentling, TL, Waight, C, Gallaher, J, La Fleur, J, Wang, C & Kanfer. A 2000a, 'E-learning: A Review of Literature', Knowledge and Learning Systems Group, University of Illinois: Urbana, Champaign.

——Waight, C, Strazzo, D, File, J, La Fleur, J & Kanfer, A 2000b, 'The Future of E-learning: A Corporate and an Academic Perspective', Knowledge and Learning Systems Group, University of Illinois: Urbana, Champaign.

Werkman, RA & Boonstra, JJ 2002, *Lessons in Survey Feedback: Interactive Reflection, Sensemaking and Learning in Organizational Change Processes*, University of Amsterdam: Netherlands, viewed 10 October 2002, <http://primavera.fee.uva.nl/PDFdocs/Boonstra2.pdf>.

Whetten, DA & Godfrey, PC (eds) 1998, *Identity in Organizations: Building Theory through Conversations*, Sage Publications: Thousand Oaks, CA.

Whitby, R & Bowles, M 2003, *Development of a Transport Integrated Learning Information Service (TILIS): Learning to E-learn Case Study 7*, Unitas Company Ltd: Hobart, Australia.

Whiteman, J 2000, 'Learning Environment for the Next Generation', ERIC No. ED441158.

Wiig, EH & Wiig, KM 1999, 'On Conceptual Learning', Working Paper 1–99, Knowledge Research Institute.

Wiley, DA (ed.) 2001, 'Connecting Learning Objects to Instructional Design Theory: A Definition, a Metaphor, and a Taxonomy', *The Instructional Use of Learning Objects: Online Version*, viewed 19 July 2003, <http://reusability.org/read/chapters/wiley.doc>.

Wiley, DA (ed.) 2001, *The Instructional Use of Learning Objects: Online Version*, Association for Instructional Technology and the Association for Educational Communications and Technology, viewed 19 July 2002, <http://reusability.org/read>.

Williams, P 2001, 'Learning Area Network: Information Dissemination and Online Discussion in an Education Environment: The Capabil-IT-y Project', *Aslib Proceedings: New Information Perspectives*, vol. 53 [3], pp. 99–107.

Wilson, P 2003a, *Norway, NKN E-learning and Competence Reform: Learning to E-learn Case Study 8*, Unitas Company Ltd: Hobart, Australia.

——2003b, *New Zealand's PROBE Project and E-learning Strategy: Learning to E-learn Case Study 9*, Unitas Company Ltd: Hobart, Australia.

Wood, B 2002, 'Engage your Customers by Offering New Services that Anticipate Customer Needs', *CRM Project*, vol. 3, October, viewed 1 January 2002, <http://www.crmproject.com/documents.asp?grID=187&d_ID=1474>.

Woolfolk, A 1993, *Educational Psychology*, Allyn & Bacon: Needham Heights, MA.

Woolner, P & Lowey, A 1993, 'A Developmental Model of the Learning Organization', paper presented to the Chicago chapter of the American Society for Training and Development, Chicago.

Yukl, GA 1989, *Leadership in Organizations*, Prentice Hall: Englewood Cliffs, NJ.